A Beginner's guide to

CHANGING
THE
WORLD

ISABEL LOSADA

HarperSanFrancisco
A Division of HarperCollins*Publishers*

For Tibetans, both inside and outside Tibet.
And for their friends and supporters all over the world.

HarperCollins books may be purchased for educational, business, or sales promotional use. For information please write: Special Markets Department, HarperCollins Publishers, 10 East 53rd Street, New York, NY 10022.

HarperCollins Web site: http://www.harpercollins.com
HarperCollins®, 🏰®, and HarperSanFrancisco™ are trademarks of
HarperCollins Publishers.

FIRST HARPERCOLLINS PAPERBACK EDITION PUBLISHED IN 2006
Designed by Joseph Rutt

Library of Congress Cataloging-in-Publication Data
Losada, Isabel
[For Tibet, with love]
A beginner's guide to changing the world / Isabel Losada.
p. cm.
Originally published: For Tibet, with love. London : Bloomsbury, 2004.
ISBN-13: 978–0–06–083452-4
ISBN-10: 0–06–083452-8
1. Tibet (China)—Politics and government—1951– 2. Losada, Isabel—Travel—
China—Tibet. 3. Tibet (China)—Description and travel. I. Title.
DS786.L67   2005
951'.505—dc22   2005040448

06 07 08 09 10 RRD(H) 10 9 8 7 6 5 4 3 2 1

All that is necessary for the triumph of evil is that good people do nothing.

Edmund Burke: 1729–1797

Whatever you do will be insignificant, but it is very important that you do it.

Mahatma Gandhi: 1869–1948

CONTENTS

THE QUEST

Sometimes you just have to do something, don't you? Sometimes an injustice comes along and you think, "No, this cannot be," and—rather than just sigh, switch off the TV, or throw away the newspaper one more time—you know it's time to act.

If you or I decide to take an action for a cause beyond ourselves, one in which we have no historical reason to become involved, will we be greeted with cynicism and become a laughingstock? Perhaps. But I enjoy making people laugh. So that's the first problem solved.

It doesn't matter what the injustice is that's got you hopping about. It could be the destruction of the rain forest, the war in the Middle East, or the drug addiction in your neighborhood—it's all the same. It's making a difference I'm playing with here.

And I know these are serious topics, but I say "playing with" on purpose because I believe joy has to be a part of it. I want to be persistently joyful and joyfully persistent, even with the most difficult of tasks, because we have a limited number of heartbeats left. I believe that it's OK to want to make a difference and have fun . . . as you'll see.

I look around the world, and the escalating violence is so bad that I know I'm not the only one who wants to do something. What can you and I do about the war on terror? I'll tell you: We can observe that terror is not the way that we want to go. So we ask, "Who is the world's leading proponent of nonviolence?" Most people when asked this question say, "The Dalai Lama." He asks for what he wants for Tibetans but insists on nonviolence. He's the man for me.

Why is the world fighting terror with terror and yet not supporting a man who has spoken for nonviolence for fifty years? Why are we ignoring the sanest voice on the planet? And can one crazy, misguided woman who lives on Battersea Park Road in London do anything about it?

For many years I have carried with me the famous serenity prayer:

> *Grant me the serenity to accept the things I cannot change*
> *The courage to change the things I can*
> *And the wisdom to know the difference.*

This will be my guide.

So here is my quest. To understand the prayer—to learn to have just a small amount of serenity, courage, and wisdom. And perhaps to change the world.

PART: THE FIRST

—mm—

Grant Me the Serenity to Accept the
Things I Cannot Change

THE BEGINNING OF
THE BEGINNING

This being the twenty-first century, "the man who moves a mountain starts with one small click." Whatever it is you want to do to change the world, the first step is now to switch on a computer. My computer skills are of a fairly basic kind, but I know that there is a butler somewhere in my machine, called Jeeves, and I can ask him anything I want, from "Is there life after death?" to "What shall I do on Friday evening?" I don't really see Jeeves as a political activist, but he's a mine of information. So I asked him, "What can I do about Tibet?" and he told me that on Wednesdays between 6 p.m. and 8 p.m. there is a demonstration against the Chinese occupation outside the Chinese embassy, just down the road from the BBC in Portland Place, London.

I couldn't remember the last time I'd demonstrated for or against anything. My last book, *The Battersea Park Road to Enlightenment,* is an exploration of personal happiness. Happiness is a great subject, and being happy ourselves is perhaps the best contribution that we can make to the world. On the other hand, I realized that the critics who had accused me of tummy-button gazing were right. I know about the world inside me, but I have no experience in trying to change anything not sporting my navel. Reflecting on this, I was filled with shame. As a student I'd joined a march with The Campaign for Nuclear Disarmament (CND) and the anti-apartheid movement, and since then I've written two letters for Greenpeace. Perhaps there is a balance, but I'd leaned over so far one way I'd fallen asleep. Standing outside the Chinese embassy for two hours may not be doing much, but it would be more than I'd done for the last ten years.

When the day came, I found myself wondering what you wear to demonstrate. Don't sigh. I don't mean the right Ab Fab fashion. But there is a dilemma. If you wear clothes in which you can sit on the pavement and keep dry if it rains, you soon look scruffy and fit far too easily into a category where the Chinese officials and the police can just see "troublemakers." So I arrived in shorts and a white top on my trusty two-wheeler, to find a very small crowd in anoraks and raincoats. If you can call eight people a crowd.

Should you ever venture down Portland Place early on a Wednesday evening, you could be forgiven for being confused. Apparently there is an international law that protects embassies in all countries. If you want to demonstrate outside an embassy, you are obliged to stand on the other side of the road. Fortunately for the Chinese, it happens that Portland Place, where they are lucky enough to have their embassy, is a very wide road. So what you see is a group of demonstrators outside the Royal Institute of British Architects. Car drivers stare curiously at them, presumably thinking that there really are some ugly buildings in the United Kingdom, but what could the vexed individuals be demanding?

Meanwhile, the night that I cycled up, peace reigned in the building opposite. No flag was flying to indicate to passersby that it was an embassy. The windows were closed, and the shutters were down. It looked totally deserted.

A delightful character with a long beard and long straggly hair arrived and pulled out his homemade banners from a bag that he carried on his back while wobbling along on his bike. The banners said, "Free Tibet," "China out of Tibet," "Free the Panchen Lama—the World's Youngest Political Prisoner," "Stop Enforced Birth Control in Tibet," "Stop Nuclear Dumping in Tibet," "Stop Human Rights Abuses in Tibet." Huge issues painted with poster paints on old pieces of cardboard.

"Hello. Which one would you like?" said the bearded character.

I rather liked "Beep Your Horn for Tibet," but someone else took that. "I'll take that big Tibetan flag on the bamboo pole, please," I said. "Thank you."

I looked at my fellow demonstrators and considered the might of the continent of China. One or two ladies in their sixties. One wore a T-shirt—"Don't kill the elephants." The other looked like a member of the Women's Institute or the Mothers' Union. One man wore a large straw hat and had a horn that, he informed me, he'd bought at the Notting Hill Carnival. He wore sandals that were falling apart, and most of the buttons had long since parted company with his shirt. I smiled at him, and he leaned towards me and whispered in a conspiratorial tone, "I've heard some bad news . . ."

"Oh?" I said, noticing his flushed red face and swollen stomach.

"About Colombia . . . but don't tell anyone . . ."

I said, "I don't know anything about Colombia. So perhaps you'd better not tell me."

I looked at him, and he honked his horn. No one else spoke to him.

In fact the demonstrators didn't seem to talk much to each other. One very tall and thin man gave off "don't talk to me" vibes with every ounce of nonverbal communication that a human being is capable of. He looked very uncomfortable and avoided my eye as I attempted to smile at him. Two women talked between themselves; they seemed to have been demonstrating for many years and maybe they were tired of people who turned up once and never came back. They didn't approach me, so I didn't approach them.

Then the remaining lady said, "Hello. I'm Paula." She must have been in her forties or early fifties, long hair and a relaxed friendly look about her. I held out the hand that wasn't holding the flag. "Pleased to meet you. I'm Isabel." She explained that she was the one who brought a flask of tea every week and distributed it to the banner-wavers. She seemed gentle and lovely.

"Have you been involved in the Tibetan cause for long?" I asked, feeling as if my powers to ask interesting questions had deserted me for the evening.

"Yes, I first taught English to Tibetan refugee children in India about ten years ago."

Then a "shout" started. The long-haired man called out, in an impressively loud voice, "China, China, China," and the assembled crew replied, "Out, Out, Out." Then he called, "Free Tibet!" We responded, "China Out!" He said, "China Out!" and we said, "Free Tibet!" It was good clear communication. But was anyone listening?

I glanced at the embassy. The might of China was unmoved. The closed eyes of the shuttered windows didn't blink. A solitary police-woman, posted by the front door, must have been glad of the entertainment we were providing.

I waved my Tibetan flag and decided to stroll across the road. I smiled at her broadly as I approached.

She smiled back, "You aren't allowed to stand on this side of the road with that flag. You know that."

"No, I don't actually. This is my first time."

"I see."

I smiled at her some more and stood with my flag on the wrong side of the road. "So what happens if I sit on the embassy step with my flag?"

"I'd have to ask you to move."

"And if I didn't?"

"I'd have to call the local patrol, and they'd move you."

"I see. My name's Isabel, by the way." And I held out my hand. She shook it.

"Sarah. How old are you?"

I laughed. "Why do you ask that?" I didn't tell her. "How old are you?"

"I'm twenty-eight," she said. It's very strange, meeting police who are younger than I am.

"So what else am I not allowed to do?"

"You aren't supposed to be standing here with that flag!" She laughed.

"I won't get you into trouble, will I?" I asked.

"No, don't worry."

So I raised it a little in the direction of the camera above the door of the embassy.

"What else can't I do, then?"

"You can't lay flowers on the steps of the embassy. They used to do that all the time in memory of the Tibetan dead."

"So I could get arrested for laying flowers."

"You'd be cautioned, I suppose. You don't want to get arrested, do you?" She was a bit wary of me.

"I was thinking of it. Do you know anything about Tibet? The Chinese occupation? The destruction of the culture and the environment?"

"Not really."

"Do you see the picture of that boy on the banner?" I pointed to a black-and-white photo of a beautiful boy of about six.

"Yes?"

"That's the Panchen Lama. He's a political prisoner, and no one knows where he is. He's a teenager now."

"I'm going to have to ask you not to stand here," she said.

"I understand, yes." I didn't move. I just went on smiling. "Do you enjoy working for the police force?" I asked.

"I love it."

"I'd find it hard, I think."

"Why?"

"I'd never want to lock anyone up. Don't you find it hard, with kids, for example?"

"Sometimes, but some people just don't care . . ."

That morning I had spoken to a supermodel. What a difference. I told her, "This morning a model told me she hated her job and she didn't know any happy models. She said they are all insecure and have terrible relationships because the men like them for their looks. Never, in ten years, had she met a happy model."

"Well, tonight you've met a happy policewoman. You're not really going to get arrested, are you?"

"I'm just doing some research right now. But thanks for the information."

Then from nowhere a tall elegant Chinese official appeared. He walked up to us and, ignoring me and the flag, he directed his eye to Sarah and spoke to her quite pleasantly as if I didn't exist. "Have they changed the rules?" he asked. "Are these people allowed on this side of the road now?"

"No," she said, seeming embarrassed herself by the way he had ignored me. I attempted to smile at him, but he walked away to join an anxious-looking wife and a baby in a stroller.

"That's OK." I smiled at her. "I'll go now. The demo is over now anyway. It's been lovely meeting you."

"And you, too . . ." She obviously wondered if this was the right thing to be saying. "What's your second name, Isabel?"

"Losada. Why? Are you going to write a report on me?"

"Yes, we have to write notes on anything that happens, for the person who is here next week."

I see. I thought I'd give her more useful information. "I live in Battersea, and I have a ginger cat."

The demonstration was ending. The banners were put into bags, and the flags rolled up. The long-haired leader of the "shout" who painted the banners smiled at me. "Do you go to the pub now?" I asked. "Can I buy you a drink? I have vouchers for free coffee in Starbucks." Some of the women glowered at me. "I know they are an evil multinational bent on world domination," I attempted my defense feebly. "But I happen to have vouchers. I'm not going to give them money." Silence. "How about a glass of wine, then?"

"Sure," said the beard. "I don't normally, but why not? My name's Simon Gould."

We trundled into the local pub, nearly removing the eyes of several innocent bystanders with our flagpoles and banners.

"So is it dangerous, all this?"

"Not really. I once had my phones bugged, and I've had a couple of bruises."

He obviously enjoyed himself.

"How did you know your phones were bugged?"

"The ringing went all strange. Instead of the usual two 'bringg, bringgs,' I'd just get one very long 'briiinnngggg,' and I once heard talking in the background."

I laughed. "So what did you do about it?"

"I said lots of cool, calm things like 'No, we're not planning any action during Jiang Zemin's visit.' Which of course we were. And Scotland Yard once asked me if I'd received any anonymous phone calls or death threats."

"Had you?"

"No. But I think they had to ask that as a part of a legal process that justifies bugging me 'for my safety.'"

"So you think it was Scotland Yard that was bugging you and not the Chinese?"

"Of course I don't know, but I'd guess so. The security around the time of Jiang Zemin's visit was so tight that even Scotland Yard has now admitted it was illegal. The British government didn't want him to suffer the indignity of seeing a Tibetan flag."

"So didn't you wave flags anyway?"

"We tried, but we were forced not to. At one point my pedal bike and I were both put into the back of a van. And on another day they pulled me off a wall. The two policemen were terrified they'd hurt me . . ."

I love a good story.

"I was standing on a wall about six foot high by the river with the Tibetan flag unfurled where we knew Jiang Zemin was due to pass. The policeman said, 'I must ask you to step off the wall, sir, for your own safety.' I said that I felt quite safe and wasn't going to fall, thank you. He said, 'I must insist that, for your own safety, sir, you step off the wall.'" The long-haired, long-bearded character was smiling at the memory.

"May I ask how old you are, Simon?"

"I'm fifty-four. Anyway, the policeman was obliged to grab me and force me off the wall. They expected me to resist, but I didn't. I just went floppy like a rag doll when they pulled me off the six-foot wall. I was in a heap on the ground, bundled up in the Tibetan flag, with my T-shirt over my head. I could tell they were worried. I was winded but OK, so I said, 'That's it! No more friendly relations with the police,' and I heard a voice say, 'Oh, don't be like that, sir.' It was friendly enough, but they had obviously been told to do whatever was necessary to ensure that no flags were to be seen. So much for the right to peaceful demonstration."

"How long have you been doing this?"

"Since 1989. The Tiananmen Square massacre. I started with the Chinese radicals. Not many people realize that most of the demonstrators wanted pure Communism."

"I thought the students were pro-democracy?"

"That's the way it was reported in the West, but some were radical Communists demonstrating against the corruption. I know this because I met so many of them. My son, who was seven at the time, became friendly with the Chinese kids as we all used to demonstrate together . . ."

"Do you have Chinese people who demonstrate with you now?"

"Yes, sometimes. The ones who have come to understand what their government has done in Tibet. And is doing."

He suddenly looked pensive and far away. "I've had about six hundred letters from Tibetan refugees in India, asking me to continue. It's very moving."

"So what's next?"

"We are starting a demonstration opposite Downing Street on Wednesdays between 1 p.m. and 4 p.m. Will you come?"

"I'm not sure . . ."

"I've got to dash now. Here's my phone number."

He put his bag of banners on his back and staggered out under the weight to get on his bike. I was still holding a Tibetan flag.

"Would you like to keep that?"

"Yes. I think I would."

"OK, then. Bring it next week." And off he wobbled.

I too had a bike but only one flag. I decided to unfurl it and ride home with it flapping in the wind. I'd heard people were sent to prison in Tibet for waving a Tibetan flag.

My silhouette looked like one of the early propaganda posters for Communism under Stalin. Suddenly I wasn't an individual anymore. I imagined what it would have been like to have been a member of the Hitler Youth Movement or to have been swept up by the Communist Revolution in China. The waving of flags has all those associations in my mind. And I'm probably not alone. I hope nationalism is dying as we all become internationalists. I'm an optimist. Probably a cockeyed one.

It was early evening in midsummer as I rode along Oxford Street, through South Kensington, down the King's Road, and over the bridge, and I certainly turned heads. A woman in shorts with a flag flapping in the wind. I watched as eyes went from me to the flag, and then people turned to the person they were walking with. I could guess what they were asking. What was this flag? What country? And no one knew.

SHORT HISTORY LESSON

I read somewhere, "If you want to know something, don't read a book. Ask someone who knows." This works very well for me. It's not that I don't enjoy reading books, but when you're reading a book you can't ask stupid questions. Also I love meeting people, and it's amazing who will agree to meet you if you write them a letter that fits on one page.

Dr. Isabel Hilton was described by the *Spectator* on the back of her latest erudite epic as "one of Britain's very few home-grown top-grade China specialists." I'd discovered that her doctorate was honorary and had been awarded to her for services to international relations. If there were a stylish way to acquire a PhD, this was it. She also had her own radio show and wrote for the *Guardian,* the *New Yorker,* and every other publication with intelligence and class. She knew everyone and had written about everything. She is also the only person I've ever heard of who actually receives phone calls from the Dalai Lama when he wants to ask a favor. But in spite of having what the Americans would call "kick-ass" qualifications and a track record to die for, she was fantastically relaxed.

"Come over round about six, and I'll do some cheese and olives and bits. That OK for you?"

"Yes. This is so kind of you . . ."

"It'll be a pleasure."

I arrived at her front door to hear her speaking quite clearly. She was making a speech of some kind, but the house appeared to be empty. I stood outside the door listening, but there was no one there. Finally I exclaimed, "OK. I give up! I can hear you, but I can't see you."

And then, lo! there appeared on the roof, back-lit by dazzling sunshine, an angel on a mobile phone.

"Hello!" said the angel.

Then the door opened, I blinked, and in front of me stood Isabel Hilton. The woman seemed to have miraculous powers.

"You're an angel!" I said in some confusion, pointing at the roof. "Or at least there is an angel on your roof, speaking with your voice."

"Shhhhh!" said the mystical form on the roof. Waving frantically, it had now become an agitated angel.

Isabel Hilton stepped outside the door, and her face assumed the appearance of an army sergeant. "My daughter," she explained. "She knows very well that she isn't allowed on the roof. She'll kill herself." She stepped forward and peered up at the roof. "I thought you were doing your homework? I've told you before . . ." But the angel on the roof had dematerialized. And all this before I had stepped over the threshold. Isabel smiled at me wearily.

I grinned. "I have one of those." I recognized the curious habits of the species *teenagera feminea*. "Do you find them scary at this age?"

"I do," she said. "I wonder what happened to my daughter."

"But at eighteen they transform, overnight, back into humans. For years I didn't believe it—but it's true."

The form of music favored by the younger *teenagera* could be heard from the top of the house. An older version of the disheveled male *teenagerus* passed on the stairs, smiled politely, and said "Hello" in the same disarmingly friendly manner in which the angel had spoken earlier. "My son Alex," Isabel explained.

She showed me through her home and into her study. It was just what you would expect. Four walls lined with books from floor to ceiling. More books lay in boxes, and on top of those books sat some books. She seated me in a comfy seat and herself at her desk. I tried to remember why I was here. She smiled at me.

"You wanted to ask me about Tibet?"

OK, time to speak with clarity and precision.

"I just wondered if you could tell me . . . what I don't understand is . . . it all seems so black and white . . . well . . . why do the Chinese think that . . . er . . . the place no longer called Tibet belongs to them?"

"I can tell you what their argument is. Whether they believe it, is another matter."

"Really?"

"Their argument is a historical one. There are a number of points they make that they claim show that Tibet was 'always part of China.' Which is not the case. Exactly as the Tibetans believe."

So I think I could work out where Dr. Isabel stood, then.

"The first point is the marriage of the Chinese princess Wencheng to a Tibetan king."

"Ah!" I remembered this story from somewhere. "Isn't this a Tibetan king who also had a Nepalese wife?"

"Yes."

"So according to Chinese logic Nepal is also part of China?"

"Or the Nepalese own Tibet. Or the Nepalese own China. Take your pick."

"When was this?"

"This was in the seventh century. She was a Chinese princess sent as a bride to a barbarian king."

"Was it a love match, then?"

"Not at all. It's something that the Chinese only did when the barbarian king was very powerful and you had to appease him. There was no other reason to send a Chinese princess, and she would have considered it a hardship posting. Chinese poetry is full of unhappy princesses sent to foreign lands, complaining about the conditions."

"So Tibet was a kingdom to be appeased?"

"That's it exactly. It's a dubious argument for China to use as it shows that at this time Tibet was an independent powerful kingdom. But Wencheng played an important role because she and the Nepalese wife between them converted the Tibetan king to Buddhism."

"So it's China's fault that Tibet is a Buddhist country? That's rather ironic considering the efforts that Communism has put into trying to stamp it out."

Torturing Buddhist nuns and monks to endear them to the principles of Communism, for example.

I glanced up and noticed a shelf of books in Chinese.

"Do you read and write Chinese too?"

"I do. Anyway . . ." She hurried on before I questioned her on her casual achievements.

"The next case the Chinese make is that there was a Mongol conquest. Which there was. Briefly. They argue that because the Mongols conquered Tibet and then the Mongols conquered China that therefore Tibet belongs to China."

"I see."

"It's a pretty ropey argument, too. They then established the Yuan Dynasty, of course."

"Of course, yes." The blank look on my face must have given me away.

"That was a large and important dynasty that lasted from 1206 to 1368. The dynasty that immediately preceded the Ming."

"Ah! Yes . . . right." I couldn't believe she actually knew these dates from memory.

"You've heard of Kublai Khan, the grandson of Genghis Khan?" A vague memory of a poem?

> *In Xanadu did Kublai Khan*
> *A stately pleasure-dome decree . . .*

Literature is so much more beautiful than history.

"Well, Kublai Khan didn't go on ruling Tibet. These arguments are very tenuous. But you asked me what they are . . ."

"Yes . . ." I scribbled notes on to a large pad.

"The final argument they give is to do with the Qing Dynasty. In 1644 the Ming fell to the Qing Dynasty. The last emperor hanged himself on Cole Hill as the Manchu hoards poured into China to establish what was to be the last imperial dynasty. The Manchus were a Central Asian tribe, they came from Manchuria, and before they conquered China they conquered quite a lot of Central Asia. They conquered their neighbors essentially. So they were quite big and powerful before they conquered China."

"And they conquered Tibet?"

"No. They didn't. But they were Buddhists. Tibetan Buddhists."

I hope you are following this.

"I'm sorry . . . Manchuria is where?"

"It's roughly northeast China. Would it help if we looked at a map?"

"I doubt it."

"If you look at a map of China in the Ming Dynasty, it's about half the size of China today. That part is core China. Han China. China within the Great Wall."

I wished very deeply that I'd read a Ladybird book of Chinese history before ringing her doorbell.

"China is bigger today because the final dynasty was a Central Asian dynasty, and they brought with them the territories that they had conquered previously, like Manchuria."

"But they hadn't conquered Tibet?" Obviously the relevance of this would become clear eventually.

"No. But they had a relationship with Tibet that was known as the priest-patron relationship. Because the Qing emperors were Buddhists, specifically they were followers of Tibetan Buddhism, they owed a spiritual duty to the Dalai Lama. They regarded him as their spiritual superior. So when the Dalai Lama visited the imperial capital, the emperor would get down off his throne and come to the gate to meet him."

"And the emperor wasn't in the habit of doing this for any old visiting VIP?"

"I don't know if he got off his throne for anyone else. It wasn't what emperors did."

"But he did it because the Dalai Lama was his spiritual superior."

"Exactly." She encouraged her student effortlessly. "And in turn the Dalai Lama could rely on the emperor for protection should he need it. So if the Gurkhas invaded, as they did from time to time . . ."

"He'd email the emperor and say, 'I've got trouble with the Gurkhas again.'"

She smiled. "And the emperor would text some soldiers to go

and sort the problem out, and when they'd sent the Gurkhas back to where they belonged they'd get a message telling them to come back home again."

"And what century was this?"

"This was about the seventeenth and eighteenth century. It was a relationship that worked very well. The Tibetans went on doing what they did, and the Qing Empire went on doing what it did."

"Sounds chummy enough."

"It was very cordial, yes. The emperor would send gifts to the Dalai Lama, and the Dalai Lama would send gifts to the emperor. Distinguished lamas would go to Beijing to teach, and palaces would be built for them as they were always treated with great reverence, and then they'd go home again."

"Not like that now, sadly."

"There was no Chinese military presence in Tibet apart from a couple of imperial officials who were Ambans to the Dalai Lama's court."

"Ambans?"

"They were like ambassadors. So there was no mechanism at all that would suggest to the dispassionate observer that Tibet was part of China."

"But they were friends?"

"Yes, there was a close relationship because of the common religion."

"And China now claims that at this time Tibet was part of China?" That is what I was trying to understand.

"They do. And then finally the West started to cause problems. There was a period of political instability they called 'the Great Game.' It was a kind of competition for Central Asia between the British Empire, which of course held India, and the Russian Empire . . . and in the middle . . ."

"Was Tibet."

"The British were interested in getting into Tibet because they wanted to keep an eye on the Russians. The Qing emperor was very concerned that nobody should get into Tibet, so they put a lot of pressure on Tibetans to close off Tibet from the outside world."

"And didn't the British invade Tibet for some bizarre reason?" Never let it be said that I know nothing.

"Yes. Francis Younghusband invaded Tibet in 1903 because the British were concerned that the thirteenth Dalai Lama was being influenced by the Russians. They didn't stay. But it was enough to upset the Chinese even more. I won't go into all the complications, but the very unfortunate thirteenth Dalai Lama was forced into exile several times."

"And this was . . . when?"

"The Qing Empire fell in 1912, and by that time the priest-patron relationship was out of date because the later Qing emperors weren't interested in Tibetan Buddhism, and they wanted greater security."

"So they rewrote the history books?"

"Well, they began to talk up their influence in Tibet and to see themselves as emperors of Tibet, and Tibet as a tributary state of China. And this in turn was parlayed into the modern relationship of 'it's ours.' So when the Qing Dynasty fell, every subsequent Chinese government decided that Tibet had always been part of China. But if you look back before the Qing Dynasty on the map, then this is clearly not true."

"And that's it? That is their justification for what they've done to Tibet?"

"That's about the sum of it. If you'd like a more detailed version . . ."

She smiled and waved at a shelf of books.

"I promise I will read the history books. Are there any you recommend?"

"Tsering Shakya's book, *The Dragon in the Land of Snows*. He is a truly independent historian. He's Tibetan, but his book was criticized by everyone—the Chinese and the Tibetan government-in-exile. I think he is fair to both sides."

I resolved to purchase it on the morrow.

"Is it any more simple the other way around?" I asked.

"What?"

"I mean, why do the Dalai Lama and the Tibetan government-in-exile believe that Tibet is not part of China?"

"That is simple. The Dalai Lama knows the history of Tibet. The Dalai Lama knows that he was the king of Tibet. The Dalai Lama knows that the thirteenth Dalai Lama explicitly declared the independence of Tibet when the Qing Dynasty fell. As did the Mongolians. That they issued postage stamps and had their own currency. That they had a diplomatic representation from Britain."

"Seems to be a fairly strong case."

"And he knows that when the Chinese invaded Tibet they signed what was essentially a peace treaty with the sovereign country of Tibet. It was called the Seventeen-Point Agreement on Measures for the Peaceful Liberation of Tibet."

"You mean it was signed between one nation and another?"

"Well, why would you have to sign such an agreement if Tibet had always been part of China?"

"That sounds like a rather stronger argument."

"The Chinese don't seem to have much of a case really, do they?"

"I can imagine my daughter saying, 'It's bollocks, isn't it?'"

"Personally, I would agree. Many Chinese historians who are starting to have access to their own history would agree with you, too."

"Really?" I wondered what the Chinese people thought aside from the government. "I mean, isn't there a whole Chinese generation that genuinely believes that Tibet is part of China?"

"Yes, but any Chinese historians who make it their business to find out can now discover otherwise. From the fifties onwards dissent has been dangerous in China."

"So you still can't have an unofficial view if you're Chinese?"

"You couldn't. But one of the things that is happening now, which I find very interesting, is that it is breaking down in the

Chinese universities. After this dreadful period of being shut away from the outside world and shut away from their own past."

"Really?" I heard myself beginning to sound like a parrot.

"Previously the position of the Chinese government was essentially: 'Everything before 1949 is bad, and everything after 1949 is good.' Now students are finding out that there was more individual freedom . . ."

"Under the old-fashioned dynasties?"

"Yes. There was more justice, there were often fewer taxes, there was more commerce. They are finding out all these things about their own past that they never knew."

So did this mean there was hope for the Tibetans?

"And are they also finding out that there was a time when Tibet wasn't part of China?"

"I'm sure some of them are. Yes. They wouldn't say it very loudly. But I've talked to many Chinese, whose names of course I couldn't mention, who are absolutely clear about it."

"You amaze me. I thought the Chinese all believed their government's propaganda?"

"Many do, but you have to remember that the party has told so many lies to the people that any thinking person, nationalistic or not, is likely to be skeptical of the official version. Why should they believe when so little has been believable?"

"So you see hope?"

"I think the problem will diminish as people have more access to their own history. One of the things that happens in a totalitarian state is that parents are afraid to tell their own children what they know. Because if the children tell anyone else, then everyone gets into trouble. So there are whole generations that don't know their history."

I don't think I'd ever realized how important history was until this moment. "Do the Tibetans think they are part of China?"

"I'm sure some do. But you often meet Tibetans, particularly in exile, who have come out of Tibet, and when you talk to them you

find that one of the great moments for them in finding their freedom is the discovery of their own history. They realize for the first
time that they are a conquered nation. That they were a nation and
that they were conquered. And they know the truth. It's both a liberation for them and an uncomfortable discovery."

"How so?"

"Because they then often feel that they have to do something
about it. And that is dangerous for them and for their families and
friends back in Tibet."

I sat and stared at the piles of books.

"If the Seventeen-Point Agreement was signed under duress by
the Tibetans because their country was being invaded, why didn't
anyone help them? I mean, didn't you say that Britain had an official representative to Tibet at one time? Surely Britain knew that
Tibet was an independent state? Why didn't they do anything? Or
India? Surely India knew? And the United Nations just sat by and
let China walk in and start bombing the monasteries?"

"No one did anything. When Tibet tried to get the UN to de-
fend her against the Chinese invasion in November 1950, a long list
of countries declined to support her—the UK, the U.S., and India
were the parties chiefly concerned, and they all declined for their
own reasons. There was one country that drafted a resolution and
argued strongly for it to be debated."

"And, as a matter of interest, who . . ."

"El Salvador."

"So why . . . ?"

"You really would have to read the history books to have that
question answered. I could answer it, but how long do you have?"

"Why didn't America help?"

"America tried to help, but it was hard for them to do anything
without the Dalai Lama specifically asking for assistance, and apart
from the fact that there were no phone lines and he wasn't the easiest person to reach, he couldn't be seen to ask for help as the Chinese were claiming that they were protecting Tibet from the West.

It was impossible for Tibet to accept help from America as it would justify Chinese 'protection,' and America wasn't offering much anyway. Nobody really cared. Tibetan culture, although unique, wasn't considered important, and the Tibetans couldn't protect themselves against the Chinese invasion as the Chinese were too strong."

"And what about the story that it was the CIA that smuggled the Dalai Lama out of China. Is that true?"

She smiled. "Where did you read that?"

"Er . . . I think, possibly, my daughter's history teacher . . ."

"No. It's not true. The Tibetan government got the Dalai Lama out because they were afraid for his life."

"Do you think he did the right thing—leaving?"

"Yes, of course. But this isn't Tibetan history you are asking me about now."

"There are so many things that I can't get my head around. . . . This morning a friend sent me a link to an article in a Chinese newspaper in which the writer had said that he had researched views of the Dalai Lama and could not find anywhere the slightest evidence of his commitment to Buddhism."

She laughed. "Substandard Chinese propaganda."

"I did wonder if he perhaps didn't have access to the Internet because on amazon.com there are about five hundred books that the Dalai Lama has written on Buddhism."

I don't think I was telling her anything that she didn't already know. Where had she found such calm in the face of all this? She smiled, "When the Dalai Lama announced the verification of the new incarnation of the Panchen Lama, the Chinese accused him of breaking the rules and of not abiding by the correct procedures. So you have a situation where the Communists know more about reincarnation than the Dalai Lama."

"And are 'protecting' Buddhism."

"Generous of them, isn't it?"

"Why do the Chinese distrust the West so much?"

"That's a good question." I smiled idiotically. "You have to remember that, in the nineteenth century, Westerners went into China and broke down the system and government and the economy for their own interests. The West sent several military expeditions, forced China to trade, and established territory and enclaves like Hong Kong at the point of a gun. So when foreigners start saying to China, 'Ah well, you don't have a very strong case on Taiwan really, do you? And frankly your case on Tibet . . .'"

"Sucks."

"'And Mongolia is none too clever either. And what about Xinjiang? It was never really part of China' . . . then they think that the West is up to its old tricks again."

"And just trying to break up China?"

"Yes. China. The center of the universe and the most powerful and civilized nation on earth. You are out to prevent the great Motherland from becoming strong and powerful, so you'll do anything."

"I see. So they don't like us supporting Tibetan independence."

"Not independence, autonomy. Even the Dalai Lama gave up his struggle for independence in 1988 and is prepared to compromise with the Chinese."

"So how can I be pro-Tibet without being seen by the Chinese government as an enemy to China?"

"That is a very good question. Good luck." She looked up. "So are we done? Would you like some wine?"

We went down into the kitchen, and three identically dressed *teenagerae femineae* scattered from the room, leaving the telltale boxes of opened cereal and sundry Coco Pop droppings—the usual evidence that there has been a gathering.

We sat and drank wine and talked about the delights of parenthood during the great end of school exams and invitation rites. She mentioned her son's particular commitment to French grammar, and I agreed that my daughter had also found this aspect of her education to be most enthralling. A book lay on a table in the kitchen. *French Grammar: A Revision Course*. It looked unruffled.

A large cat flounced through the room and sat on me as the conversation drifted into a haze of wine and coffee. I felt very at home. "Who plays the piano?"

"I do."

"And who feeds the cockatoos?"

"My daughter."

I looked amazed. "A teenage daughter who does chores?"

"Well. She does it most of . . . some of the time."

The stability of my universe restored itself.

We then started to conform to the expected behavior of the *adulta feminea*. The subspecies that eats excellent cheese and posh olives and drinks only red wine. How could she be so lovely and so clever? She wasn't a bit like the stuffy academics that I'd met at university.

When talk turned to men, she came up with an excellent suggestion that I'd like to pass on to you in case it comes in useful.

"I've thought of a new variation in the case of a man who wants to prove true love. Just like in the old fairy tales, you set three tests. The first needs to be very, very easy, to encourage him and give him confidence. The second harder, but still achievable by any ordinary mortal. And then when he comes to you for the third, say that he must install the Dalai Lama in his palace at the Potala in Tibet and bring back proof that he has done so."

I wanted to turn her into my fairy godmother. To tell her my life story, and my daughter's life story, and seek her advice on love, life, my future, and anything else I could think of. Instead I dragged myself out as I knew I had to. Out into the night. Home to read my history books.

So now, a little later and with the benefit of study, for any of you who are still lost: The Chinese invaded Tibet to enforce their claim of historical dominion—a dominion that had never actually existed. They had invaded to "liberate" Tibet from the "influence of Western imperialists." The Tibetans' response, that since there were no imperialists in Tibet they did not need liberating from them, was irrelevant. International governments stood by silently and let the Communists take over.

From that day to this, the Dalai Lama has continued to put the case for Tibetan freedom by following the Buddhist path of nonviolence. The world has given him a Nobel Peace Prize. And then ignored him.

WAKING UP IN KATHMANDU

This morning I woke up in Kathmandu. Which is strange because I could have sworn I went to sleep in Battersea.

And then it came back to me. A thought had entered my head and refused to go away. It had sat there. In fact it had placed itself right in the middle of the front row of what few other thoughts I had, until everything else was obscured from view. To some small degree I wanted to know for myself what I was talking about. I needed some personal experience. I needed to see Tibet for myself. Go to Tibet. There it was.

Not one of the most practical thoughts I've ever had. Voices of sanity warned of the impossibility of the task. The Chinese authorities only allow groups being shown approved locations by a Chinese propaganda spokesman—er, I mean "guide." Without officially forbidding it, they make travel by individuals virtually impossible. All visits to the "Tibetan Autonomous Region of China" require special permits, on top of the visa, for every 200 yards that you want to travel, and they are known for changing the permit requirements every forty-nine seconds.

The Lonely Planet guide stated that although the Tibet Tourism Bureau Permit was a necessity, no one had ever actually seen one. The permit is only good in theory—but in practice, apparently, whichever permit you have it will never be the right one. Your permit would be for a piece of road that has now become officially "closed" and may not be used until next spring. You could be forgiven for thinking I'm exaggerating here.

"I thought the Chinese were trying to encourage tourism?" I would ask innocently of various travel agents in London.

"Only if you want to see the Great Wall of China or the Terracotta Warriors. Are you sure you wouldn't like to see the Great Wall? We do a very nice package, and it's discounted this month."

"Thank you. I'm sure the Great Wall is very, er, long." I didn't wish to appear rude. "But," I repeated my only thought like a mantra, "I want to go to Tibet."

"We can't help you then," they'd add huffily as if I were a personal affront to their profession.

One day I'd wandered into one of those shops designed for people who want to kill themselves. Ropes, strange rock-climbing tools, and tents for temperatures of −50° hung about. I'd wandered in hotfoot from meeting a "man from the BBC." I was wearing a pink silk dress and high-heeled shoes. I approached a tree-sized hulk.

"Hi! My name's Todd," he enthused. "What can I do for you today?"

"Well, I want to go to Tibet." I waited. He looked at me quizzically.

"What do you need?" he screwed his eyes up.

"I was hoping you could tell me."

"What's the altitude? How high are you going exactly?"

"I have no idea."

"I see. Hold on a moment." He wandered off to consult a colleague. They looked at me and talked out of the corners of their mouths. "It's over 5,000 meters in places," he said. "You'll need one of these." He pointed at a range of jackets designed for Michelin men. I put one on, and my arms stuck out at the side.

"Do you have anything slightly less, er, puffy?"

"Not for 5,000 meters. You'll need that. You have thermals?"

"No."

"You have boots?"

"No."

"You have a backpack?"

"I don't have anything." He was beginning to warm up. I vaguely wondered if he was on commission. I felt like a confused version of Julia Roberts in *Pretty Woman* who'd wandered into the wrong shop.

Eventually I'd struggled out with a lighter credit card. I couldn't carry everything in my heels so I was now wearing a pink silk dress and jacket, extra thick trekking socks, and boots. I felt very silly and very happy.

Now I needed some good advice. I went home, switched on my computer, and found Jeeves. "I want to go to Tibet," I typed in, and he bombarded me with organizations I should contact. I phoned a couple and found a girl called Emma at the Tibet Information Network. She was full of helpful tips. "You need to know not to squat down in the bushes on the Nepalese side of the Himalayas. I was caught short and while I was doing what every girl has to do, a leech attached itself to my thigh. I only discovered this when I looked down and my leg was pouring with blood."

"Well, thank you. That's a useful tip, then. Anything else?"

"Yes. You'd better come and see us."

So I made an appointment. Time to wise up.

They didn't sugar the pill much.

"Tibet is an occupied country. If you take pictures of the Dalai Lama and give them to people who ask for them, you are putting their lives in danger. You wouldn't give out illegal items in this country and expect to get away with it, so don't do it in the 'Tibetan Autonomous Region of China' either."

It was less "advice" than a formal briefing.

"If you want to go to prison in China, we suggest shouting 'Long live the Dalai Lama' or 'Free Tibet' in the center of Lhasa. If you want to endanger the lives of others, just find a public place to ask them their views on Tibetan independence. Several years ago there was a TV journalist living in Britain who wanted to do a documentary about how bad the human-rights situation is in Tibet. She interviewed local Tibetans who trusted her and spoke honestly and courageously about what they knew. Of course she made efforts to disguise them. She blacked out their faces and even used some distortion of the voices to protect them. But inevitably the Chinese found out who they were. We heard that six Tibetans were arrested as a result of her visit to Tibet. One of them was a nun who was held for six months and was tortured. And there are other stories about the carelessness of journalists asking monks if they are really loyal to the Dalai Lama. Of course they are but they can't say so."

The gist was that if I said or did anything unwise, I would be putting people's lives in danger. Even accepting simple hospitality or friendliness was unwise.

"The Tibetans are naturally hospitable people, but they are not permitted to let you stay in their homes unless they have a license, and very few licenses are given. If you are on the road and you accept a ride, you may be risking severe consequences for the person who gives you a lift. The right to pick up passengers requires a Chinese license."

This was a variation on "Have a good trip."

"Tibetans may want to tell you their stories in the belief that if Westerners know what is happening, things will change. But if you tell their stories, you may risk condemning your friendly host to imprisonment and torture."

"Anything else?"

"Yes. Don't give anyone pictures of the Dalai Lama. They are illegal."

"You mentioned that."

There is a wonderful irony here. Depending on your perspective, the Dalai Lama is either a living incarnation of the quality of compassion or, to take a less spiritual view, he is a monk whose job is to be the living incarnation of compassion. All his life he has been a student and a teacher of wisdom, compassion, and nonviolence, and yet the Chinese government forbids anyone to follow him. The official Chinese position is therefore: "He teaches compassion. Don't listen to him."

He has always instructed his people to give love in return for the horrors inflicted on them by the Cultural Revolution and insisted on cooperation with the Chinese authorities, asking only that people be left to practice their religion. He was so venerated that his photo was once the proud centerpiece of every home. I had intended to take in some photos, knowing how the people longed for them and the risks that they would run to own one. But I decided to heed the advice given to me and leave them at home. I didn't want anyone sent to prison because of my stupidity.

I left my Tibetan advisers with a heavy heart and walked out into a warm and sunny London.

A bus awning flashed by me: "Over 90% of accountants recommend Sage Software."

My mobile phone rang, and a friend announced that she had decided to have breast implants. She wasn't asking me what I thought. Just telling me. I descended into the Underground and levered my way into a train. The man next to me pressed himself against me in a way that felt decidedly inappropriate. Voices and images swirled around in my head. Snatches of conversation overheard across the car. I half listened, but my mind was a blur. I still had only one actual thought. I wanted to go to Tibet.

If you decide to do anything different in your life, Job's comforters appear. They are the "Be Careful" brigade.

"It's very dangerous."

"You're not doing this alone, are you?"

"The altitude sickness can kill you."

"What a crazy time to travel."

I have one wealthy and generous friend. I can tell why he has done so well in life. His voice always stands out from the others with a ring like a church bell on a frosty morning. "It's a wonderful idea. If you want to go, I'll give you the air miles."

I was humbled and amazed. I'd never traveled with anything before except "fourth-class super-double-cramped, don't try breathing in these seats" tickets. But when I boarded for the eight-hour flight to Delhi with the ticket my miracle friend had organized, I was shown into business class.

"What? This seat?" I stared at the bed-sized luxury recliner with buttons that adjusted it to every possible position.

"Yes—by the window."

I laughed. "You must be joking."

"No, madam. Would you care for an aperitif or some champagne before dinner?"

I thought of Mahatma Gandhi always traveling third class to be with the people. They brought me a bottle of red wine and asparagus tips for starters. Shame about the spiritual progress.

"Anything else we can do for you?"

"A manicure and pedicure would be nice."

He didn't know how to reply. I saw one of the other passengers smiling. "Reflexology?"

"Not today, madam."

So, alas, no pedicure. I'd have to make do with the four-course à la carte meal and the Cointreau. Then I fell asleep. Can't think why. And when I woke we were over Iran.

An entire landscape of brown and barren-looking hills. Not a touch of green as far as the eye could see. I just had to tell the other business-class passengers.

"Look! Look! Have you seen the landscape?"

"Yes," said an important-looking Indian executive. "We'll be passing Tehran soon. I do this trip once a month. Long, isn't it?"

"What? Have you seen down there?" I glued my face to the window.

"Mmm . . . ," he said, and fixed his eyes to his paper.

I stared down and wondered what percentage of all the people who have ever lived get to see the clouds from the top? How many struggle to stay alive in the desert, and how many fly through the sky above them? How could I do something with this position of extraordinary privilege that somehow I had been born into?

Why had I done almost nothing for my fellow creatures since being born on the planet? Did I really think that my £10 a month to Oxfam and my £10 to Greenpeace made a difference? I could probably feed a village on what I spent on coffee alone. Was this really all I was? Another consumer of capitalism on the King's Road? A follower of the "because you deserve it" school of justification for the best ever pair of boots? I wanted to have my perspective blasted away. I wanted to be so altered by all that I saw that the next time I saw great boots I would know I didn't need them.

In the meantime I was enjoying this flight. I was the recipient of another person's generosity.

I walked into the cockpit. (So much for security.)

"Hello," I said to the weary characters in the front with the stripes on their jackets. "I just wanted to tell you that I've never flown over anywhere except Europe before and I think this land is just amazing, and thank you for flying the plane."

"The plane flies itself. It's all automatic." It was true that they weren't touching anything. "But it's a good thing you are enjoying the view because it'll be dark in five minutes." I thought it always got dark slowly. And then it was dark.

I had to slope back to my seat and drink some more Cointreau. I pressed a button, and the footrest extended. I pressed another, and the seat lay down for me. I pressed a third, and a smiling man in a suit with shiny buttons appeared.

"What can I do for you?"

"Just some water, please. Mineral water, yes. French mineral water naturally carbonated and bottled and served just for me in a glass with ice and lemon."

And so it was that I came to wake up in Kathmandu.

MEETING KHENPO LA

I opened the door of the little room I seemed to be in, and there was a courtyard with benches and a square of grass. Three boy monks in orange and deep-red robes ran by. They had hitched up the long skirts between their legs so they could run more easily, which made it look as if they were wearing large red diapers. They all looked the same with their shaven heads, sunburnt faces, and huge carefree smiles. They were evidently playing hide-and-seek. I'd been given the name of a guest-house run by a monastery. The sound of deep horns, bells, and chanting started to echo out of the monastery. It was a strange, eerie sound. I wasn't at the convent of St. Mary the Virgin anymore.

There are lots of Tibetan monasteries in Kathmandu, and Tibetans have been escaping over the Himalayas to India and Nepal for fifty years. Here they have been able to study Tibetan Buddhism without also having to indoctrinate themselves with the teachings of a certain little red textbook.

I crossed the garden and stepped out into the tiny narrow streets with rivulets of mud flowing down the center. Old wooden houses leaned towards each other affectionately from either side of the road. The entire population seemed to be out in the street, already buying, selling, or simply surviving. Beggars aged two to ninety stared at me as I passed and held out their hands. One woman with stumps for lower limbs pulled herself through the dust like a lame dog.

Fantastically beautiful children with blue-and-white school uniforms linked arms and carted their satchels on their backs like children everywhere. Smiling Hindu women in bright saris floated by, looking decidedly middle class. Others, not so blessed in their births, sat in the gutter and sold vegetables. Everywhere Tibetan monks and nuns sat or walked, chatting and smiling.

I turned into a café in search of something resembling coffee. The menu offered cappuccino, so I sat down immediately. I felt rather out of place. It was five Tibetan monks and myself. I smiled at them. They smiled back and then went back to their chatter. They were curiously asexual. It wasn't like being in a room with five men. Not a leer, not a smirk, no eyes going up and down. No suppression and trying not to look either. I've met more than my fair share of Christian monks. Some of them were like this—comfortable with themselves—and some had fear written all over them as if I'd had a tail and horns and every inch of me a living incarnation of temptation. But not here. Here I had become an interesting part of the wallpaper. A postcard from an unknown location. One of them found some English.

"Where are you from?"

"London. England."

"Oh, England? Very good." Smile smile.

I morphed into a postcard of Tower Bridge. And that was it. They smiled, bowed, and left.

The little path that counted as a road, but was too narrow for anything except pedestrians and dogs, led to the Boudha Stupa. The postcards told me this was "The Biggest Stupa in the World." A stupa is a representation of the Buddha's mind. Or, if you are attempting to describe it, then it's a large bell-shaped construction with various levels that you can climb up and on while hundreds of passing pilgrims spin prayer wheels and light candles in front of numerous exotic Buddhist statues.

The prayer wheels are full of manuscripts of prayers, so spinning them is a bit like cheating on a Roman Catholic rosary where you have to say a thousand Hail Marys. In this case you can say one hundred and spin the rest. There are huge prayer wheels that you spin by pushing them as you walk around. On every rotation a bell rings and you hear the bell ringing all day long as the faithful walk the prayers while saying the prayers while spinning the prayers.

On top of the stupa the huge painted eyes of the Buddha look out in four directions. The whole edifice is layered with multicolored prayer flags. Some pilgrims do prostrations around it. They have wooden blocks on their hands, and they bend down and slide the blocks forward until they are flat out on the floor. Then they stand up and walk three steps to the point that was reached by their outstretched fingers. Then the next prostration. It's slow progress.

I walked around with everyone else and suddenly became part of the endless cycle of birth and rebirth. According to some Buddhist teachings, none of it is real. It is all a creation of our mind, and even our mind itself is unreal. That is why, as far as I had learned, even attachment to our own identity is futile. We don't take that with us to the next life. My life would go by as quickly as I could walk around. It took 347 steps to walk around the stupa. I thought of prostrating myself to slow the pace down a little and make my life longer. But perhaps not.

I stopped and opened the only Buddhist book I'd brought. *The Dhammapada*. It begins, "What we are today comes from our thoughts of yesterday and our present thoughts build our life of to-morrow: our life is the creation of our mind."

For an hour, perhaps two, I sat and watched the people. Most would smile at me as they passed, their lives interacting with mine for perhaps a second. Beggars, too. Faces that pointed at their mouths, saying, "Eat, eat." I had no change so I said no and then realized later that I had been denying them the equivalent of one penny. Five pence would have bought them a meal, and I had said no.

I tried to wander back to the guest-house and got lost. Retracing my steps I began to laugh at my hopeless sense of direction. I knew it was not five minutes from where I was standing, so I walked up and down, looking for anything familiar. None of the streets had names, and all the shops sold Buddha statues. I asked some shop-owners standing in a doorway, and a monk appeared from nowhere. "I'm walking that way. Would you like me to show you?"

"Thank you," I said, and he walked ahead of me, not speaking. I thought how odd this was, but when we reached the garden he sat on a bench to chat with me. His English was almost perfect, along with his five other languages.

"Your English is so good. Have you lived in England?"

"No, but I think it is important to speak English. I don't like American or cockney, and I especially don't like some accents from the north of England. I met some people from Manchester once, and I couldn't understand them at all."

I laughed. My friends in Manchester would love that. "Don't worry. I can't understand them, either. But where did you get your BBC English?"

"From books with good pronunciation guides. I'm self-taught, but I read a lot. If you would like to discuss the works of Shakespeare, I'd be glad to talk about them with you."

"Really?"

"I'm afraid I wasted a good deal of time reading English I could have spent in study of the dharma."

"Well, perhaps nothing is wasted."

"No. Quite right. As you say. Perhaps not. So how long are you staying in Kathmandu?"

"I hope to leave as soon as possible. I'm hoping to go on to Lhasa."

"You want to go to Tibet?"

"Yes. Do you know anyone who could assist me? I have a contact address for a travel firm, but I don't know where it is."

"Show me. I know this place. I can take you. We will need to take two buses and a rickshaw."

"Thank you. That is very kind of you. How fortunate I am to have met you."

"I am the only English-speaking monk in my monastery. There are thirty-six monasteries around the stupa, and very few monks speak English. Except to say, 'Where are you from?'" He assumed a heavy Nepali accent and made me laugh.

"Then God is good to me. Ah, but you don't believe in God, do you?"

This was evidently the funniest thing he'd ever heard.

"No, no. Quite right. We don't believe in God."

"Yet people do prostrations and light candles to give thanks and ask for things. I don't understand. Who are they asking?"

"It is complicated. But do you have a Chinese visa?"

"Yes. I got it in London. I pretended I was traveling to see the Great Wall."

"It's very difficult to get to Tibet. And the roads are very dangerous."

"I've heard there will be obstacles of many kinds, but I've got this far."

"Here it is warm, and you will not get sick here. You don't want to stay in Kathmandu?"

"It is beautiful here. But no."

"Very well. I'll help you. I will show you in the morning where to go. I will come here at 9 a.m." He got up.

"That is really very kind of you."

"Oh, I am a very kind person." He laughed. "But I have to go now. I have to teach a class."

"Can I come?"

"No, you cannot. You are not a monk."

Blast it. He was right. I wasn't a monk.

"Will you tell me tomorrow what you taught?"

"I will." And he was gone.

That night, sitting in a local café, some of the European residents in Kathmandu were, to say the least, a little skeptical about the "kindness" of my new friend.

"He'll be after a Western wife," said Rodney, a resident New Zealander.

"Or a sponsor," said Steen, a resident Danish film director.

"How do you know?"

"You see a lot of it when you live here."

"What?"

"I'm just a poor monk, and I have my parents and ten brothers and sisters to support." And the Westerner says, 'How much do you need, O wise monk?' and the monk says, 'Five hundred dollars a month should cover it.' They say some of them have many sponsors and can become quite rich."

They began to get into the swing of their storytelling.

"And single American women think it's a great idea to marry a monk. So he gets out of here to the West, which is what they all want, and she gets an interesting husband with lots of Buddha points," added the Kiwi.

"Or he may just be after sex," added Hans the beer-drinking German.

"Is it also possible that he's just being friendly?" I suggested radically.

"Unlikely, I'd say," said the Dane. They all thought me charmingly naïve.

So the following morning when he stood there in his maroon robes at 9 a.m., I was a little more guarded. But he came with me on the bus and translated for me until we had arranged all the travel to Lhasa.

I would go with a group on a seven-day tour and then lose the group as soon as I could when I arrived in Lhasa. Once I was there, as I had a long visa, there was little the Chinese authorities could do unless I gave them a reason to throw me out, which I didn't intend to do. We would travel there by "land cruiser." It sounded like a boat, but turned out to be a battered four-wheel drive. I asked for the super-economy version, but apparently the four-wheel option decreased my chances of death quite considerably. I would have to sit in the back as an "elderly American woman" was traveling in the group. So now I just had to hand over my passport with a small fortune in dollars and wait, much to my dismay, for another five days.

My monk took care of me. "Don't forget your receipt. That's your only proof that you have given him your passport."

We left the agency and climbed into a rickshaw—a seat on wheels attached to a tiny motor scooter. It chugged along for about fifteen minutes and then broke down.

"Would you like to have some lunch? We are just by a restaurant that sells good Nepali food."

I was very keen to spend some time with him. He couldn't have made the scooter break down, and he just seemed friendly to me. I couldn't believe he had any of the motives that the Europeans were so keen to suspect him of. And, I found myself thinking, he does have the most gorgeous eyes. But wait a minute—where did that thought come from? Surely I couldn't be that predictable? Unless of course I could. So what was going on here? I thought I'd broach the subject immediately.

"I met some resident Europeans, and they told me that you would be looking either for a sponsor or a wife."

He looked at me with a fabulous monklike grin.

"I don't think you are rich enough to be a sponsor. You are not Chinese and from Hong Kong. And I don't want a wife."

"Why not? I'm told Western wives are the fashion here."

"Wives bring problems. They divide you. You have to think everything twice or three times. Wives are not good. Then if your wife has problems, you have problems. Some monks leave and marry, and they always come back and tell us all their problems."

I listened and smiled back.

"I am a khenpo, and khenpos do not marry. Also it is not my habit—I have been a monk since I was eight, and I value my privacy. I love to be alone. I could not tolerate to have someone with me all the time. I do not want that."

I almost believed him. "Never?"

He smiled.

"Not in this lifetime."

I was completely fascinated. So was he real, or were the European locals right?

He was smiling at me quite comfortably, so I thought I'd follow an old workshop teaching: "Be outrageous."

"But tell me—and please forgive my curiosity—you study the Tantric tradition, don't you?"

He smiled, laughed, looked away, looked back at me, and then looked away again.

"We do. Yes."

Why not get to the heart of the subject immediately? "Isn't Tantric practice more fun with two?"

"The Tantric practice is not about feeling pleasure. It is possible to feel pleasure so that every hair stands on end. But it's not that."

"No?" I gathered he was referring to the spiritual aspects of the practice.

"Many men do not know how to give women pleasure, and many women do not feel much at all." I couldn't believe I was hearing this.

"But . . . ," he continued, looking around the restaurant with a seemingly inordinate interest in the decor. "Let's eat lunch."

I wanted to say, "No, I'm most interested. Please go on." But his manner did not invite contradiction. He was a man who was used to saying, "Let it be so," and it became so. Suddenly I was a novice. So I shut up and ate lunch. I found his company confusing and fascinating. He seemed to be completely uninterested in mine.

I looked up at him. "Do you have any questions that you'd like to ask me?"

"No."

Shucks, and there I was thinking that I may have learned something of value in my lifetime that I could have passed on.

"What do you enjoy doing most?" I asked, still trying to figure him out.

"Reading and studying."

I would have expected him to say meditation.

"Do you meditate?"

"Not much."

He seemed lonely to me, but I was so confused I couldn't tell if that was a projection of my loneliness onto him and whether he was in fact perfectly centered. Was it him who was lonely, or was I?

The eyes of the Buddha at the stupa are said to reflect whatever the viewer experiences. Some say the eyes are angry, some sad, and some compassionate. My new friend felt like this to me. As if, to use a Christian phrase, he had "died to himself" and just become a vehicle of kindness. He was laughing and smiling, and yet I felt as if he wasn't there. Even his name, Khenpo, is not a name but a role—the closest translation or academic equivalent being Professor. It was as if a Western doctor just called himself Doctor and was so fully identified with the role that he ceased to have a self-identity beyond it.

I found him impossible to connect with because he didn't identify with what we in the West call his "self." And if he was not himself connected with himself, then how could I connect with him? His beliefs taught him that identity was an illusion, and so it had no meaning for him. He was there and yet not there.

How many Zen masters does it take to change a lightbulb? Two. One to change the bulb, and one not to change it.

"Would you like ice cream?"

"Yes," I smiled. "That would be lovely." We walked along, the monk and the Western woman, and I had to remind myself not to link arms. All eyes turned in our direction, but I couldn't decide which of us they were staring at.

We clambered into a local bus where his earlier request that I not touch him was useless. He chatted in Nepali and made everyone on the bus laugh. Another man spoke to me in English. Then suddenly the khenpo said, "This is Boudha. You get out here. I'll see you later."

"Oh. OK. Thank you. And thank you for helping me with the tickets."

I went back to my room for a ten-minute nap that lasted three hours.

YAK TEA WITH THE RINPOCHE

I didn't see "my monk," as I began to call him in my head, for a couple of days after that. I went climbing in the hills and riding through the dusty streets on the back of the Danish film director's motorbike and met other weird and wonderful characters in the cafés around the stupa. It was easy to make friends.

Then one morning there was a tap on my door. It was 9 a.m., and I was still in bed. I staggered to the door sleepily. The khenpo stood smiling at me. No wonder he was amused. His day started at 5 a.m. I felt ridiculous in my pajamas.

"Hello. Would you like to eat breakfast?"

"Yes, thank you, Khenpo. Can you give me five minutes?"

"I can give you ten."

I showered in three and appeared, trying to look as if I'd been meditating or something.

"You want to eat Tibetan bread?" And he strode off while people bowed to him as we passed. "Khenpo La," they'd say. *La* is a term of respect and honor. We ducked into a café but were still followed by a monk, making a long speech and bowing profusely.

"What is it?" I asked.

"He wants me to write letters for him. He can't write. I'll do it for him. I do it all the time. I need a secretary and an office."

We ate breakfast while the itinerant monk continued to make supplications. I dearly wished that he would go away. He eventually did—only to be replaced by a second, better-dressed monk, also bowing.

"And what does this one want?"

"He is asking me to go to the hospital with him. There are some people there who need help. I'll go tomorrow. He's happy now." More bowing.

Eventually they all went away, and he looked at me. He seemed to invite intimacy.

I put my hand up towards him, not touching him but with my elbow on the table with my palm facing him. I was inviting him to do the same—to leave a space if he liked or to touch my hand if he wanted to. My nonverbal communication was lost on him. Instead he peered at my hand. Then he began to stare intently at it. Then he burst into a joyous laughter.

"What is it?" I laughed, too.

"You could have made a great deal of money when you were twenty-six or twenty-seven, but you missed the chance." He chuckled.

"Oh well, I'm glad that amuses you. May I touch your hand?" I asked.

"She is so naughty." He looked away, enjoying it all the same.

I moved my hand away and smiled at him.

"I think you are quite naughty, too."

"Oh yes. I have 105 faults."

"You've counted them?"

He suddenly looked at his watch anxiously. "I have to go now. I will come to see you later."

"OK." And he was gone, followed by a monk who appeared from nowhere.

I asked myself why I'd wanted to touch his hand. Was I being disrespectful? But it was he who had invited me. What were my real motives by that gesture? Would I invite him to visit me in London?

I ordered some more tea. I was confused by this attractive, funny, and rather lovely monk, whose celibate state mirrored my own. His was chosen, and so, at this point in my life, was mine. I had no "significant other"—any more than he did. I suspected that I was confusing him, too. His decision not to complicate his life with women felt absolutely solid. And yet he still wanted to see me in every spare moment that he had. I would have to gather a little of the serenity I was here to find. This man, however attractive, was a monk, I reminded myself. And I must not ask to touch his hand.

That morning a distraction had been arranged. The film director had suggested that I go and visit a local Rinpoche. This is an honorific title meaning "precious one" that is given to a monk in the highest position in his monastery. This one was famous for his way with Westerners. He had been "studying the Western mind" for twenty-seven years. As a result of this he was an abbot, not only of his own monastery but also of a huge school of Buddhism that attracted hundreds of students annually from Europe and America. There were genuinely holy men, I'd heard, and then those who had found out how to make money from the spiritually starved Westerners. Then I suppose there were those in the second group who considered that they were also in the first. I was curious to go and have a look at one for myself.

I found his monastery easily and entered a room where a small man sat on a slightly raised platform. Around him sat two monks, about six students with a range of interesting faces whose places of birth I couldn't even guess at, and an American woman of about my age.

I was supposed to come with a question. But I had no question.

He had plenty for me. "How did you hear of me?" I was unwilling to tell him about the Danish film director, so I simply smiled gently and said, "I heard that you have been studying the Western mind for twenty-seven years and that I should come and meet you."

"But how did you know this?"

"Hasn't everyone heard of you?"

He smiled. "Are you from the BBC?"

"No. I'm not."

"Some people came from the BBC, and they asked me, 'What are all the holy places in Buddhism?' So I listed the towns where the Buddha was born and where he traveled. And they asked, 'How do we get to those places?' So I said, 'You can fly or get a taxi, but a taxi is very expensive.'"

We all laughed. He explained that the interviewer should have been asking about the spiritual journey of Buddhism and how you travel. But as the question was asked in a literal form, he replied in a literal form.

"Anyway . . . ," he continued, "I forgot about this rather silly interview, but some months later wherever I went people would say "I saw you on television," and they were very excited. Finally a year later I was very honored to be invited to a conference where I was to meet His Holiness the Dalai Lama. I was so overwhelmed and so full of devotion, and you've guessed the first thing he said, haven't you? 'Ah it's you! I saw you on TV.'"

He turned to me again. "Are you from Oxford?"

"No, I'm not from Oxford."

"I studied in Oxford, you know."

"Oh really?" I have heard that, on first meeting, it takes any old Oxford student a maximum of five minutes to mention that they studied there. So this was true to form.

"Oxford is very prestigious." He imitated an upper-class English accent and put his nose in the air for the entertainment of his tea party. He was funny.

"What did you study there?" I asked.

"Science and mathematics."

So much for Buddhist philosophy.

"In England," he continued in an upper-class accent, "they are very interested in class. They know what class someone is from after they speak one sentence. Isn't that so?"

I could not deny it. "Often this is so, yes."

"What about you? You seem to be high class."

"No, not me," I said. "To be high class you have to have family. My mother and father were not married, so I'm certainly not high class. I'm what they call 'middle class.'" What an absurd conversation.

"But you are very beautiful," he went on. I wasn't sure where this was leading. "You are beautiful like the flowers in that vase there. But come back in two weeks and see how the flowers look." He turned to his audience. "You see I will make her angry."

"No," I said. "You won't. You don't have the power to make me angry unless I give it to you. And I do not give it to you."

While I said this I noticed that his assumption that he could make me angry irritated me. So I suppose he had already succeeded. His admirers chuckled. He switched to Tibetan, and while he was in full flow I whispered to the American woman, "Do you speak Tibetan?"

"I'm learning."

Then swapping back to English he explained that it is considered rude in England to speak in a language that not all those present speak if you are able to speak inclusively.

He turned to me again. "What do you do in London?"

So even Buddhist abbots who are called Rinpoche ask that question. I hesitated.

"I'm a mother. And I write a little."

"Oh, are you a journalist?"

"No, I'm not a journalist."

"Are you studying Buddhism?"

"No. I'm traveling to Lhasa."

"You are going to Tibet?"

"Yes." For the first time everyone in the room looked impressed.

"What are you going to do in Lhasa?"

"Look. See. Be. I shall 'be' in Lhasa."

"When you get there, find a statue of the Buddha, sit in front of it, and let your heart become calm and kind."

"Thank you. I'll do that."

"And be sure not to be kicked by the Chinese police."

More laughter.

"If they kick me, I shall smile at them."

I was presented with a cup of yak-butter tea. It tastes really horrible, but I had been warned that the only thing worse than hot yak-butter tea was cold yak-butter tea. So I drank it quickly.

Then food arrived. But it was for the students, not for the American lady or me.

"Thank you for coming." He handed me some information about his school. The American lady was a student in her fourth year. Her course was eight years.

I invited her to join me for lunch. We were both full of questions for each other.

She began, "How come you didn't ask Rinpoche questions? Most people go with questions."

"I thought that whatever I asked the answer would be 'Have more compassion.'"

"What do you mean?"

"What is the most important thing you have learned? 'To have compassion.' What should I ask you? 'About compassion.' If there was only one thing I could learn from you, what would you want it to be? 'To practice compassion.' Love, kindness, compassion—isn't that what it's all about?"

"I suppose so."

"So I thought I'd just go and see what happened."

"I see."

"Can I ask you some questions?"

"Sure."

"How would Tibetan Buddhism define enlightenment? Sorry, I know that's a bit of a cliché, but it isn't the same as being happy and at peace, is it?"

"That's part of it. But no. We all have the Buddha nature within us, but it is masked as clouds mask the sun. Our path is to remove the faults that obscure the complete manifestation of our Buddha nature."

"Are all our faults the same?"

"In a sense. Our chief fault is our idea that we have a fixed and permanent identity."

"Don't we?"

"No. It is an illusion. You need to get past the idea that you have a permanent self."

"But don't I?"

"No. Think about it. Are you the same person as you were when you were six? Everything about you is different. Every cell in your body. Every thought in your head."

"And what about the part that goes with us when we die? What Christians call the soul?"

"There are different parts of the 'self.' There is the form, the feelings, the perception, the emotions and habitual tendencies, and the conscious intelligence. The personality and the form do not reincarnate."

"But if my personality doesn't survive, then I've died, haven't I?"

"That depends on who you think you are. Are you your thoughts?"

"No. I know I'm not what I think because I can watch my thoughts come and go. I suppose I think that 'I,' the real me, is the part that watches. What part is that?"

"Now that, as we say in the U.S., is the million-dollar question. If you are not your body, your thoughts, or your emotions, who are you?"

I suppose I had always had some vague notion that this "higher self" or "soul" or the spiritual bit of me was just present. I'd never given much thought to what this part of me was. Or was not. It's a rather scary thought to think of only parts like our habits and attachments reincarnating. But it does explain child prodigies. How could Mozart play the piano and write music at four years old? Possibly because he had spent his previous lifetime with music and somehow remembered?

"I understand one thing better now anyway." I'm a slow student.

"What's that?"

"I've always wondered why everything in Buddhism takes so long. If you have to practice all the disciplines until all your faults are gone, I can understand that might take some years. I sometimes think that this very patience stands against justice for the Tibetans. They have such hope, and the world does nothing."

"Exactly."

"Have you ever met an enlightened person? One who completely revealed the Buddha nature?"

"I believe so. I met the late Khyentse Rinpoche. He was one of the Dalai Lama's tutors. If I have ever met an enlightened person, it was he. But I'm not an expert."

"But you can say what you think."

"I can, but if someone who has studied very little art says, 'This is the most beautiful painting in the world,' would you believe them?"

"Did you ask him about enlightenment or about Tibet? Could I meet him?"

"Not the version of him you want. He died, and his reincarnation is a young boy. I have to go now."

"I hope you have a good life or a good many lives."

"Thank you. You, too."

I wandered through the dusty streets, having decided to give money to all the beggars I met. I gave them each the equivalent of ten pence—a generous gift by local standards. Enough for them to buy a meal and for me to ease my conscience a little. I wandered back to my room and tried to think about who I was not and remember that I was not myself; of monks and nuns who were not their thoughts, traveling through the mountains to try to reach freedom to think as they pleased. I fell asleep, leaving my form as an offering for the evolved mosquitoes of Kathmandu.

SHE IS SO NAUGHTY

I was woken by a gentle tap on the door. Oh joy! It was my fascinating and inscrutable monk. Why was he visiting me? Maybe he just wanted to practice his English? He was utterly compelling.

"Do you want to eat something?" he asked.

In a second I was thrown into a delightfully subtle turmoil about my behavior and motives. From one moment to the next I couldn't work out whether I wanted something from him or whether he wanted something from me and if so, what it was for either of us, and if not, what exactly was the nature of our friendship? Should I feel flattered that he was spending his time with me? Was I being irresponsible by flirting with him or allowing him to flirt with me? Was this harmless fun between two human beings who obviously liked each other? Did he just want money, sex, or marriage like the cynical local Westerners said? Or was he a genuinely holy man whom I was confusing by making him laugh?

I couldn't answer any of these questions. But I did know that I wanted dinner.

"Can we go somewhere where people won't know you?"

"I am known everywhere in this place."

"What about the American cafés?" I asked.

"I never go to those places."

"Yes. Exactly."

"And they are expensive."

It's all relative. Dinner for two—fifty pence.

"I'll pay."

"I don't want you to pay."

"Don't be silly."

I turned into an American restaurant. He had no option but to follow. It was full of Westerners and mercifully free of monks. We found a quiet corner.

I wanted to learn a little about him, so I asked him about his day. It had started at five with prayers, then study, then more prayers, then teaching, then "helping people," which seemed to take up every afternoon, then more prayers, then teaching the monks again.

"And now I help you."

It was so perplexing. Was he seeing me as a lost visitor that it was his religious obligation to help, or was he enjoying my company? If it was the second, then why did he say, "I help you."

I told him about my morning visit to the Rinpoche. He began a speech.

"All we Tibetan monks are very grateful to that Rinpoche. He leads many hundreds of Westerners into the way of the dharma." Pause. "And that is good."

I listened.

"So we are grateful to him."

"That's nice."

"On the other hand, he has two Mercedes."

"Really?" I was genuinely shocked.

"But I should not say these things."

I laughed.

"There is so much suffering here, and the monasteries often do nothing for what is here. This afternoon a woman came to me, crying because her husband beats her. She is a low-caste Hindu woman. She is begging with three children and a tiny baby. The men here are terrible. They should be . . ." He stopped and laughed. "But I should not say these things."

I looked at him.

"Why is she looking at me?"

"Because you are so funny."

"She looks for the guest-house and I show her, and she is going to Tibet and I help her. She asks all these questions. She is so funny."

"Hey!" I said. "Are you talking to me? We have a quaint tradition in England of using the second-person singular. You know. The 'you' form."

"She is so funny."

I kicked his foot under the table. Then I did it again more gently and started to shock myself again.

"If I do this without trying to hurt you, it is called playing footsie. You can play it better if you are not wearing shoes."

He threw back his head and laughed. "She is so naughty."

He had a roundish face looking quite Oriental. When I asked him where he came from, he was forced to draw me a map because I'd never heard of Sikkim. When I think of a "Tibetan," I imagine the Tibetan nomads with their burnt brown skin, their bright clothes, and their huge smiles. The man opposite me looked nothing like this. He had what I'd describe as a flattish face with shining brown eyes and more an olive complexion than the burnt faces of Tibet. I looked at him. He had the wickedest twinkle.

But what was I thinking? Was I being drawn into some devi-
ously clever escape plan of his? Who was the cat, and who the
mouse? I forced myself to stop flirting.

"Tell me about your mother and father."

"My father is a little bit weak man with big heart. My mother is
very strong woman, also with big heart. They look after many
people. They sent me to the monastery when I was eight. So now I
look after them. I was an investment."

"But surely they loved you and sent you believing it would be
the best thing for you?"

"Not so much. My brothers were not very bright, so they sent
me. My younger sisters, they study and get good education, and I
support them."

I waited for him to say, "So a check for five hundred dollars a
month would be useful . . . ," but he didn't say it.

His conversation was like his gaze and jumped all over the
restaurant. I found his habit of not looking at me when he spoke to
me totally bewildering. I'd also catch him looking at his watch.
"Am I boring you?" I asked. He threw back his head and laughed
again. A deep open laugh.

"She is so funny."

Then he paid the bill. I pleaded with him.

"Excuse me. Could you not do that, please? Won't you let me
pay?"

"That's OK," he said. "So you have to pick up your passport and
tickets tomorrow? I will come with you. You want to eat Tibetan
bread for breakfast? I'll meet you at ten."

"Thank you. That would be very kind." By now I knew my way
around the area where I was staying, but the center of Kathmandu
was another world. We walked back to my guest-house. He had another unnerving habit of walking ahead of me all the time. I just
noticed it and let it be.

Then we sat on a bench and chatted for about an hour, and his
hand touched mine. And our fingers stayed touching, hidden under

the strips of deep red cloth that made up his robes. It felt wonderfully illicit. We laughed. And I was still wondering whether I was the cat or the mouse.

The next morning I was up at six, writing, thinking, and walking around the stupa. I watched the faithful "crossing themselves" the Buddhist way. They touch their head, mouth, and chest—thoughts, speech, and heart—and they walk around and around.

After I'd walked around three times, I was ready to call on the Danish film director for coffee.

"So? Has he proposed to you yet?"

"You are *so* cynical."

"Yes. But I have lived here for some years. I could tell you some stories."

"I'm sure you could."

"Incidentally, I meant to tell you to buy Diamox. It's a drug that may keep you alive at altitude. Loads of people die every year, you know. Traveling in Tibet."

"Everyone keeps telling me. And some people come back safely, I presume? My guidebook says, 'Do not take Diamox as you won't then know how ill you are and some people die because of it.' So I wasn't going to take any. Oh, OK. Write the name down."

"Diamox. Would you like breakfast?"

"Er, no thanks. Places to go, you know. People to see."

"Breakfast as well now, is it?"

"Might be."

"It must be in your karma. Most visitors come to Kathmandu and don't even find the stupa let alone meet a khenpo."

"My karma or his? For good deeds in a previous life? Or bad ones?"

"You must have known him in a previous life, or you wouldn't have met him."

"If you say so. I'll ask him what he thinks."

"Supper tonight?"

"Can I let you know?"

CLOSED GATES

I strolled through the hot muddy streets. The same beggars held out their hands. I was bored of giving money so I was giving out apples today. I gave a child the comb that had been a free gift on the flight and was still in my pocket. He looked at me as if he'd won a grab bag.

Then there was the khenpo walking down the street. "Khenpo La," I greeted him with the customary greeting of honor that I had observed everyone approaching him with.

"Do you make fun of me?"

"No. Not at all."

We ate a quick breakfast while he spoke to everyone in the room but me. Or maybe they spoke to him and he replied. I couldn't tell.

As we came out we found a man selling birds. To my horror he had green parrots, crows, budgerigars, and little tropical birds. They were all for sale for next to nothing.

"Khenpo. Wait. Is it safe to release these little birds here?" I asked.

"If we take them to the monastery garden."

"OK. How many of these little ones can I buy for £5?"

He negotiated with the bird seller for a long time. Finally he said, "Twenty-six. But I'll get them. If you buy them, he'll double the price."

So we bought twenty-six very distressed little birds, took a detour through the gardens, and released them.

He smiled as we watched them fly away. Brightly colored feathers fluttered among the leaves and disappeared. Two sat side by side on a branch, singing to each other.

"This will add many days to your lifetime."

"That's good because I've killed a lot of mosquitoes in my time."

"That's bad."

We took two bone-shaking buses into the town center. Little boys of about eight that all looked like Nepali versions of the Artful Dodger collected all the money and held on to the bus-vans at extraordinary angles.

"How many of these boys are killed every year?" I asked.

"None. It's their business. They are used to it." I produced a Murraymint from my pocket and offered it to the smiling boy monkey, who put it in his mouth immediately.

The tourist office where I was to collect my tickets was above a shop in a street with no numbers and no name. I wondered how they received any mail. "The travel place above the seventh tourist shop along in the street three blocks down from the roundabout." I was glad I had a guide. Khenpo gabbled on in Nepali. Wouldn't it be good to speak six languages?

"You need to give them your tickets back to England so that they can confirm your returning flights. But they are OK. You can trust them." So I gave them my tickets back from Nepal to London. And they gave me tickets for Tibet. My heart sang.

The last night in Kathmandu came. A local Swedish woman told me a story.

"In 1990 I made the trip to Lhasa, and there was a young German boy traveling with us. He got altitude sickness, and eventually we had to take him to hospital. The Chinese doctors said it was not safe to move him, but we all knew he needed to be got out of there. Everyone gave money for a helicopter, but the Chinese said they didn't have one. We were all desperate to do something. No one could accept what was happening. He died. He was twenty-three."

"Thanks for that."

"Many people die every year."

"Why does everyone keep telling me this? Some also get through alive, I believe?"

"That is true."

Seeing my optimism, she eventually gave up trying to warn me and went away. I hung around. I wanted to see Khenpo and not have dinner with anyone else. But no sign of him.

I strolled down the street to the stupa and went to say goodbye to the Danish film director.

"So, you leave tomorrow? Do you have Diamox now? If the bus breaks down, take it and start walking down. Or you die."

"I see." He handed me two packs of tablets. "You want to eat with my friends and me tonight?"

"No. I mean—no, thank you. I have an appointment."

"An appointment?" He laughed out loud in a rather raucous fashion. "I see. Good luck, then."

"Thank you. And for the Diamox. And everything."

I walked out into what was now the dark. Pilgrims walked around the stupa. I joined them. I walked around repeating the prayer that was on all their lips. *Om mani padme hum.* It felt like "May I be at peace." I felt very blessed. Nervous about the journey ahead, but blessed. Elderly women sat begging. I gave them all small amounts of money. I live in the West. I can afford to. They would look up in surprise and delight if I gave the equivalent of ten pence.

Back at the guest-house and still no sign of my friend. Maybe I had imagined . . . imagined what? What did I want from him? What did he want from me? Still I didn't have an answer. Then there he was. All smiles.

"Have you eaten?"

"No." Trying to sound nonchalant.

"OK. We go eat, then. Are you ready? Are your things in order?"

"Yes."

"Good."

So we went and sat in a little café in the back of nowhere. For about three minutes we were alone, then an elderly couple arrived. They bowed profusely at my companion and smiled profusely at me.

"This man did the painting on the walls of our monastery."

"The whitewash or the figures?"

"The characters. He is an artist."

I bowed at the old man and his wife while an enthusiastic three-way conversation began. In Tibetan.

Thirty minutes later we had all finished eating. The couple got up to leave. They bowed. I bowed. We all bowed.

We ordered black tea. I said nothing. I figured if I didn't, he may eventually say something.

"I hope she has a safe journey."

I smiled. He went on . . .

"I hope you have a safe journey."

What a shift. Suddenly he was not talking about me, he was talking to me. I looked at him. He looked at me and continued.

"I like you very much."

My heart leapt inside me. I should say nothing more often. I continued to keep quiet.

"You are pretty. You have a good heart. You are funny. And you impress me because you are not good at counting money."

"You like it that I'm hopeless with money?"

"Yes. So many people have always their calculators. You don't do this."

I didn't like to admit that I'm pretty well innumerate. I looked at him.

"Thank you, Khenpo. I like you, too. You also have a big heart and a good one, and you too are funny. And I like it that you calculate everything in your head."

"You could turn my life upside down, but I do not open the heart gate. I follow my head. I am a khenpo."

"You choose when to open the heart gate and when not to?"

"Yes. I do not open."

"That is OK. I don't open mine either then."

And we looked at each other. Him from behind his gate and me from behind mine.

HEAD IN THE CLOUDS

BREATHE IN, BREATHE OUT

The journey started at six in the morning on a bumpy bus. We bounced along while dry, dusty, and beautiful Nepal flew by outside. When we started it was flat, but very soon the bus began to climb up brown hills and through the scraggly villages with dusty faces, dusty roadside stalls, and dusty cows that stood in the middle of the road. The bus driver smiled and honked his horn at them.

When we reached the border it was still early afternoon. I knew the overnight stop was only just beyond the border so I thought we had made good time. I had of course imagined that it would take less than four hours to get through the border. After relaxed and friendly Nepal, the Chinese officialdom was almost comical.

"Stand there! Make a line! Wait!"

And wait we did. We were numbered and sorted and divided into groups of eight and then renumbered and made to queue up in the order in which our names appeared on their lists. We filled in forms. Then more forms, then more forms.

A box hung on the wall for "Complaints at the Border." We laughed about it, and one young Frenchman joked about dropping in a Dalai Lama picture or an anonymous note saying, "You are ridiculous." But perhaps not.

Meanwhile I was concerned about who was about to be forced onto whom for the next five days. One woman looked completely out of place among the sundry backpackers and potential Everest trekkers. She was dressed in lively colors and pulling a suitcase and was, er (how can I put this nicely?), surprisingly overweight. She peered up over the border.

"Gee, is that Shangri-La?"

"No," I said, being rather a killjoy, "that's what they call 'China.'" It began to rain. More Chinese officials arrived and herded us, sheeplike, into a construction resembling an oversized municipal bus shelter.

We were all asked to produce our visas, passports, tickets, proof that we were in a group, details that showed where the group was going, and details of our departure, including air tickets out of China. Several of us, including me—as I hadn't anticipated needing these tickets for weeks—cursed while pulling sundry personal items out of knapsacks for everyone else's entertainment. Pink pajamas?

After a further inexplicable hour's delay in which the officials presumably looked for any reason they could find to turn anyone back and various trekkers were seen bursting into tears, our group of eight was herded through to the final checkpoint.

"Visa!" said a uniform with a woman's face above it.

"Visa, please," I said, with a big smile. No reaction.

"Where did you get this visa?" I had just written this information down twice.

"In London. At the Chinese embassy."

They couldn't understand how I had obtained the right to be in Tibet for up to thirty days. I decided not to explain. "I said I thought the Terracotta Warriors would be very nice at this time of year."

She scowled at me.

"Plane ticket!"

My unsolicited lesson in courtesy had been lost on her. I smiled sweetly and handed her the ticket.

"What will you do in China?"

"I'm going to Lhasa," I said. I didn't really consider that Lhasa was China anyway. But perhaps she wasn't the best person to try to influence with my thoughts on an analytic approach to the study of history.

I added, "To see the Potala Palace."

She went on looking at me. I was obviously trouble, but she had no reason to detain me. Under "Profession" I had written "Mother."

I decided to reassure her. "I'm sightseeing. I'm a tourist."

"You go!" I was hustled forward by an official in a manner that would probably be called "assault" in California. But I was through. One more bridge, and I'd be in Tibet. My heart smiled as I walked over the bridge. On the other side was a large plaque in Chinese with some translation. It read: "Brief Moment of Friendship Bridge."

I think the irony had been lost somewhere. I thought this genuinely funny and pulled out my camera. A uniform appeared from nowhere. "No photo! No photo!"

"Of the bridge?"

"No photo!"

It was no photo, then.

Rows of tacky shops lined the border on the Chinese side, selling reproduction paintings in huge frames and brightly colored washing-up bowls. I didn't see anyone stop—"Ah yes, just what I needed." Bored shop-owners all sat and watched their color TVs, on which some violent fighting seemed to be taking place. Chinese music blared out from loudspeakers. So this was my first sight of the deeply Buddhist and devout Tibet.

From among the crowd, faces that were to be our guides for the next five days were trying to find out which sheep had been assigned to them.

"Eeezibeel Londone?" said one.

"Yup. That must be me."

"My name is PJ. I am your guide."

I had insisted on a Tibetan guide, saying that I'd rather not come than have a Chinese guide. He looked relaxed and interesting, with an American baseball cap worn back to front.

"You're not Chinese, are you?"

"No. I'm Tibetan."

"Interesting Tibetan name you have there, PJ."

I was delighted. My insistence had paid off. I'd been told that out of about 450 guides working in the whole of Tibet, more than 70 percent were Chinese, and more Tibetan guides were being replaced each year. No reasons were given for their dismissal, and there was no chance to take anyone to court in this country. They just didn't have jobs anymore. So I'd been lucky. As had the American lady with the suitcase. She would be sharing the jeep. And a young Dutch couple. The driver, into whose hands we were about to place our lives, looked about eighteen.

PJ looked at the motley crew that was to become his responsibility for the next five days. "We are two on the front seat? Sit with me?" It was me or the lady behind me.

"I don't mind sharing the front seat," I said and turned to her. "You don't mind the back?"

"I'm certainly not sharing my seat with this young man."

"OK, then." It was intimate. I either had to put my arm around the stranger or end up on the driver's knee. The land cruiser started its long journey up. It got colder and colder, and outside it got darker. We made very slow and bumpy progress along, well, it could not be described as a road. "Scary, thin mud track" might be closer. Amusingly the Chinese have named it the Friendship Highway.

"We call this Hell Road," said the guide cheerfully, while the lady in the back said, "Oh gee, this is bumpy," approximately every four minutes. Eventually the track flattened, we turned onto a road that led into a village, and stopped. It was bitterly cold. Since the start of the day we had climbed 2,000 meters. I felt nauseous and frozen. I silently thanked the smiling Todd in London for selling me an absurdly puffy jacket.

The guest-house had one heated room in which the tourists ate. The rest was unheated for "everyone else." I felt an instant desire to eat with "everyone else," but the piles of yak meat and clouds of cigarette smoke drove me in with my fellow travelers.

People who travel always complain, don't you find? It's a bit of a mystery to me. Why go to a remote area of Tibet and then moan that things aren't like they are at home?

"Have you seen the toilet? It's just a hole in the floor! Isn't it disgusting? And there's no hot water, you know."

I began to alienate myself from the group with skill. "There is hot water. It's in the huge thermos in the corner of the room. Those flasks keep the water hot all night long."

"I should think so. I shall tell my travel agent when I get back home that the rooms aren't heated, because she didn't mention that in Hamburg."

Outside, local boys tapped on the window, with big smiles, shouting, "Pen?"

"I hate to see children begging," said the young Dutchman, and he drew the curtains. I thought that if I were a boy of eleven and lived in this village I'd be there smiling and saying "Pen?"

I sat and ate vegetables and rice and wondered why I seemed to disagree with almost everyone I was traveling with on almost everything. I was feeling too sick to eat. But I had pens. I had been given 300 by friends in London to give to local schools, as the Lonely Planet guide suggested. I thought the schools could spare a few. I got up from the table and walked outside and was giving out pens just as the young Dutchman passed. He tutted audibly. Perhaps he was right, and I was encouraging begging. I felt more inclined to go home with these boys than step back into the guest-house. But I was about to turn into ice. I clambered up the three flights of stairs to the freezing bedroom, climbed under all the covers I could find, and lay wondering whether everyone else felt as ill as I did. I was breathing but with the curious sensation that no air was entering my lungs. I was OK if I kept completely still. Eventually I fell asleep.

An hour later I woke up. My body seemed to know something was wrong. I was warm now, but I was breathing fast, and my heart was pumping like a baby's. I tossed and turned in bed, convinced illogically that some better position would feel OK. I thought of sunny days at the seaside in Devon, of people I loved. Somehow I fell asleep.

BRING ME SUNSHINE

I dreamt I was living with the British comedians Eric Morecambe and Ernie Wise. Aren't dreams strange? I never met either of these men. Yet there they were in my dream as real and as vivid as the people I know best. And they were so funny, so sweet to me, and so kind. I was conscious in this place, perfectly aware that I was dreaming, and surprised to be with them. I said, "Thank you for looking after me. For making me laugh." And they smiled at me with so much warmth and affection and shrugged it off as if to say, "All in a night's work."

And then I woke up. My head was aching. It was 4 a.m. The walk to the hole in the floor demanded a drop in temperature that I didn't want to estimate. I got back to my room, shivering violently. I lay down. As long as I didn't move I could breathe OK. Somehow I slept again. 5 a.m. 6 a.m. . . .

At 7 a.m. I stood up and tried to roll up my sleeping bag. I felt very queasy and much to my surprise was very sick. (There were three bedroom bins that I suspect may have been left in the room for this purpose.) I looked in the mirror, and a strange green alien stared back.

I wondered whether everyone was feeling like this. Downstairs at breakfast the lady from San Francisco was consuming an American-sized breakfast.

"Did you sleep OK?" I asked.

"Sure did. Always do. I take lots of sleeping tablets."

"I see. And you're feeling OK now?"

"I had a headache when I woke up so I took two extra-strong aspirin. I feel fine now. You?"

"I've been sick already this morning."

"Oh, I'm soo sorrryyy. I have some tablets here. They should settle your stomach. You ate something?"

"No. I think it must be altitude sickness."

"Take these anyway."

I swallowed her tablets with mineral water. The others started to arrive and eat hearty breakfasts. "You do not look too well this morning," the Dutchman informed me. Obviously I was struck down for having given away pens inappropriately. The guide and driver dug into their yak-meat breakfast. I bolted outside and was sick a couple more times. Entertainment for the locals. The guide fetched my gear for me, sat me on the front seat, and then held my hand. It was strangely comforting.

The landscape became harsher as the morning went by, the colors browner, the road steeper. We saw the last trees that we would see for days. The track curved and bumped, and while the three in the back shared cookies I sipped water and told myself I was feeling OK really. The land-cruiser stops were named for the Tibetan driver who spoke no English. He had been taught "pee-pee stop," "photo stop," or "breakdown." The pee-pee stops were interesting as there were no bushes with which to maintain any modesty. The girls looked enviously at the boys. We had no option but to squat in front of everyone each time. I suppose I came partly for new experiences. Every time we turned a corner and another mountain peak capped with snow came into view, we would all say, "Photo stop, please," and the guide would smile patiently and say, "Later." Breakdowns were to be one a day.

The higher we went, the more precarious the bends. The drop was inches from the wheels, and the valley was thousands of meters down. We peered over the edge to see if there were many four-wheel-drive trucks containing skeletons in hiking gear, but they seemed to have moved them.

"Driver, would you please keep your eyes on the road?" said voices from the back. PJ would laugh openly, as the driver didn't speak English. Going as fast as possible round these bends and scaring the tourists was obviously a local sport. I was feeling too ill to mind. They did this trip every month in the summer and still seemed to be alive, so I suppose we had to trust them.

"How old are you, PJ?" I asked.

"Twenty-one."

"And the driver?"

"He is twenty-four."

I tried to remember the words of the Hail Mary and regretted not having been raised a Roman Catholic.

Then we reached the first summit for the day. The peak of Tong-la rose to 5,000 meters. My companions got out to take pictures. I looked around in four directions at views of snowy mountains and deep rocky valleys that no camera could ever capture. Prayer flags fluttered in the breeze, the ground was holy, and I was sick on it. Not quite the offering I would like to have brought. The wrinkled face of an elderly nomad couple looked at me sympathetically. I smiled and uttered my only two Tibetan words: *Tashi delek*.

They smiled and nodded obligingly.

"It's so beautiful, PJ. I don't think I've ever been anywhere more beautiful. Please can we go down now?"

"Oh yes. Only one more pass today. You are not good color. You drink water."

"But it's not staying down."

"You drink water."

So I did what the boy said. We sped down past little Tibetan villages and yaks munching tufts of brown. Women were out in the fields, stacking barley onto carts with pitchforks. Tiny children helped or played beside them. I was watching a way of life that had been unchanged for hundreds of years. As we passed they lifted their heads and waved. Their clothes were bright and cheerful, and despite the bitter cold, their faces all had smiles. I gazed at them with wonder and admiration. And drank water.

At regular points along the road the land cruiser would stop. PJ would jump out of the front seat and jam himself in next to the three in the back. "Checkpoint," he'd explain. And sure enough, around the bend would appear an umbrella, a desk, three or four chairs, and three or four very bored Chinese officials in green military uniforms with red stars.

They looked about sixteen years old. "Passport!" they would bark. And PJ would patiently gather up all the passports and visas and tickets for them to examine.

"If this is not an occupied country but just part of China . . ." I asked PJ, "then why do we have these checkpoints every two hours?" He smiled at me and said nothing. The Dutchman in the back reprimanded me again. "You must not ask him questions like that." He was quite right, of course. At one checkpoint, when neither guide nor driver were looking, I pulled out my camera. I knew they would take my film if they saw me, but they didn't see me and I couldn't resist snapping at the young boys sitting in the middle of nowhere for no apparent reason. "You're mad," said the young Dutch girl. "Yes, I know." I smiled at her. It was about the greatest risk I'd be taking on the trip. It hardly felt radical.

The second pass of the day was again over 5,000 meters above sea level. It was too high too quickly. As long as the land cruiser kept moving I ached but I was OK, but as soon as it stopped I was sick again. By the time we reached the stopping point for the night, at the lower height of 4,000 meters, I was in a really bad state. Reality was beginning to distort. My head throbbed, my legs ached, and I hadn't kept down anything for twenty-four hours. I was shivering despite being in five layers of clothing. I couldn't walk steadily, and my heart was pounding.

"I'm really feeling bad, PJ." I sat and shivered. "Have you got a thermometer?"

"What?"

"For taking temperature."

He put his hand on my forehead for one second. "You not have temperature," he said.

"Then why am I so cold?"

"You OK."

I opened my Lonely Planet guide to read about altitude sickness. It was not reassuring.

> Acute mountain sickness may become more serious without warning and can be fatal. Symptoms include . . . confusion, breathlessness, headache, lack of co-ordination . . . vomiting and eventually unconsciousness. These symptoms should be taken very seriously. . . . Those experiencing them may not be in a position to recognise them. . . . Severe AMS can strike with no warning.

I turned to the American, the Dutch couple, and some Germans who had caught up with us. "I'm worried about how ill I feel." I tried to joke, "I mean, if I die in the night it will ruin your holiday. I can't keep water down."

A friendly German man with a red face said, "It's true you look in a bad way, and he is being rather blasé about it. But what can he do? It's up either way out of here, and they are hardly going to get a helicopter."

I wondered whether to cry, but I didn't have enough spare breath. I wondered about taking the Diamox, but again my guide-book was adamant: "Diamox can reduce the symptoms and there-fore the warning signs. Fatal AMS has occurred in people taking Diamox. We do not recommend its use."

I had promised myself I'd only take some if immediate descent was possible. Tomorrow we were, once again, going up. The only chance of a helicopter out would be from Lhasa. Lhasa was four days away.

I didn't know whether to try to persuade my mind to wake up and switch to red alert and say to everyone, "Help! Please get me out of here now!" or whether to give in to the haze that seemed to be taking me over. I swayed over to PJ. "What do I do?"

"You sleep. You want a room on your own?"

"No. I want someone there, please."

"OK. I put you in the room next to me. Come. You go to sleep now."

He helped me up some steps to a freezing room. "Where is the toilet?" I asked. He pointed across a courtyard to an open-roofed brick room. I started to cry. I felt so weak. "But I can't walk all that way. I'm so cold, PJ."

He looked sympathetic for the first time. "OK. I get you bowl." I lay down under the covers. He looked at me. "You take off your jacket?"

"No. I do not take off my jacket."

Did this twenty-one-year-old have any idea? I lay in bed shaking, realizing that my life might genuinely be in his hands. If I became unconscious in the night, the decisions he made might mean life or death for me. I thought I'd better ask him. "What happens if I get worse in the night? What happens if I get much worse?"

"We take you to the local hospital. They have oxygen tents. Don't worry."

"Are they far from here?"

"No. Not far. You sleep now. In the night if you have problem you call me, OK? I come later here." An open door lay between my room and his.

"OK."

He went back to his yak meat.

Was he lying to me? I'd seen no local hospitals, and why should they have oxygen tents in a place where they didn't have pens? If I got worse in the night, I'd be unable to help myself. I thought of my daughter at college. I had lost my own mother at eighteen. Now my daughter was eighteen. I really did not want to die.

The friend house-sitting for me in London, who was more nervous about the journey I was making than I was, had forced me to leave instructions in the event of serious accident or death. At the time it had felt ridiculous. But I'd thought, if I died, who should bring this news to my daughter? And I'd left a name. But I didn't want that call made. I tried to reason with the muddle in my head. How ill was I?

I had been sick eighteen times that day (I'd started counting at five), I ached all over like a full-body migraine, but I was still breathing. With all my clothes, a down sleeping bag, and three covers, I was still shivering.

The ground swayed beneath me. My head went woozy. It was like being engulfed in an internal haze, like treading water in an invisible sea. I didn't feel panic but just as if I were being pulled under, pulled down, and I thought, "Drowning must feel like this." There was no oxygen. So I stopped treading water and lay very still to see if I would float to the surface. I couldn't tell—was I floating up or sinking down?

And then, very quietly, almost imperceptibly, not out loud but in my head, I heard a male voice I didn't recognize as anyone I knew. It said, "You are going to be OK."

And I wondered where it came from. The invisible undercurrent released its hold on me. I started to feel warmer. And I fell asleep.

THE EYES OF THE BUDDHA MAITREYA

The three most important figures in Tibetan Buddhism are the Dalai Lama, the Panchen Lama, and the Karmapa. They are seen to be incarnations of different aspects of the nature of Buddha. Our friend the Dalai Lama is the Bodhisattva of Compassion. That is, if you like, the quality of compassion in human form. The Panchen Lama is a manifestation of the quality of wisdom or, to be specific, the faculty of perfect cognition and perception. The Karmapa is a whole other book.

The life of the last Panchen Lama (the tenth) was not a happy one. He was educated and brainwashed by the Chinese government to such an extent that when, in 1956, he became joint chairperson, with the Dalai Lama, of the Preparatory Committee for the Autonomous Region of Tibet and vice chairman of the China People's National Congress, he was considered by most to be merely a puppet of the Chinese. But he was not a stupid man. The true consequences of the Chinese occupation were before his eyes each day in the form of the Tibetan people who told him their stories. In 1961 he presented Mao with a 70,000-character catalog of Chinese atrocities against the Tibetan people and a request for greater freedom. In reply, he was asked to denounce the Dalai Lama and become himself the spiritual head of Tibet. He refused. They threw him into jail, where he was abused and tortured for fourteen years. By the time they released him, they had persuaded him to keep quiet, but shortly before his death he was again critical of the government, arguing that the Chinese occupation had brought nothing but misery to his people. Many think that he died not of a heart attack but because of some old-fashioned poisoning.

In 1995 a six-year-old boy, Gedun Choekyi Nyima, was identified by the Dalai Lama as his new incarnation. For centuries it had been the job of the Dalai Lama to identify the Panchen Lama's reincarnation. Within a month the boy was seized by the Chinese government, becoming the world's youngest political prisoner. This was the little boy whose face I had first seen on a banner outside the Royal Institute of British Architects.

Then a different, "government-approved," choice was found. The son of a Communist Party member, he is now being carefully indoctrinated, or rather "educated," under the control of Beijing. The government is very interested in his educational progress because it will, one day, be his job to identify the Dalai Lama's next reincarnation. This boy is referred to by the Tibetans and in the West as "the Chinese Panchen Lama."

Meanwhile, the boy who is considered to be the true eleventh Panchen Lama has spent over half his young life under house arrest. It is rumored that their "policy" towards him is to be kind but to deny him any knowledge of Tibetan Buddhism, his mystical tradition, or who he is. He will certainly have been given a true muggle education.

You may wonder why I'm telling you these tragic stories. I wanted you to know more background to the first monastery we visited at Shigatse, our next stopping point, than all my fellow travelers put together. Tashilhunpo Monastery in Shigatse is the home of the Panchen Lamas, and Gedun Choekyi Nyima comes into this story again later.

I woke, after my night of concern about the likelihood of my continued status as a living person, with nothing more than a headache. For some reason my body had decided that adjusting to the high life was a possibility after all. After another day of "photo," "pee pee," and "checkpoint" and different members of the group vomiting their thanks onto holy places, we emerged from the bus into one of the few monasteries that was left relatively unharmed by the Cultural Revolution.

Now, if I say "monastery," you probably visualize a building of some kind. But for a Tibetan Buddhist monastery you need to think of a village. The small and tidy living quarters of the monks usually surround the main temple, and there may also be libraries, classrooms, burial chapels built over the bodily remains of former incarnations of important lamas or over the ashes, buildings for the hand-printing of scriptures, and buildings for the making or mending of robes. There will certainly be endless small temple buildings housing ancient statues of the confusing panoply of Buddhist deities. Below the monastery in the valley there may be a stream or a small river while the monasteries themselves are usually in remote areas that hug the hillside as if attempting to keep out the bitter cold that blows down from the snowcapped mountains all around. Yaks, cows, goats, sheep, and dogs all wander about, shivering and looking for something to eat. None of them will ever grow fat, but as long as there is food the monks will feed them.

The simplicity of the monks' single-story (often single-room) dwellings contrasts with the elaborate temples and shrines, which may be two or three stories high with gold-plated roofs that gleam in the brilliant sunshine. The outside walls are washed ("sloshed" would be more accurate, as that's how they get the paint on) with white, black, and red. Here everything has meaning. White is the color for compassion, black for power, and red for wisdom—but think brick, not fire engine. Around the windows of Tibetan buildings the woodwork is painted in brilliant primary-school colors with ornate decorative patterns. Hangings with ornate Buddhist symbols are displayed from every windowsill and every doorway.

The tourists made an amusing bunch. Denied of what the lungs consider to be an adequate supply of oxygen, we stood to rest every five steps and watched as pilgrim grannies, who looked well over eighty, zoomed past us up the endless flights of steps with their prayer beads, yak-butter offerings, and enduring smiles.

In the first building I ventured into, I was greeted by a 26-meter statue of Maitreya, the Buddha of the Future. He took nine people four years to complete and has 300 kilograms of gold coating on him. His face is serene and beautiful. I looked at him and he looked at me, and I knew the lack of serenity in my own heart. I held my eye contact with him and tried to absorb his influence. Tibetans believe that he will return to preside over the world when we have all earned our deliverance from suffering. I hope they are right.

A group of ten tourists bustled in and started clicking their cameras at him. Then a monk appeared and pointed at a notice: "To take photograph 20 Yuan" (about £2). He started to collect money. Somehow I felt that this was not quite the series of events the ninth Panchen Lama had intended when he commissioned this statue. I felt angry with the tourists, angry with the Chinese government for taking 80 percent of the money given to monasteries by tourists and pilgrims alike, angry with myself for judging everyone and everything. I looked at the Buddha of the Future. He went on look-ing serene. Maybe he knew something I didn't. Everyone else there seemed happy enough with the way things were. Maybe I could just join the tourists? I sighed, took out my camera, snapped an image, and paid my twenty yuan.

The next building was the tomb of the tenth Panchen Lama. He had spent his life struggling for the rights of his people against Chi-nese policy and here he lay, in death, as a tourist attraction. A photo of him had been crudely pinned up. He looked round-faced and friendly but somehow also distant and sad. Numerous yak-butter candles flickered in front of the images, and dusty pilgrims from re-mote villages far away across the mountains prostrated themselves on the cold stone slabs before him.

Some tourists arrived and took photographs of the pilgrims. Some went on with their prostrations and tried to ignore the cam-eras. Some stopped and covered their faces. How were these tradi-tionally friendly and open people to respond to the intrusion? Some had spent weeks walking to reach this place.

I watched the scene. The face of the tenth Panchen Lama watched, too. I did not take photographs.

The centerpiece of the monastery is the Kelsang Temple building, where the monks congregate to chant their way through "puja" ser-vices, which can last anywhere from two hours to seven days con-secutively for eighteen hours a day. At the death of the ninth Panchen they said prayers for days to ask for his early reincarnation. The assembly hall is one of the buildings in Tashilhunpo that sur-vived the destruction of the Cultural Revolution and dates back to the founding of the monastery in the fifteenth century. In the center is the throne of the Panchen Lamas. Here they would sit and address the monks, teach them, and give audiences and blessings. This is surrounded by rows of deep-red cushions for the monks to sit cross-legged. The walls are hung with *thangkas* or material pictures, with images of centuries of incarnations of the Panchen Lama.

Only the present Panchen Lama, as you'll remember, isn't there.

The Chinese government says that the boy is "alive and well." But no one has seen him since his arrest in 1995.

Neither is the Chinese Panchen Lama there. Apparently even if they could persuade the monks to accept him, the Tibetan people would not. A twenty-four-hour guard would have to be provided for him, and the unfortunate adolescent would have to listen to whispered (or not so whispered) accusations that he is a fraud. It would all be a trifle embarrassing.

I looked at the faces of the men in maroon robes. Their numbers are now severely limited so that Tashilhunpo, which before the Chinese "liberation" of Tibet held 9,000 monks, is now said to be allowed closer to 700. Some sources say that they are merely "puppet monks." There are even claims that many are not real monks at all but Chinese officials paid to wear monks' clothes because they speak English and can check that no tourists give out pictures of the Dalai Lama to the faithful, ask the wrong questions, or express controversial opinions. To be less paranoid but more cynical, I could have concluded that these were the monks allowed to remain by the Chinese to take money from the tourists and maintain the buildings. I hoped I was wrong.

Outside in the sunshine children begged among the tourists and the pilgrims. They held up tiny hands. "Allo, money." "Allo, money." The nomad pilgrims gave money. Once more the tourists did not.

At the end of the designated tour was the customary gift shop of Chinese propaganda. The history of the Tibetan Autonomous Region written by Chinese scholars whose viewpoint would perhaps have been a little biased. I wasn't feeling too unbiased myself. Smiling Chinese businessmen in suits sold postcards to Chinese tourist groups in matching red baseball caps.

I looked out over the breathtaking beauty of the monastery buildings, and I wondered whether to take a photo or to sit down and cry.

THE FRIENDSHIP HIGHWAY

One of the successful results of naming the road from Kathmandu to Lhasa the Friendship Highway is that it sounds like a safe place to travel, don't you think? But as we shook along the next stage of the mud track we all said more prayers that we would not suddenly end up in a valley. Now, don't misunderstand me. I'm not complaining. The fact that the track is there at all is a truly remarkable feat of engineering and sheer hard toil. In many places you see the labor that is going into creating it; remarkably to Western eyes, young teenage girls break up the rocks with pickaxes.

Funny thing, that. We've heard a lot about equality of opportunity, haven't we? Women who want to be judges or vicars or go into the military and fight at the front. "We demand the right to kill the enemy!" we women have shouted. But have we ever demanded the right to dig up the road? I've never been wolf-whistled by a woman as she pulled up her oversized trousers and wiped the sweat and dust from her brow.

But here women wear beautiful-colored clothes, dig up the road, and sing. I had to resist the temptation to take photographs of colorfully dressed girls younger than my daughter swinging the pickaxes and singing with high and amazing joyful-sounding voices.

The road required faith. Not faith in the Buddhist gods who are manifestations of inner qualities. At times like this it's the Christian God you need. Someone outside yourself who is ever loving and there to help if you've got yourself in a tight corner. Or on a tight corner every two minutes. As the twenty-four-year-old driver continued his game of taking ridiculously dangerous turns at hair-raising speed and the others went back to reprimanding him in sundry languages that he didn't speak, I found myself addressing the creator deity I'd learned about in confirmation class. "Er, Lord . . . hello, remember me?"

An hour later the driver fell asleep at the wheel, and we reeled off the track. But into a ditch and not over a cliff. It took an hour, a lot of nomads, and a yak to rescue the land cruiser, but we were all alive and unhurt. I'm not suggesting here that my rather unpious prayer protected us. But, as is always the case with a could-have-died experience, I felt very glad to be alive, and I certainly thanked any invisible beings that may have been about that we weren't lying at the bottom of the cliff to become lunch for the vultures. The driver looked as though he was in shock, but all we could do was give him a pat on the back and offer him a pack of Polo mints. The Dutch couple took photos of the damage to the land cruiser, and the American lady took a sedative.

When we started off again, the bent metal was rubbing something that was moving, but driver and guide insisted that it was not important, and we sped off. The trip was certainly not for the thin-blooded or the fainthearted. I seemed to have got over my altitude sickness, but the young Dutch girl was now feeling very ill, and we were all wondering what we would do if the land cruiser broke down on a high pass a five hours' drive from the nearest town.

But the landscape was so dramatic and powerful it was hard to mind about the danger. And then we skidded around another hairpin bend on two wheels, and there was a lake. Not a lake in a valley, but a lake high up in the peaks. Somehow they have high mountain lakes. They are true turquoise blue and so clear that around the edges where it isn't too deep you can see to the bottom. A shepherd appeared leading a flock of sheep by the water's edge. We pleaded with the driver, and he stopped. I leapt out, sat on a rock, and tried to take it all in. My heart was singing, "Thank you, Isabel, for bringing me here." This was Tibet. The land of snows. And the struggle to live and to be joyful in this frozen and beautiful land was what had made the Tibetan people who they are. Their faith is not in a God outside themselves who will change their circumstances for them—but is a faith in the qualities within themselves that they have to develop in order to live and be happy in this place. So every day the focus is on peace of heart and mind and the development of compassion.

I read once that the Dalai Lama has said that Buddhists are good at talking about compassion but Christians are better at taking action. This may be so, but in the West it is rare to find people who really have Christ's teaching at the center of each decision they make. In Tibet it is rare to find people who do not have their faith central to their lives. They are a deeply religious people, and over two million are said to have died for the right to practice their faith, even though it threatens no one. Chinese government policy just doesn't like it and considers Buddhism an old-fashioned superstition that needs to be stamped out in the name of "progress." It was a mystery to me. Torture and kill people whose beliefs can be summed up in one word: *compassion*. Where is the logic in that? Why are they still locking people up and torturing them despite their new policy of "religious tolerance"? Why does the world let them get away with it? Serenity to accept what I cannot change? I supposed I would need some of that. Some things should be left just as they are, like people, like the khenpo. Sometimes I needed to do nothing—like the night before—and life would still go on. But as to what I could do, what I could change? I stared out over the lake, wondering what I could do next. And then, as usual, the answer came from the place I least expected it.

"Isabel, time to get back in the van," said the American lady. Sometimes life is simple. That was the next step.

WHO ARE YOU?

The next town we arrived at on the long, long road was Gyantse. The Lonely Planet guide is forthright in its opinions of towns in the Tibetan Autonomous Region: "Gyantse is one of the least Chinese-influenced towns in Tibet and is worth a visit for this reason alone."

Wonderful that we can write what we like in the West, isn't it?

It is indeed a stunningly beautiful town, with a wide main street that leads up to the Pelkor Chöde Monastery. This monastery is dark and gloomy and made me glad that I didn't come here to worship four times a day. But next to it is one of the most remarkable buildings that I've ever seen. In fact, I take it back—it is the most remarkable building I've ever seen. I mean, where else could I count? I once went up the Leaning Tower of Pisa and heard an American tourist, not unlike the lady I'd been traveling with, say, in all earnestness, "When you've seen one view, you've seen them all." The leaning tower was as beautiful and delicate as the Eiffel Tower is . . . er, tall. But the Gyantse Kumbum is extraordinary.

You couldn't really call it a tower, although it is a round tower-shaped building that is six stories high. It is a *chörten* (What's a *chörten,* you ask? It's Tibetan for stupa) that is—well, they are all different. This one isn't the least bit like the one I told you about in Kathmandu. This one has four central chapels on each floor, which are surrounded by what feels like hundreds of smaller chapels. A clockwise route spirals upwards, and as you walk you pray in each of the chapels. Or if you are a tourist, you peek into each of the chapels and say, "Gosh," as the face of another amazing statue looks at you. A white Tara (the female goddess of compassion), a green Tara, and then suddenly a wrathful protector deity. They have faces that are designed to scare you, and they are certainly not the kind of people you'd like to meet in a nightmare. They were there to trample over obstacles to enlightenment. I hoped I wasn't an obstacle. The statues hypnotize you after a while with their focused eyes and endless unspoken challenges. I'd look at them and ask, "Who are you?"

"Who are you?" A strangely powerful stare comes back. I can't answer, "I'm, er, I'm Isabel." That's just my name. But as for what I represent? This Buddha represents compassion, and I represent, well, nothing particular. "I'm a tourist," I'd say, in my ridiculous imaginary conversations with the statues. "You need to think about this," the statue would reply. "Be quiet—you're a block of wood," I'd say. "And you are skin and bone," came the immediate response. It was true, but I had a camera. I took a photo.

After a while they start to gang up. *Kumbum* literally means "100,000 images," and after looking at the first thousand of the paintings on the chapel walls, my head was starting to spin. Guiltily, I skipped a floor and walked up to the golden roof, where the eyes of the Buddha looked out like the stupa in Kathmandu. I stepped back ridiculously close to the edge to take a photo. No safety barriers here. "That was very stupid," said the reprimanding Dutchman, who was following behind me. "Yes, it was, wasn't it?" I smiled at him merrily.

The view over Gyantse is beautifully unspoiled, the way I imagine all of Tibet could have been. Above the old town is a steep hill, and on it—and *perched* would be the right word here—is an old fourteenth-century fort. Between the view from the Kumbum and the fort was the tiny town itself with its traditional Tibetan buildings and, I'm delighted to say, more carts than cars. There were remarkably few people to be seen. I made my way down the Kumbum and declined the taxi ride back to the hotel, preferring to walk back through the streets. Schoolchildren came up to me. "Pen? Pen?" I laughed. Is it turning children into beggars? I still don't know. I gave them pens. Tied up outside the houses were the animals. I imagined keeping a goat and a cow outside my house. How unimaginative of me to keep a cat.

Then a curious sight appeared. A group of about twelve children stood precariously on a table, peering through a doorway. I looked at them. They had obviously been there for some time although it didn't look particularly comfortable. They were all quiet and staring intently at something. Whatever could be happening in the house? I approached cautiously and heard what at first sounded like a fight going on. I was surprised and horrified. I hadn't heard a raised voice since leaving Britain. But this time it wasn't even the Chinese government policy that was influencing these children to abandon everything their parents had lived for. It was a television set. They were watching *Terminator*.

I walked rapidly past and tried not to imagine these Tibetan children acting it out in their school playground the following day. I would like to have stopped and delivered a short homily: "Listen, kids. Actually your parents are right—killing people isn't a cool thing to do." Luckily for them, I only have two words of Tibetan. They mean "Peace be with you."

I turned into a restaurant and sat down to dinner. It would be vegetable momos—like stuffed pasta but not made of wheat and not tasting like stuffed pasta. (How do you think I'd do as a food writer?) The restaurant was deserted apart from the bowing wait-ress. I took out the only books I had with me. *The Dhammapada,* the Lonely Planet guide to Tibet, and my own notebook intended for writing noble words about my trip.

The Dhammapada is described on the back of the Penguin Classics edition as "a collection of aphorisms that illustrate the Buddhist Dhamma or moral system." It goes on, "Probably compiled in the third century B.C. . . . among the greatest spiritual works of the century." I thought I'd read a little before writing myself. I opened the teachings seemingly at random and read: "Better than a thou-sand useless words is one single word that gives peace."

I closed the book again. It was certainly interesting advice for a writer. I put my notebook away.

I opened the guide to Tibet. We had the high passes Karo-la and Kamba-la left. Two hundred and fifty kilometers to go. The first pass was another of the highest, at 5,000 meters. Then we'd no doubt freewheel down to the town of Nangartse at only 4,500 me-ters. Then, just when we were feeling well, we'd go up again to the next pass, which was just under 5,000 meters. And then—I turned a page excitedly—then we would travel down and down and farther down until, no longer feeling sick, sometime tomorrow evening, at only 3,500 meters, eventually, we would arrive, by the grace of all the Buddhist deities, in Lhasa.

So close. Celebration was called for. Turning to the bowing wait-ress, I asked her, "Do you have coffee?"

OFFICIAL VISITS

Here is a tip if you ever decide to go to Tibet. Get a Chinese visa before you leave home. For some reason I was the only one in our group who had done this. This meant that after this long journey everyone else had two days of compulsory sightseeing, in a large group, and then they were obliged to leave the country. But I didn't have to go. I was grumpy enough that they had given me only nine days instead of the two weeks I'd wanted. But nine days was more than two days, and at least I was free to do as I pleased for seven of them. I didn't like compulsory visits.

On the first day they took us to the Potala. This was, and could still be, the winter palace of the Dalai Lama and the residence of the Tibetan government. If you've ever seen the film *Kundun* or even Mr. Pitt in *Seven Years in Tibet,* you'll remember the young Dalai Lama describing how, as a boy, he was taken to this magnificent but huge and dark palace and given the bedroom of his previous incarnations. As he was kept apart from other children, his main companions in his room were the mice who would run over his bed as he slept, occasionally wetting him and leaving him little gifts.

The Potala has been described as one of the wonders of Eastern architecture and was placed on the UNESCO World Heritage List in 1994. It is thirteen stories high and apparently has over 1,000 rooms. Work began on the palace in 1645, and the fifth Dalai Lama moved there in 1649. Since then it has been the home of each of the Dalai Lamas, most of whom were poisoned or bumped off in sundry ways at an early age. In the late eighteenth century they decided they wanted somewhere a little more sunny, and a "summer palace" was built. The current Dalai Lama describes in his autobiography how, as a boy, he would long for the day each year when they left the Potala and traveled to the summer palace, which had gardens and animals and which he loved. But in the winter they would all return. As the Potala has its own chapels and schools for the religious training of the monks and tombs for the previous Dalai

Lamas, there was no need for him to leave until the following spring.

As I walked around the Potala I tried to imagine the impression that these thousands of statues would have made on him. The elderly monks who made up his government shuffling along, and the thousands of yak-butter candles burning endlessly in the tombs. There was no doubt in anyone's mind that he was the incarnation of the thirteenth Dalai Lama. There is a story that when he arrived for the first time at the Potala Palace, he ran up to a cupboard and shouted, "My teeth! My teeth are in there!" The amazed attendants opened the locked cupboard, and there, sure enough, were the teeth of the previous Dalai Lama. Skeptical? Or not?

In the Potala today it is difficult to summon up the atmosphere of those years. The Chinese have installed electric lights and put up signs everywhere. The statues have been enclosed behind glass, and there are ropes, as in any other museum, telling you where you can and can't go. This is what the Potala has become: a museum. The guards in their Chinese military uniforms, now familiar from the endless checkpoints, sit about looking bored.

I noticed with amusement a large display of fire extinguishers in a locked cupboard. They could have had another notice: "In case of fire, go and look for the key."

Apart from our little group, the Chinese guides were everywhere. They would deliver history lessons to the groups, and the phrase "great Motherland" echoed endlessly across the chapels.

We turned into the Dalai Lama's Throne Room. This is the room where official guests have been received for generations. A large photo of the thirteenth Dalai Lama was up on the wall. The matching photo of the current Dalai Lama was conspicuous by its absence. As indeed was he. This was all stolen property. It didn't belong to them, and I began to seethe under the injustice of it all. Pilgrim nomads brought their candle wax and tried to worship amid the guided tours. I was one more tourist seeing what the government wanted me to see.

Then I walked out onto the roof and was suddenly transported again to another time and place; the roofs were untouched, the hills were still there, the air was as cold and the sky was as blue as it always had been. This was the confusion: rage one minute and exhilaration the next. It was stunningly beautiful, and I couldn't get out of there soon enough.

I had one more day of compulsory visits to endure. In the morning we were taken to Drepung Monastery. *Drepung* translates as "rice heap" because there are so many little white buildings that make up this monastic community that some clever person thought it looked like blobs of white rice spread out over the countryside. At the time of the Chinese takeover in 1951 there were 10,000 monks at Drepung, the largest monastery of the Gelugpa order. Today there are about 600.

I'm not going to describe Drepung Monastery to you because it's not what I remember of the visit. What I remember is an old monk. I say "old." I think "very old" would probably be more accurate. He hobbled down enthusiastically and greeted PJ with a smile. They were obviously old friends. He laughed and joked. He smiled at me and posed for the camera with a childish sense of fun. Everyone wanted to photograph him. He had a face that had to go on a wall somewhere. It would have seemed criminal not to photograph him if he allowed it. He must have been ninety. I watched him smiling and laughing with the tourists and wondered what he had seen and what he had lived through. He opened the Lonely Planet guide and pointed at a photograph of another elderly monk. "This one, nirvana now!" He laughed. He was full of joy, and his laughter was the way I've heard the Dalai Lama's laughter described, a belly laugh from a place deep within. And I wondered how the human spirit can suffer so much and yet not be broken. I wondered if his joy frustrated the Chinese guards who watched us. They couldn't take it from him.

In the afternoon we were promised a chance to glimpse a lost culture in action. Sera Monastery, the second of the largest monasteries of the Gelugpa sect, had once housed 5,000 monks. The numbers are now confined to several hundred, but the agenda still promised us an opportunity to see a form of debating unique to Tibetan Buddhism.

But when we arrived we found that the debating was not taking place that week at all. The monks were repainting the monastery, and all other activities were canceled. They stood about with white aprons over their maroon robes and splashed whitewash over the walls of the buildings. I wondered why they could not afford local labor to do this job, but then I recalled rather cynically where the money brought by the tourists went. Not to the monastery, evidently.

So here it was again. The disparity between what should have been here and what was here. The buildings were teeming with children begging, with pilgrims in their brightly colored clothes, and with tour groups with video cameras and Chinese guides. I'd had enough. It was like an emotional overload. I abandoned my group once again and sat down in the sunshine. Reading about the monastery education, I learned that at the head of each college was an abbot, or khenpo, and that the position of khenpo was chosen by the Dalai Lama himself. To reach this position it was necessary to be awarded the highest degree of monastic studies.

I thought of my khenpo back in Nepal and wondered if he ever thought of me. Was he engrossed in the teaching of his monks, or was his mind sometimes distracted from the dharma by thoughts of a smiling English girl? I wished that he was with me to explain all the symbols and the rich meaning of everything I saw around me. Why was the Tara, the goddess of compassion, sometimes personified with a white face, sometimes with a red face, and sometimes with a blue face? And what would his answer be to the important questions: Why were the Chinese guards here, and why was Tibetan Buddhism being so effectively wiped out? I got up and went to make paper planes with the children. I couldn't give them all money, but I could teach them how to make paper planes that would fly farther and put the Chinese leaflet about Sera to good use.

Back at the official tour hotel that night I lay in bed reading the instructions for the room: "Excessive drinking and making trouble are not available here. Do not make noise in case of disturbing others. Gambling, fighting, promiscuity, drug taking and watching or propagating obscene film is prohibited." Oh dear, and there was I about to film my neighbors through the bedroom keyhole.

"Do not eat the food or smoke offered by others in case of being poisoned and cheated." There was obviously more going on in this hotel than met the eye. "Dangerous articles, such as inflammable and explosive materials are not allowed to put in the room."

If you are ever in the Kailash Hotel in Lhasa you can check this out yourself in the little booklet marked "Welcome to Foreign Friends." Except in room 118, where I've helped myself to the instructions.

But there is a TV with about one hundred channels. All in Chinese. I sat back to watch "This is China," which appeared to be twenty-four-hour propaganda about how wonderful China is. Pictures of happy brides, in white, Western-style wedding dresses, kissing their new husbands in expensive hotels in Shanghai; professors in white suits, looking into microscopes; and endless Chinese businessmen securing deals with international corporations who are eager to expand into the huge potential Chinese market. Then back to pictures of dancing peasants smiling about the glories of the Motherland. It was quite fascinating, even though I couldn't understand the words. Was it possible to combine the old-style Communist propaganda machine with the twenty-first-century greed to make money and embrace capitalism? Evidently it was, and I was watching it. I flicked off the TV and opened *The Dhammapada*.

"For hate is not conquered by hate. Hate is conquered by love. This is a law eternal."

So I thought about love, and the face of the elderly monk at Drepung Monastery, and remembering his sad, gentle eyes, I finally fell asleep.

WHAT DID YOU DO IN LHASA?

The following morning I was free. I waved goodbye to the tour group, kissed the lovely PJ, and checked out of the Chinese hotel.

I checked into a Tibetan hotel and breathed a sigh of relief. Now my time was my own. I didn't want to do anything. I just wanted to be. To be in Lhasa. Leaving my camera and my notebooks, I went out to walk the streets. I had no desire to explore the 95 percent of the city that was now full of modern Chinese buildings. I was heading, as everyone seems to, for the Jokhang temple. Not to go inside but just to sit on the ground and people-watch for a couple of days.

Outside the temple, rows of pilgrims do prostrations. They bring along a thin bedding roll or cardboard and lay it out on the ground in front of them. In their hands they may have blocks of wood or just pieces of cardboard. They take off their shoes and lay them to one side carefully. I sat quietly and watched. There were mainly old people, it was true, but also some in perhaps their thirties or forties and even some teenagers. The women all wear their hair in long black plaits with elaborate beads threaded into their headdresses. The beads are turquoise, amber, or brightly colored stones. The clothes are similarly ornate, with the traditional woven aprons of the Tibetan costume. The belts and buckles are intricately decorated, and the cloaks look warm and very heavy. Not ideal for making prostrations. After about twenty minutes, with perspiration breaking out on their foreheads, they would rest and come and sit down on the stones. They would look at me curiously and smile. And then I'd smile back, and that was all the communication that was needed. When I'd been sitting for a couple of days I was accepted as part of the scenery.

On the fourth day of sitting and being, I bring my pen to write, and a large group soon gathers around to watch the squiggles it makes on the paper.

A man with stumps for legs sits begging about two yards from me. Seeing his disability, people are kind to him. They stare at the tips of the stumps, which are red and raw. Monks pass and give him money. A Tibetan nomad woman cannot contain herself—she just stares at his stumps in horror. Well-dressed Chinese boys stare, too.

Then something wonderful happens. One of the local Chinese police arrives. I have grown to dislike them as they strut about controlling people. But this one has a smile on his face. He obviously knows the beggar because he hits him about a bit playfully and then takes out a Walkman. He puts the earpieces in the man's ears, and the beggar begins to sing a delightful tuneless ditty. He's happy now, and we all smile.

He and I attract almost equal attention. But eventually I draw a larger crowd. The sight of a Western woman sitting on the ground, moving a black pen over white paper, brings most people over to look. A row of children stare at him, but I have a crowd of all ages staring at me. I regret that I can't talk to this man who sits so close to me. He's heard these songs before, and so sings in his loudest voice. Today he is happy with his life, and so am I. The sun is warm, and it shines on us both.

More people come and stand by me and use me as an excuse to stare at him. It seems that here no mother ever said, "Don't stare, dear—it isn't nice." Then he speaks to me: "I am Dawa. Hello, how are you?" I say, "I'm very well and . . . ," but he has already gone back to his singing. A woman comes and offers him two cartons of yogurt. He offers one to me. I say, "No, no—for you."

I'm touched by the kindness of all these people towards him. When I was in New York some of the beggars there were also handicapped, but the New York attitude despises them. People walk past, giving nothing, and I did the same. It was as if we thought that to have no legs was somehow the fault of the person themselves. As if they had sawn off their own arms for the purpose of extorting money from people. Or was it more subtle? As if, without quite believing it, people thought they were using their disability to get money "and that ain't right."

I notice here that the only people who don't give him money are the tourists.

A woman approaches me and asks me to write, and then another wants to look at my postcards, another at my books. They pass my possessions around, but I have no fear that anyone will grab them and run. They give them back, and then one of the nomad women beckons for me to stand up and follow her.

They are walking around the temple. So we walk the pilgrim route around and around. There are no tourists here except me. I am surrounded by heavy clothes and dusty faces. The yak-butter candles flicker in the dark, and as we walk we spin the prayer wheels. I try to empty my mind of everything except the images around me. The shuffle of boots, the stone floors, the sweet smell of the wax, and the chanting that has been heard for centuries. "*Om mani padme hum*" repeated and repeated in endless eternal circles of life and death. I walk around with them until eventually they stop and start to make prostrations. I am obviously intended to join in. They look at me. I speak to them in a strange tongue: "Oh well, why not?" I leave my bag and jacket but as I lack the strips of cardboard I'm only putting my forehead on the ground in the direction of the Buddha. I don't even attempt the full flat-out version. The nomads watch approvingly. Half an hour later the old woman in front of me finally stops. They look at me and I look at them, and they all speak to me at the same time and in Tibetan. Then they start walking around the temple circuit again. Ten more rotations later they are ready to go.

I make signs indicating that I'd like to buy them something to drink. Two of them tag along until we get back to my guest-house. The member of the staff is amused when we walk in.

"Where did you find these two?" he asks me.

"In the square—I've been with them for hours."

"They are nomads. From Amdo."

"Where is that?"

"A long way away. They live in the mountains in tents. It's so cold. None of us would be able to live there."

"Tell them please that I'm glad they are joining me for tea."

"I don't speak their dialect, but I'll try."

They talked for some time while tea and cake was served.

"They keep yaks, and when there is no more for them to eat, they move the tents. They are very good people. Very honest. There is no lying or cheating where they come from."

They stared at the cake and biscuits. The younger of the two women tried some biscuits, and then pulled a face as if she were being poisoned.

"It's very difficult to communicate with these people." But they were having fun just looking at me. Just I was enjoying their smiling burnt faces.

"I'd like to give them a gift," I said.

One of the other guests spoke.

"If you have a picture of the Dalai Lama, you'll see them cry they will be so grateful. That's all they want or value."

"But I don't have one," I said. For the first time I was ashamed that I had listened to all the good advice in London. I didn't believe I could have endangered the lives of illiterate nomads by giving them a picture. Surely even the Chinese army would not arrest people like this? But maybe I was naïve.

I bought a pack of the most beautiful postcards of Tibet that I could find and gave them to the older of the two women. She looked at them like treasures and was amazed when I indicated that she should keep them. They had cost £2. If I'd given her money instead, they could probably have eaten for a month. But the food would go, and the pictures would be kept.

Part of me wished I could go with them and look after the yaks.

I tried to imagine six months without a shower, without a telephone, and living on yak meat, and I was glad that the authorities had fixed my ticket out. I'm often unable to resist a challenge, and if they had invited me home with them I might just have said yes and learned an obscure Tibetan dialect the hard way.

Halfway through October is a good time to sit in the Jokhang square. This is the time when the nomads come from all over Tibet, and there are very few tourists here. The visitors are both the very poor and the not so poor. Some of the women are evidently wearing all they own, but the colorful clothes are worn by the richer as well as the poorer. Western clothes, worn by the Chinese and some of the Tibetans, are unbearably drab beside them.

A young monk sits down beside me and tells his tale. I have no reason to doubt him.

"Are you from England? I would like to go to England."

"Yes. I'm from England. Maybe you will go to England one day."

"No, I can never go. Even if I had money."

"Why not?"

"I have no passport."

"Can't you get one somehow?"

"No. I go away Tibet and go Nepal. Very long travel. Nepal police find me and give me to China. I nine months in prison. Now I not go back to my monastery."

I'd heard this. Monks who got in trouble with the police were forbidden to return to their monasteries. It is not the monks who won't have them, of course, but the government that will not allow them to return. So they lose all that they know and end up as displaced beggars.

I gave him a pen and felt pathetic.

One day I had to give up writing because I had fourteen people around me and two children climbing on my lap and wanting to use the pen.

Some of the people who come and sit with me don't smell too good, but I wouldn't have spent these days any other way. I am wonderfully happy sitting among the beggars and the monks while the Chinese tourists walk around at a distance with their telephoto lenses.

An old man who must be eighty comes and sits right next to me. I offer him some Kendal mint cake. He declines. His joints are horribly swollen, and I see him rubbing them. Perhaps if I give him a little money he can buy some medicine. I give him twenty yuan. It's nothing, but the crowd has to persuade him to take it. One woman speaks a little English. "Please ask him to take it," I explain to her. "This is nothing for me. I can afford it." They look at me in surprise. One student, who also speaks English, says, "Either you are very kind or very rich."

"No," I say, "really I'm neither. I spend more than this to go on a train in England. I spend this to drink coffee." Coffee and a muffin in London coffee shops is more than £2. I feel ashamed. Not for the first time. They talk among themselves for a while, and the old man takes the money and hides it away in some inner pocket.

Finally, unnoticed by my companions, the sun goes down and the temperature starts to drop. I give away the remainder of the things in my bag. Combs, toothbrushes, more pens, postcards. I take off my thick hiking socks and give them to an old woman doing prostrations in socks that no longer have soles. She smiles and accepts them gracefully. I leave before I give away my boots.

Some days in the square people would gravitate towards me who wanted to practice their English. On two occasions young men brought me their essays to mark. And I'd sit there for hours explaining the use of the infinitive or the essential requirement of a period. Both these young men were Tibetan and wanted to become tour guides. They were studying for exams that the Chinese government is making ever more strict so that they know which version of history they had to repeat at the various tourist locations. To pass these exams they had to learn both Chinese and English. For the Chinese guides, Tibetan is not a requirement, only English.

One day I chatted to a young man I met on the street who was working as a guide. As it was late October, he would have no work until the following year. He explained, "Every year they make it harder for the Tibetan guides. They fire us for no reason. They are trying to get rid of Tibetan guides, but not officially, so they make it impossible for us."

So the facts, which had once been only statistics for me, were verified.

"So what will you do if they don't let you be a guide anymore?"

"I don't know. Really I'm something of an expert as I've been guiding tourists round Tibet ever since I was eighteen, and I've been everywhere and I know most things. I've seen many things. In the north they are mining so much. They are digging up everything, and there are factories. I even do the most difficult routes, and of course I know all the history, too."

"Can't you get another job?"

"It's almost impossible to find good work if you don't read and write fluently in Chinese, and I don't even speak Chinese. Only a few phrases."

"Will you leave?"

"For me that, too, is impossible. I was educated in Dharamsala, as many of us were. I had to come back because my mother was ill, but I don't have a passport. She's dead now, but I can't travel as I have no legal status here."

"So what will you do if they don't let you work as a guide anymore?"

"I do not know."

He must have been about twenty-five years old. He was attractive and full of energy. I didn't like to tell him what he'd be earning in the States for the difficult work he does. A twenty-four-hour day in dangerous conditions with responsibility for large groups of people. He wouldn't be sitting on the ground with the beggars and the tourist.

"I hope your predictions are not accurate," I said rather weakly. "All the tourists want Tibetan guides. Maybe the Chinese will come to appreciate the importance of having local Tibetan people who know and understand their own country."

"Aren't you forgetting one thing?" He smiled.

"What's that?"

"This is China."

"Oh yes, you're right, I was forgetting that."

Then, as we sat there, right on cue a Chinese policeman appeared and made everyone stand up. He forced the pilgrims to get up and "move on."

"What is he doing?"

"Tibetans are not allowed to sit down in the square. Of course those who come from far away don't know."

"But why can't they sit down on the ground?"

"I don't know. I think the control office thinks it looks untidy."

He went on making people get up. No one complained. They all did as they were told, meekly. Except me.

"Why?" I asked. "You go away." I was playful but insistent. Behind his back I pulled faces and pretended to kick him away with my boot. The nomads all laughed. I pushed him away playfully, keeping a huge smile on my face, and indicated for the nomads to sit down again. More laughter. It was easy fun, and the official was powerless. He couldn't arrest me for entertaining the crowd. But he was losing face. He pointed at my bag. A hush fell on the crowd; they were probably assuming I had nothing but Dalai Lama pictures within it. He rifled through it: a pair of socks, a toy yak I'd bought to bring home, a toothbrush, and a T-shirt that did not say "Free Tibet." He was obviously disappointed. I indicated apology that there was nothing he could arrest me for. The crowd was enjoying the spectacle. Finally he gave up and walked back to his control office, looking irritated. I gestured grandly for the nomads to

take their seats. More laughter. Then one of the elderly nomad women took my hand and ushered me off. She dragged me across the square, with her two friends. I wondered where we were going. We went down a back street and around a corner. Finally we arrived in a little shop that took photographs. She stood me in the middle while she and her friend stood on either side. I laughed while they took a photo of me. Unless she was a Chinese government spy, I was their souvenir of a day in the Jokhang square. It was the best honor I ever remembered having achieved.

As we walked back to the square they chatted to each other and then pointed at my watch, indicating seven. Seven o'clock I was to come back to the temple. I nodded. What would they have in store for me?

I returned at seven to their smiling faces. They walked me into the temple, and I realized that there was some kind of ceremony about to take place. The monks were all sitting making the curious atonal sound that they make when they chant. The temple was full to bursting. Around the back was a huge queue, and the pilgrims clearly intended that I should join them. I was hugely happy among these people. Even though this was Lhasa, it couldn't have been further from the atmosphere in the Potala. The temple was alive with hundreds of the faithful. I stood among the dusty robes, plaited hair, and smiling faces; old men mumbled their prayers as the beads that each person held were turned endlessly. The queue edged forward, but as I noticed with amusement, it moved very slowly. People were endlessly jumping in and going to join relatives and friends at the front, but no one seemed to mind.

I wondered what would happen in my church in Battersea if, when people were queuing for communion, people barged to the front. You can be sure that despite the solemnity of the occasion someone would pipe up: "I say! Look here! You can't just go barging to the front like that . . ."

We edged forward. It was all the more exciting for me because I had no idea what I was waiting for. Then the Dutchman from the trip suddenly appeared. I'd thought he had left Lhasa, but he obviously had extra days on his visa as well. He walked up to me. Once again it seemed I had offended him.

"What are you doing?"

"Er, I'm not sure. Waiting for a kind of blessing, I imagine."

"You can't do that. You're not a Buddhist. You're not a believer—it's not right."

I was astounded. Did I need to explain to him that I'd been invited by the people around me who were now smiling at him and looking at me with question marks on their faces.

"Well, it's true I'm not a Buddhist. But I'm not sure that means I'm not a believer. I think I am a believer."

"You're not a Buddhist." And off he went. Everything I did had offended him. It was so strange. I felt such joy in this place, in the middle of a ceremony that was unchanged for hundreds of years. I pondered his words, but Buddhism is not a religion that you need to join formally like the Roman Catholic Church. I had been invited to be here, and that was good enough for me. The queue shuffled forward. I shuffled, too.

About an hour later we came to the chapel of the Buddha Avalokiteshvara. The gates of the chapel, normally closed, had been opened for the occasion. I observed what happened. Each pilgrim stepped forward and laid their head on the statue, kissing what would have been the feet were they not covered in piles of *kathaks*, the traditional scarves used for making an offering. After a couple of seconds, if the pilgrim was tempted to rest his head for too long, a monk would unceremoniously pull the back of his clothing to indicate that the time was up. Then everyone was walking around the back of the statue and repeating this on the other side.

After I'd watched the process twice, I was ready for my turn. I glanced up at the serene eyes of the Buddha and walked towards him. I stepped forward and laid my head on his lap for perhaps three seconds. I felt the whole area of my body behind my breastbone go warm. I got up and walked around and laid my head down on the other side; warmth flooded through me. I lifted my hands and laid them across my breastbone as I walked away. I had felt something quite clearly. What was this? My intellectual mind went into overdrive. What was I feeling? Was I suddenly prone to suggestion? I was definitely not imagining the feeling. I am familiar with what Chinese and Indian medical maps of the body call the "heart point." It's the part in the center of your chest that aches when someone you love goes away. But sometimes it seems to move. What they call the "heart point" seems to have sensation all of its own.

The warm glow spread outward through my body. I felt touched and strangely tearful. I looked round to the people who had invited me, and they smiled at me.

They could see that I was moved, and it evidently pleased them. This was their way of thanking me for entertaining the pilgrims. I bowed to them the way they bow to lamas, and they laughed. Then I gave them hugs, European fashion, before they walked off, smiling at me through the crowd. These were friends that I would never see again.

Outside in the square it was dark and cold. Very early tomorrow morning I had a flight to Kathmandu. I walked past the Jokhang Square Control Office and in my freshly blessed state felt nothing but warmth for the men who worked there. They were far from home, and apparently no Chinese person likes to be stationed in the Tibetan Autonomous Region. So much paradox in this place. So much pain and so much beauty. Somewhere hundreds of political prisoners were still being called "dangerous separatists." Then the Chinese official who had been so kind to the beggar saw me and waved with a big smile.

I would have been glad to have spent another year in Tibet just learning about the realities of life here. And I was also glad to be flying back to the freedom of Nepal.

A Gentle Friendship

I walked out of the airport into the polluted but blissfully warm air of Kathmandu and looked around for a bus. I figured I knew the name of the place I was heading for, and there had to be one. It would be cheaper than the price that taxis would charge me as soon as they saw my rucksack.

But then somewhere out of the corner of my eye I saw red robes and did a double take—surely I was not being met? And then there was a laughing face that had grown so familiar and, I realized in an instant, so dear to me that it was as much as I could do to avoid throwing my arms around this strange man.

"Khenpo La. I can't believe you came. . . . How did you know what flight I was on?"

"I arranged tickets for you. Did you forget?"

"I am very touched that you have come to meet me."

"I take your bag."

He discouraged the beggars in one language and arranged a taxi in another.

"You leave tomorrow. So today I have lunch with you."

"It's lovely to see you. How are you?"

"I am good. How are you? Did you get sick with the altitude?"

"Yes, actually." Didn't think I'd trouble him with the details.

"What did you do in Lhasa?"

"I sat down."

He looked out of the window and not at me and launched into a long conversation with the taxi driver. Why trouble to come and meet me and then not talk to me? In two seconds I was bewildered again. But it was amazingly good to see him. I tried to remember the last time a monk had met me at an airport.

He paid for the taxi. "Hold on a minute," I said, pulling money from my purse in three currencies. . . . He smiled. "You don't have enough."

"Well, OK, you win, but you must let me buy lunch."

We walked from the taxi. Him walking ahead once more as if to disown me. But then he checked me into the guest-house and said, "Where would you like lunch?"

My head spun. A journey that had taken a week in one direction had just taken a couple of hours in the other. "Khenpo, Tibet was wonderful. And it's good to be back."

"Where would you like lunch?" Perhaps he thought I hadn't heard him the first time.

"Anywhere. You choose. No—somewhere without monks who will want things from you."

"I try. You like Nepali food?"

"Anything."

So he weaved us through the busy streets. So different from Lhasa. Everyone seemed happy, which was of course absurd—there was civil war in this country. But there was no enemy on the street. No guards in uniforms trying to control everyone.

And the familiar face of the Dalai Lama smiled down from every shop doorway.

We stopped in a little café.

"So?" he asked.

"There was something I wanted to ask you."

"I answer if I can."

"Last night in the Jokhang temple, I went to a service of some kind. I kissed the feet of the statue, and I felt something quite distinct. A change in me. The statue is just a block of painted wood, isn't it? So am I crazy or deluded or open to suggestion or what?"

"Yesterday was the feast of the medicine Buddha. That is what you went to."

"But the statue?"

"When it is built it is just wood or metal. It is like a symbol. But we put mantras inside and say prayers and do rituals, and a high lama gives a special blessing, and then it is transformed."

"So it has power because it has been given it by the people?"

"It is given by the mind of the meditator. You invite the Buddhas of past, present, and future to be present there and never to leave that place as long as the five elements don't destroy the statue."

So somehow it was more than suggestion. In Catholic churches where the statues are said to have miraculous powers it is thought that they have been given them by divine intervention. Skeptics believe that if miracles do occur it is because the gullible nature of the minds of the faithful are experiencing a psychological cure because they believe in the power of the statue. No more than the placebo effect. The Buddhist viewpoint seemed to be something quite different. They were not suggesting that an external God had given the statues power, but that somehow the energy in the prayers themselves and the minds of the high lamas had been passed into the statues. This had given them power and made them more than wood and metal. This was in total keeping with some New Age theories I'd heard about objects bringing the energy of a place with them. They say that if you inherit a chair from someone who has been very lonely and sat in it for many years, do not be surprised if some of the loneliness comes with the chair. Does this sound unlikely? I'm not so sure. I knew what I'd felt when I'd touched the statue, and I've never had any kind of supernatural experience.

The Nepali restaurant owner stopped to have a long conversation with Khenpo.

I raised my eyebrows slightly.

"He says he remembers me when I was a child. He's crazy—I didn't come here till I was an adult. I pretend, and I make him happy."

I smiled and ate lunch.

"This afternoon you need to rest," he informed me. "Tonight we will eat?"

"Thank you, I'd like that."

After we'd eaten we strolled around the stupa, and he bartered for me while I bought gifts to bring home.

Then while I was supposed to be resting I made notes about a few remaining questions I had.

As we sat down to dinner I got out my notebook and said, "I've some questions I'd like to ask you. Would you mind?"

"Ask." I don't know what he was expecting, but these were evidently easier questions for him to answer than the ones about Tantric spirituality.

"What I don't understand is why, if people can live in Tibet in relative peace, so many are still making the journey to try to escape. Why are they prepared to risk their lives?"

"Eighty-five percent of men escape because they want to become monks and they can't do that in Tibet because the numbers are restricted."

"How many people are still trying to escape?"

"There are six million Tibetans. Two hundred and fifty thousand of them live outside Tibet. About 150,000 are in India. About 2,000 to 3,000 a year escape from Tibet."

"You sound like an encyclopedia. How do you know all this?"

"There is a reception center in Kathmandu, and I speak Tibetan so they ask me to go there sometimes. I hear all the stories. There is a hospital, too. Many of them get frostbite and lose limbs. There was a young boy there, and I translated for him. He was very bright, about nineteen. He had to lose both his legs because of frostbite. It was incredible. I didn't see his face sad. Somehow he accepted that."

"Why do they come in winter when it's so cold?"

"It's impossible in summer because of the monsoon and the landslides. Also in winter there are fewer Chinese guards. But it is always terrible. Some lose their way and die, some are shot. Even when they get here the Nepali police are very corrupt and they take everything. Even the few rupees that they may have. And the Nepali police hand them back."

"I met a monk in Lhasa who this had happened to. He crossed the mountains only to spend nine months in a Chinese jail."

"In the last two or three years fewer people come because they have so many checkpoints, and they know if they are caught they will be treated terribly by the Chinese. Even the United Nations and its Commission for Human Rights are asking the Nepali government minister not to hand them back to China."

"They are so desperate they will risk their lives?"

"They want to become monks, and they want to see Dalai Lama, and they want to study."

"Surely they can study there?"

"In the monasteries there they have to learn the Red Books that speak of 'the Motherland.' Everything is 'the Motherland'—the brainwashing is incredible. People would rather risk their lives than say these things. They have killed over a million people."

"Yes . . ."

There was a pause. I suddenly didn't want to ask any more questions.

In this gentle and placid monk I had uncovered rage. He ate his food. I ate mine. Finally he spoke again.

"They are controlling with brute force. They are trying to destroy Buddhism. Like Inner Mongolia. Three million Mongolians and between six and seven million Chinese. Mongolian has become a second-class language so the culture is dying."

I knew nothing about Mongolia.

"It's absurd to say Tibet is part of China. Not a single word of the language is similar. Tibetan is based on Sanskrit, which is an old Indian script."*

I listened, and finally he stopped and smiled. "I'm sorry. It is difficult."

"I know."

"I missed you." I looked up. Didn't he just say, "I missed you"?

"Sorry?"

---

* Khenpo was right in that Chinese is a tonal language whereas Tibetan is alphabetical. However, Tibetan script is not actually based on Sanskrit but derives from another Indian language branch called Gupta script.

"When you were away. I think you are very warm person. You have many good qualities."

"Thank you." I paused. What was I to make of this simple phrase? This was a monk I was talking to. I suddenly wanted to kiss him, but I could hardly tell him that. I hesitated.

"I missed you, too."

"I will come with you to the airport in the morning."

Suddenly I started to sound very English.

"No, really. There is no need. I'm sure you are very busy and have many things to do."

"I will come to the airport with you."

Maybe he wanted to be sure I caught my plane.

"Thank you, Khenpo."

I sat and looked at him. "Do you have any friends here? Anyone you can talk to—about meeting an English girl?"

"No. I will tell no one about you."

"Do you meet many people like this? Tourists?"

"Never."

"Could you ever come to London? To visit me?"

"I don't know. I have many relatives who I have to give money to. They are simple people, and they have no income."

I didn't like to ask where he got his income from.

"Would you like to come?"

"Maybe. We will see what happens in the future."

What on earth did this mean? We walked back under the gaze of all of Kathmandu, and he dropped me at the gate to the guest-house, under the gaze of the guest-house staff. No chance of even pecking him on the cheek.

In the morning he appeared at my door while I was searching helplessly for the lid of a water carrier that had chosen to disappear into thin air. I felt profoundly stupid as I'd promised I'd be ready. I looked up and saw him smiling. "I've lost a lid. I know it must be here somewhere." I crawled around on all fours while he stood in his robes, a picture of elegance and composure.

"I brought you these for your journey. From the garden here." And from behind his back he produced four white roses.

"Roses? Why, thank you. But you know roses are considered very romantic?"

"I pick them in the garden this morning," he said, giving me no answer to my question at all. What did he want? The locals had said, "Marriage, sex, or money." What did I want of him? Whatever it was, we were on our way to the airport. I gave up on the stopper. "Would you like a water carrier?" I asked.

"Yes, that would be useful. Especially as I have a stopper here that matches it. A boy brought it to me. Someone left it in the restaurant last night." This monk was far too clever for me.

I touched him on the arm for good measure. As I knew I wasn't allowed to.

"She is so naughty!" he said, going back to the use of the third person.

"Could he take my bag, please?" I asked.

We climbed into a taxi. The guest-house staff waved. "They will all be talking about me getting in a taxi with a Western lady."

"Your reputation in tatters? We didn't even kiss!"

"She says things!" He looked round at the taxi driver, who evidently did not speak English.

Then he became all organizing again. "Do you have everything you need? Did you check your tickets?"

"Yes, Khenpo."

"Do you have Indian rupees for Delhi airport?"

"No. I don't."

"How are you going to buy a drink or anything to eat on your transfer planes? I give you some Indian rupees."

"I'm sure I'll be OK."

"You have long wait. Take this." Once again he was giving me money.

The taxi sped on towards the airport. Somehow we had become fond of each other. We said nothing else. I could say I felt like a teenager, but as a teenager I had never had a friend like this. Someone who gave me white roses.

When we got there he said, "I have a gift for you." And out of his pocket he took a wonderful Tibetan medallion. "Inside are many strong prayers. It will protect you from difficult obstacles. And it has the Kalachakra mantra on the back. This is very powerful mantra."

I felt tears pricking the back of my eyes and took a deep breath so as not to embarrass him or myself.

"You go in now . . . take that door there." And again he became a man who was used to being obeyed.

He held out his hand for me to shake it. I shook it obediently. "Thank you, Khenpo. Your present is beautiful. I am very touched."

"You go in now." He was obviously not accustomed to saying goodbye to people that he seemed to have grown to care for.

I did as I was told and watched him linger until I was quite out of sight. I tried to summon a little serenity.

PART: THE SECOND

The Courage to Change the Things I Can

HELPING THE HELPERS?

—*mm*—

MAY I GIVE YOU THIS BOOKLET?

"The courage to change the things I can." This phrase haunted me as I pondered the whole Tibetan experience. Some argue that if anything is to be done, then it is for Tibetans themselves, within Tibet, to act. Others ask how they could act when even to sit down in the Potala square in the name of greater Tibetan autonomy will get them locked up. Surely, enough Tibetans have given up their liberty or their lives already. If I lived in Tibet, I think I'd develop many interests, possibly excluding politics.

Yet in Britain I could act and not fear imprisonment and torture. Suppose a small action does have repercussions? I don't have much wisdom, but the prayer seems to assume that there is something that can be done. "Courage to change the things I can" seems to indicate that it is possible to change things. But with a problem as huge as the Chinese desire for "progress" in Tibet, could I do anything that mattered?

I didn't doubt, to an extent, that Chinese motives were good. But so were the motives of the Christian missionaries as they suppressed native religions and of the Islamic fundamentalists bent on killing off anyone who doesn't worship Allah in the way that they think is appropriate. I could argue in my head that all these people thought that their motives were good. The Chinese government believes Tibet is part of China because they have been taught that since primary school. They believe that the Dalai Lama is a "separatist" who lies and deceives for his own political ends and is trying to bring about the breakup of the Motherland. Each demonstration in Tibet is stamped on so severely because they hate to see their precious stability disturbed.

What could I do? And if, as the prayer seems to suggest, the answer is not "nothing," then what answer could I find where Tibet is concerned? I glanced at the little card I had of the serenity prayer, crossed out the title, and wrote "the courage prayer." Wisdom could come later.

I set to work almost immediately. Getting in touch with the main British organizations that support Tibet, I soon found that they all had different ideas as to the best way to proceed and some interesting descriptions of each other. I heard the Tibet Vigil, with whom I had spent some enjoyable Wednesday evenings, described as "hopeless idealists," the Free Tibet Campaign as "a campaigning organization that just promotes itself," and the Tibet Information Network as "the crusty lot that writes the boring news reports"; a good friend of one of the TIN researchers referred to them as the "Lost Cause Information Network." Mmm—very helpful. The Tibet Society, which was supposed to have some political emphasis, was described as "well-meaning." There was also The Tibetan Community in Britain; they were described as "about 200 lovely people that have good parties."

I hoped to find a strong and clear lead coming from the Tibetan government-in-exile and the organizations working in cooperation with them.

I made an appointment to go and see the Dalai Lama's representative in London. Mr. Dorjee had a heavy accent, and I barely understood him on the telephone, but he gave me an appointment as soon as I requested one.

To open the conversation I told him that I had just returned from Tibet, and as he made polite inquiries about the journey, a diplomatic smile crossed his face. Then I launched into what was being done about the problems and specifically what the individual could do.

"We are very appreciative of the support people give to the Tibetan cause. The people who stand outside the embassy every week and demonstrate, for example—we are very encouraged by this. But of course we have no links with them. If we did have, then the Chinese government would accuse us of organizing this activity. As it is, they know that we have nothing to do with them. Support from grassroots level is not based on self-interest so it is genuine support. These people just go there, year after year. It's a wonderful thing."

It may be wonderful, but I wondered how effective it was.

"Do you think it's useful what the Vigil does and asks for?"

"We don't know what they are asking for."

He jumped around from one subject to another.

"The British government had a treaty relationship with Tibet, but now they turn a deaf ear."

I dearly wanted him to clarify some of these things for me.

"What is your government asking for?"

"We would like to open negotiations with the Chinese. But the world governments will not put pressure on them to do this. China appears huge, economically and militarily, but the government fails to realize how desperately China needs the West. Would you like some information? May I give you this booklet?"

He handed me a huge booklet: "China's Current Policy in Tibet: Life-and-Death Struggle to Crush an Ancient Civilisation."

"Thank you," I mumbled, rather half-heartedly perhaps.

"And here is another."

He handed me an 88-page booklet about the enforced "agreement" between Tibet and China.

"And are you interested in the environmental problems?"

I was handed an A4-sized book of 159 pages.

"There is the magazine of the Tibet Foundation. You will find many interesting articles there." He handed me ten or eleven different issues.

"Thank you."

I felt as if he was, quite literally, weighing me down with information on why nothing would be achieved.

I stood up before he presented me with a history of Tibet.

I was determined to find a way forward from this brief meeting, however small.

"Tell me," I asked. "Can you give me one example of an action that you feel is effective?"

"Yes, writing letters, especially about political prisoners, is very effective."

"Thank you."

"Thank you. It has been most interesting to meet you."

When I got home I rang Amnesty International and spoke to Isabel Kelly, the China specialist.

"Could you tell me, please, where China is concerned, do you think writing letters is effective? Does China listen?"

"It may not get the prisoners released any sooner, but I think it stops them being tortured."

I see.

"Could I come and meet you?"

"No. I finish here this week. After eleven years, I'm going to Tibet."

"Ah." (I didn't say, "I've just done that" and warn her that she might die.) "Can I meet you when you get back then?"

"Yes. That'll be in three months. I'm going to India and Nepal, too."

"OK, I'd rather it had been this week, but three months would be an obvious second choice."

"Did Mr. Dorjee give you some booklets?"

WAIT A MINUTE, SERGEANT

So I made an appointment with the Tibet Information Network, the first of the organizations on my list, and I started to read. I began with a list of ten books about Tibet. I didn't want to become an academic, but I had to know something.

Meanwhile the Tibet Vigil was still demonstrating outside the Royal Institute of British Architects. I had been sent an email: "Special Tibet Vigil for International Human Rights Day. To remember Tibetans who have died in prison or been killed on peaceful demonstrations, and to call for the release of political prisoners."

I was dubious about the benefits of such actions. It was worthy, of course. But opposite an empty embassy? I knew something more was called for. Maybe it was time to get arrested. I knew that if I broke the law for the first time, I would simply be carted back to the police station and told off. Given an official "caution." It would be the second or third time that I caused the police trouble that things would start to get interesting. Perhaps I could use this event as a tryout.

I rang Simon of the long hair and long beard. "I'm thinking of laying flowers on the step, where it isn't allowed, or of sitting on the step with my flag and getting arrested."

"That's great. Only you can't do that."

"Why not?"

"I've signed a piece of paper saying that we will abide by the rules of peaceful demonstration. We've agreed that we will cross the road, two at a time, to lay flowers and then we will cross back again. If you want to break the law, you'll have to register as a separate demonstration from the Tibet Vigil."

"But I don't want to do that. I don't want my own vigil. I want to support yours. Surely you can't be held responsible for the actions of everyone?"

"That's true. It would have been all right if you hadn't told me. But you have told me. I've given them my word, and I'm a man of my word, you see."

"Can't you ring them and say that one of the demonstrators may not keep her word?"

"No."

"Why not?"

"That wouldn't be fair to you."

"Do you want me to ring them and say I'm thinking of sitting on the step with my flag?"

"That's daft."

"What do you suggest, then?"

"I don't know. I've got four doors to paint. I'll go and paint them and think about it."

A day went by. He thought about it, and so did I. What were the merits of being arrested? I knew that something ludicrous was needed. I'd try anything and learn from the experience. Even if it didn't work.

I rang my daughter at college. "How do you feel about my being arrested?"

"Fantastic. Will they lock you away for long? Can I have the flat?"

"Very amusing."

"What for? Have you robbed a bank, because I'd been meaning to tell you that I need fifty pounds . . ."

"I was attempting to be serious for a couple of seconds. It's a demonstration on Human Rights Day—about Tibet. I was thinking of breaking the rules."

"That's fine. Really. I don't mind. It sounds interesting."

So that was sorted out. I had the daughter's approval. Then I asked a few other friends what they thought. The first two said, "Good for you." The third said, "And what will that achieve?"

"Not much. But I'm learning. Even if I learn what doesn't work, I feel that's important."

In the evening I rang Simon back.

"Well?"

"Yes, thank you. The doors look terrific. And no, I still don't know what's best to do."

"I tell you what, Simon. I'll come along and see what feels right on the night. I'll explain to the police that you've told me to keep the rules but that I don't know that I want to listen."

"OK. That sounds good."

I emailed a friend who had expressed disapproval and concern over the "being arrested" idea and told him that I'd be careful. He emailed back: "I have an urgent question for you."

"What?"

"If the government officials move you off the steps, does that make you Chinese take-out?"

When International Human Rights Day came, I put on some very warm clothes and stood waiting for a bus, holding the flag of Free Tibet, which blew in the wind. I did not forget the privilege of being able to hold the flag up. I couldn't really grasp the reality of people being imprisoned and tortured in Tibet for owning a post-card with this flag on it. The people at the bus stop stared. Eventually, as we boarded the rarely seen bus 344, a girl asked me about the flag.

"Tibet." I smiled. "Free Tibet."

"Oh yeah, that's the Dalai Lama's place?" She seemed to have a more accurate understanding of Asian history than the Chinese government.

"Yes, that's right." I smiled at her.

"Yeah, they tried to make it part of China. I saw Brad Pitt in the film."

"You are half right," I said. "But what happened is that they did make it part of China. In some ways there is actually no Tibet any-more. It was swallowed. Like the Nazis tried to do with Poland."

"Why did they do that?"

"Their motives have been described as strategic, imperialist, and economic."

"You mean, like money?"

"That's it exactly. Like money."

I arrived five minutes early to find that the pavement outside the Royal Institute of British Architects was filled with figures sitting cross-legged and meditating. Paula walked up to me with her usual warm smile.

"These people are members of Falun Gong. It has seventy million members in China, so the Chinese government has made it illegal."

"What do they do?"

"Meditation, a light diet, some exercises like yoga. It's a spiritual path, but it isn't Communism; that's why the government doesn't like it. They don't want anyone believing in anything that isn't Communism."

"Surely they can't lock people up just for meditating?"

"They've locked up hundreds of people so far."

Five o'clock arrived, and the gentle meditators rolled up their mats and went home. Apparently they are there all day, every day, seven days a week.

Then more Free Tibet vigilers started to arrive—a larger motley bunch than the usual. But the same bizarre mixture of the weird and the weirder still. There were even some people that looked relatively normal. And then there were the policemen—a study in normal that of course made us demonstrators seem more weird. There were four of them instead of the usual one, and two more sat in a large and aggressive-looking van. Outside the Royal Institute of British Architects, sundry old ladies stood with flowers and candles in jam jars.

Simon of the long hair, long beard, and previously bugged phones stepped forward. "I've arranged with the police that we can go across the road in ones and twos to lay flowers against the railings. While we are doing this we are going to read the names of ninety people who have died in prison. We can walk across the road as long as we don't linger and we don't lay the flowers on the actual steps."

I felt a huge desire to linger on the actual steps while laying flowers there. Simon had gotten wise to me. "Isabel, will you read out the names? Here is the megaphone."

"OK."

So while an assortment of strangers picked up chrysanthemums I switched on the megaphone and made sure I spoke into it loudly enough that anyone in the embassy who spoke English would hear.

"Lobsang Legden, aged twenty-one, a monk of Sera Monastery. He took part in a peaceful demonstration along with forty-three other monks at the Barkhor in Lhasa. They were all arrested. Outside, Tibetans started to shout for the release of the monks, and the monks began to recite prayers for His Holiness the Dalai Lama. The police fired on the monks. Lobsang was killed instantly.

"Jampa Tenzin, aged forty-nine, a monk of Jokhang temple. Was found dead with a rope around his neck in circumstances described as 'highly suspicious.' He had become the symbol of the Tibetan independence movement after he ran through flames to release Sera monks trapped in a burning police station.

"Lhakpa Dondrub, aged twenty-six, from Lhasa. He joined a peaceful demonstration, was arrested and put into Gutsa prison, where he was beaten and tortured to death."

There were pages of these stories. Each with a picture.

I kept my voice loud and clear. "Lhakpa Tsering, aged nineteen, a student. He was arrested for attempting to organize a student group in favor of Tibetan independence. He was beaten, tortured, and denied medical attention on at least three occasions. He died after less than one year in prison."

My daughter and her boyfriend arrived, all smiles. He was nineteen. The same age as the boy I was reading about. "Can we help?" they asked. Paula gave them some leaflets, and they ran in and out of the traffic at the lights, giving out leaflets. They looked so positive and so joyful. I read on.

"Sherab Ngawang, aged eighteen, a nun from Michungri Nunnery. She took part in a peaceful demonstration with four other nuns and one monk. She was arrested and sentenced to three years. One night in prison she joined with other nuns in singing freedom songs. She was beaten and tortured with electric prods, tied with rope, handcuffed, and put in solitary confinement. She was later taken to hospital, where she died."

Tears started to well up in my eyes. I ignored them. I read on, and on.

"Wangdu, aged twenty-six. A monk from Tashilhunpo Monastery, a caretaker of the eleventh Panchen Lama's stupa. Committed suicide, leaving a letter saying that he would not denounce the young incarnate Panchen Lama announced by the Dalai Lama."

My daughter bounced up. They had been chatting to the drivers, not listening to what I'd been reading. She glanced at me. "You OK?" I nodded and kept reading.

"Sangye Tenphel. Aged nineteen. A monk from Damshung Monastery. Arrested for expressing his desire for Tibetan independence in his songs and posters. Taken to Drapchi prison where he died in custody as a result of beatings and torture."

A Tibetan woman walked up to me and offered to take the megaphone. "Thank you." I smiled at her.

She took the list. I had been reading through the list for an hour. It was not halfway through. Her voice was strong. She had heard all this before.

"Kelsang Thutop, aged forty-nine, of Drepung Monastery. He has translated the Universal Declaration of Human Rights into Tibetan. He was taken to Drapchi prison for interrogation, and when he returned he could not utter a single word. He died the next morning. It was observed at his burial that his testicles had been brutally crushed."

I decided I'd hear one more, then I'd go and give out leaflets myself.

"Tenchok Tenphel, aged twenty-seven. A monk from Sakya Monastery. Government teams came to the monastery and forced monks to compose essays denouncing the Dalai Lama. Tenchok wrote an essay praising him. He was taken to Sakya county prison, where he was tortured. After fifteen days he committed suicide by strangling himself with his waistband in his cell."

I walked away and picked up some flowers. A friend had arrived, and together we walked across the road and laid flowers. I smiled at the policemen who were lined up along the step so no one could trouble the Chinese government with chrysanthemums. I walked back across the road as I was supposed to. Paula came up to me, smiling. "Here, have some chai tea," she said.

I took it gratefully. "How long has this demo been going on, Paula?"

"The vigil for Tibet has been here every Wednesday night for thirteen years. A week hasn't been missed. It's the longest unbroken vigil in the world."

"Is anyone listening?"

"I don't know—but cheer up. Simon has an idea for later that I think you'll like."

I gave out leaflets to the drivers and waved a flag. "What's the flag?" they'd ask.

"It's the flag of Free Tibet. That's the Chinese embassy there."

"Oh." More blank stares from passersby. A man in a van said disdainfully, "Thanks. Well, enjoy your little protest."

"Thank you. Have you heard of Tibet?"

"Vaguely. Some Chinese place, is it?"

"Some people would agree with you. But please read the leaflet."

Occasionally someone would say, "Free Tibet? Good for you."

Others would honk their horns in support as they drove by. Eventually the flowers ran out, and the time ran out. The names didn't. Paula sighed. "We never get through them all."

I walked up to Simon. "So what's this stunt you want to pull, then?"

"I have these two large helium balloons . . ."

"Yes?"

"And some very long twine. And a flag of Free Tibet. See those aerials up there on top of the embassy?"

It was about five stories high. "I see them."

"The plan is to tie a balloon to each end of the flag and to get the whole lot up onto the aerial."

I was all ears. "Isn't this illegal, too?"

"The police haven't expressly told us that we can't do it."

"Did you ask them?"

"Of course not. Hold this," he said, getting the twine caught up in his hair, which was considerably longer than mine. "And tie it on there. A knot that won't undo."

I proudly produced a round turn and two half hitches.

"Great, and another posh knot on this end. Now if you hold that one we can let it up."

"Has this ever worked?" I asked.

"Only once. But it's failed lots of times."

We let the flag rise way up above the buildings, but the wind was blowing in the wrong direction.

"Once it got caught on the aerial of the Royal Institute. We need to pull it down south so that it catches the through wind from Weymouth Street."

We walked up and down, pulling and teasing our rather bizarre kite. The protestors watched, but the police watched, too. They could see what we were trying to do, and they were wondering if they should let us do it or not. By this time Simon and I were at opposite ends of the Institute. But the balloons still weren't doing what we wanted. In desperation I stepped out into the middle of the road. A policeman approached me. "I must ask you to step back, madam, or you may cause an accident." There were no cars to be seen. "Wouldn't there need to be a vehicle of some kind?" I stepped onto the island in the middle of the road. My eyes were fixed on the task. I yanked. On the other side Simon yanked, too. Eventually it reached the aerials and appeared to get caught. A cheer went up from the crowd. Two policeman marched over to

Simon with scissors and cut his string. But I wasn't convinced it would hold once the string was gone. The balloons broke free, the crowd sighed, but I still had my twine. One of the policemen walked over to me. I'd introduced myself to him earlier.

"I can't allow you to do that, Isabel. That is diplomatic property."

"Chinese government property, Sergeant. Yes, I know." I kept my eyes on the flag. "Were you able to hear the voices through the megaphone tonight?" I yanked and pulled.

"I was, yes."

"Do you believe in peaceful protest in the force?"

"Yes. We do. But that is damaging diplomatic property."

"Look at those aerials. Do you honestly think two helium balloons and a piece of cloth will damage them?"

He was silent. Then he went on, "Even if they are not damaged, I can't allow you to do that . . ." But he wasn't preventing me. He was just walking beside me, telling me to stop. I wasn't stopping. I walked out into the road and back onto the island. He followed me, all the time telling me to stop.

"Give me a break here," I said. "Could you wait a minute, Sergeant? This is taking all my concentration."

The balloons wedged. I watched the wind blow the flag around the aerial. It was stuck. I smiled at him and let go of the twine. It was light and blew up the side of the building. A cheer went out from the vigilers. Simon rushed over, all smiles. "Well done!" he beamed.

"Look, we have the flag of Free Tibet flying over the Chinese embassy." We shook hands warmly. I wanted to say "Thank you" to the policeman, but I thought that might be pushing it. I could have sworn I saw him smile.

It was a tiny gesture but a satisfying one.

"Are you going to arrest me, Sergeant?" I asked rather too hopefully.

"No chance."

Shucks.

"Well done," said my daughter as she and her boyfriend appeared. "I need to ask you something though . . ."

"What is it? The nature of a totalitarian state? Hu Jin Tao's policy for economic development in the Autonomous Region?"

"I need some money. We wanted to go for a drink . . ."

I felt strangely grateful for the simple request and handed her a twenty-pound note.

"Don't spend it all at once."

But that night I'd have been rather glad if she had spent it all. She was eighteen; he was nineteen. So what if they came home drunk and watched rubbish TV till one in the morning. Suddenly I felt very appreciative of everything Western. I could go on a radio phone-in show the following day if I wanted to and say that I think the prime minister is a genius or a fool. I could stand on a box at Speakers' Corner in Hyde Park and try to induce anarchy in the nation. I could say "Bum" or "Trotsky," and no one would lock me up or torture me. And for all these years I'd not appreciated that. I went home and read Harry Potter.

The following morning I started phoning the press. I thought "Flag of Free Tibet Flies over Chinese Embassy" would make an amusing couple of lines in the Diary sections. I phoned, and Paula, the Vigil's official press person, sent faxes.

Eventually and after some perseverance, the phone started to ring. "We are going to run this story in the Diary section," said the *Guardian*. "We'll put a piece in Peterborough," said the *Telegraph*. Meanwhile I was phoning the Royal Institute of British Architects' bookshop to check that the flag was still there, which, joyfully, it was. I urged on the press gleefully, "Please phone the embassy and ask them why they are flying the flag of Free Tibet. Have they allowed the people of the Autonomous Region to vote, and are they now celebrating the independence of the Tibetan people?"

The *Telegraph* did ring the embassy as I suggested, and they apparently claimed that they had not seen the flag. But they got it down pretty quickly after the phone call. Ho ho. The *Guardian* wrote: "Bravo to the Tibet Vigil campaign for a clever wheeze which has resulted in the Tibetan flag apparently flying atop the Chinese embassy ever since becoming caught on the building's aerial on International Human Rights Day on Monday. . . . We salute their ingenuity."

What was more satisfying than this was that Paula then contacted World Tibet News with details of Simon's balloons. A heading "Flag of Free Tibet Flies over Chinese Embassy" was released to Tibet supporters all over the world. I imagined people in offices that supported Tibet smiling. Maybe even people in the Dalai Lama's office smiling. Maybe it would even be mentioned to the Dalai Lama himself? We allowed ourselves to indulge in the thought of how lovely it would be to bring a smile to a face with a reputation for smiling.

Paula and I decided to congratulate Simon by buying him a glass of apple juice the next time we saw him.

WILL YOU COME NEXT WEEK?

But however worthy this was, standing outside the Royal Institute of British Architects wasn't going to do it for me. I thought often about Khenpo and his rage and the story of the boy who had lost both his legs so that he could escape the Chinese. I couldn't decide whether demonstrating every week for thirteen years was a determined and heroic act that encouraged Tibetans and their supporters internationally or the best example of ineffective action in the history of democratic protest. It was an enjoyable evening out, and I could see myself going along occasionally. Simon and Paula were two of the most committed people I'd ever met. Serious and dedicated to supporting a cause that had nothing to do with their lives. I admired them. But no, I would not be joining them the next week.

YOU NEED TO CHANGE THE CHINESE MIND-SET

My next step was to go to meet some of the professionals. I telephoned the Tibet Information Network and made an appointment to see Kate Saunders. I liked her from the first phone call.

She arranged to meet me "in this flower shop that sells cacti and coffee."

I arrived and seated myself carefully at a table on which stood a cactus wearing a pink hat. In walked Kate with a huge smile. "Am I late?" She was not late. We served ourselves very large mugs of coffee. I had many questions.

"So what exactly is the Tibet Information Network?" This seemed an easy place to start . . .

"TIN is an independent news and research service. We give out comprehensive information on political, economic, cultural, social, and environmental issues in Tibet."

"What do you mean 'independent'?"

"We are not influenced by any governments or any campaign agendas."

I could have some fun here. "Surely," I assumed a Chinese accent, "should you not then be called the Information Network of the Tibetan Autonomous Region of China?"

She smiled at me. "No. Because the area that we research is much larger than the TAR, which was defined in 1965 and is a Chinese-imposed geographical area."

"So you are the information network of an area that no longer exists?"

"We include the traditionally Tibetan areas of Kham and Amdo, which are now incorporated into the Chinese provinces of Qinghai, Yunnan, Gansu, and Sichuan. These are areas that Tibetans in exile still define as Greater Tibet. They are huge geographically, larger than Western Europe. When the Chinese invaded Tibet, it took them a year to reach Lhasa."

"Liberated Tibet?"

"If you like, but that wouldn't be neutral either, would it? But we are not making any judgments—we are simply reporting on the news that comes out."

"So if a group of Tibetans beat up a Chinese policeman, would you report that?"

"It would depend on what the evidence was. We don't report just everything. We look more at general trends."

"What sort of trends?"

"A story came in recently about some thefts from monasteries of sacred art by Chinese officials. It had some quotes from monks but, as far as I was concerned, not enough evidence to prove what had happened. Context is very important. Because we're not operating in the country itself, it's difficult to get a rounded picture of what's going on. So subtleties and nuances become tremendously important."

"So is one murder enough?"

"You have to remember that whatever we put out will be used by the international media, Western governments, and campaign groups, so we have to be very careful that what we say is accurate. I heard that a Chinese official who shall remain nameless once described me in an Internet discussion group as a 'notorious liar,' except he spelled it 'notorious lair.'" She smiled.

"Isn't that rather irritating when you put so much time into checking all the facts?"

"Not at all. Being described as a liar by a Chinese official on matters of human-rights abuses is a great compliment. We know that the government officials read our material. If they describe us as 'splittists' or liars, we know that we have touched a nerve."

"I'd be terrified doing your work."

"During the 1980s' pro-independence demonstrations in Lhasa, photographs of Tibetan demonstrators were published in the Western media, and the Chinese government used them to identify individuals and lock them up. So we are incredibly careful."

She went quiet for a moment. Then in a change of pace she said, "One of the first Buddhist principles is 'Cause no harm.'"

"Are you Buddhist, Kate?"

There was a long pause.

"No, but I try to do my best for all sentient beings. And I try to cherish ill-natured beings and to view those who treat me badly as excellent spiritual guides."

"Oh, yes?" I smiled, recognizing this more Buddhist version of my old favorite: "Use everything for your learning, upliftment, and growth."

"But I don't always succeed."

I really liked this woman a lot. She was so open and so warm, and there was a freedom she had. She was diplomatic, certainly, but generous, too.

"How did you get involved in all this, Kate?"

"Fifteen years ago I went to India to work in a tiger sanctuary, and during that trip I met some Buddhist monks and heard their story and decided that I had to know more about Tibet, so I got involved when I got back."

"You must meet some interesting people?"

"It's true that a rather worrying proportion of my ex-boyfriends are either psychologists or dissidents in some form. What do you suppose that means?"

"That you end up taking your work home?"

"What about you, Isabel? Any romantic interest in your life?" I was embarrassed. I didn't feel like admitting that my heart was in a state of confusion and my bag full of recently developed photos of a laughing monk. "I, er . . ."

"Oh, come on," she said enthusiastically, "spill the beans."

"No, there is no one, Kate."

"Then why the hesitation?" She had seen through me far too easily.

"I did meet this man in Nepal who I became rather confused by."

"Oh, yes? And did he become confused by you, too?"

"Yes," I said, honestly enough. "I think he did."

Long pause. She waited patiently. I took a deep breath. I hadn't told anyone about him. I felt so foolish.

"He was a monk, Kate. The abbot of his monastery, in fact."

She smiled knowingly. "You aren't the first person to have been confused by a monk. At least three of my friends are married to former monks."

I laughed. "But maybe they were already ex-monks when they met. And maybe they were not the khenpo of the monastery."

"He was a khenpo? Goodness, Isabel, I am impressed."

"Thank you. But feeling myself fond of a monk who lives in Nepal and, incidentally, doesn't own a passport isn't a relationship, is it?"

"Does he email you?"

"He did at first. Now less and less. I think he loves his life there and is genuinely happy. And I'm trying to learn serenity. I wouldn't want to change him even if I could."

"So?"

"So I've decided that he is someone that I will always carry in my heart" (along with a couple of others I could mention), "and that's that. So no—I have no one at the moment. Apart from a faraway monk who is fond of me, just as I am of him."

"That's wonderful."

She was lovely. I couldn't imagine her sitting in an office, typing out dry reports of the latest human-rights violations. "I couldn't do your job." I looked at her honestly.

"Why do you say that?"

"All that giving out information and not being able to do anything about it. Nuns being turned out of their communities, primary-school children being taught to disrespect the religion of their parents and the importance of the Chinese language. Every day another attack on the Tibetan culture."

"Some people say that simply making information public is a political act. But my job is not to campaign. There are others who do that."

"May I ask you about that?"

"Ask whatever you like."

"It seems to me . . . and of course I have no real understanding of the issues, but it seems to me that all the organizations that exist to support Tibet internationally have been profoundly unsuccessful."

"Public awareness of Tibet is high compared to Xinjiang."

"Where?"

"I rest my case. Although popular awareness of Tibet is high, it isn't always taken seriously as a political issue. You have to understand Tibet in the context of the bigger global picture."

This sounded a bit like why rich countries couldn't cancel the debt of developing countries. Because those who were making these demands didn't understand the "bigger global picture."

She went on, "China is a formidable enemy for Western campaigning organizations, and I'm not sure how you can make changes there."

"Er, with Western governments?"

"That's the problem, yes. Western governments are not taking on China in the way it should be taken on because they want to maintain trade links. What they don't realize is that China needs them as much as they think they need China. Probably more."

"I have a theory about this . . ."

"Yes?" Kate said encouragingly.

"Well, it's big, isn't it?"

"China? *Big* is a good word, yes."

"I think that all the Western members of Parliament had maps of the world when they were children, and so the first thing that they learned about China is how big it is and how many Chinese people there are. So they are not prepared to say, 'Stop torturing people and destroying things and behaving like psychopaths, or we won't buy your plastic toys . . . ,' all because it's so big."

"That's about the size of it."

We stared at our coffee for a while. Then she said. "There are some chinks of light."

"Where?"

"In the development of a civil society in China. China's changing every day, but there may not be a big political shift in the next nine or ten years. Not under the present leadership. Or the next leadership. This will be men and women who are in their forties now and may have been to Harvard or Yale or come to London and who have absorbed new ideas. At the moment these people may disagree with some of the things that the old guard is saying, but they don't yet have much of a support base."

"But they may have in ten years? Perhaps? Perhaps not?"

"Things will take a long time to change. You have to understand the Chinese mind-set."

I looked at her wearily. Here I was trying to explore the question of making a difference, and she was telling me to increase my understanding. What result would that produce other than to use up a couple more of my remaining gray cells? She looked at me patiently and went on.

"I know a very successful Chinese businessman who has a home here in London. Talking to him I feel as if I'm wading through treacle. There is all the paranoia that the West is against China, and he is very proud of what China has achieved. He thinks that all the Western media is against China, and you can't challenge this thinking because it is all black and white. There are no shades of gray; there is no subtlety, no indication that anything in his mind or the minds of his peers is going to budge at all."

"Why do you think he won't consider shades of gray?"

"I think one of the terrible consequences of the Chinese Cultural Revolution in the Chinese psyche is a complete fear of new ideas that may threaten society's stability."

"So have you given up with him?"

"No, and I have seen some shift. He will admit that when he first came here he thought that all the reports that come out from TIN were 100 percent false. Now he is not so sure and thinks that some of it may be true."

I was beginning to think that possibly changing the Chinese mind-set might be more of a task than I could take up on a Tuesday afternoon.

"So what's the good news, Kate?"

"The situation with Falun Gong is an interesting one. The Chinese have attempted to portray people who practice this as members of a dangerous cult. The Chinese government is threatened by the challenge to the party that the Falun Gong represents because some members of the party are also Falun Gong practitioners, so it is like an enemy within an atheist state. They've broken up demonstrations with armed security and imprisoned practitioners in labor camps."

"But surely they don't torture Falun Gong practitioners?"

"I'm afraid they do. There have been many deaths."

I wondered what was so powerful in the teaching that the government was so afraid.

"What it shows is that the government still doesn't hesitate to use violence to implement state policy. They behave like a bunch of thugs."

"They don't allow peaceful protest?"

"They certainly don't. Those who protest peacefully and even those who don't protest at all are being rounded up and sent to labor camps."

I sighed. "Kate, er, why do they torture people? Isn't it enough to lock people up if they don't like what they are doing?"

"The violence is institutionalized. I meet people who have been in Chinese prisons. My friend Mark was in Shanghai Number One prison for four years. You wouldn't want to hear what they do to prisoners."

It was all so strange, so unbelievable, so difficult to grasp that this was still happening at the same time as the sun shone and the coffee machine gurgled in the corner. "Perhaps I need to know, Kate." She leaned over and took a book out of her bag. "Here you are . . ." She smiled. "I've written a book on the subject." It is called

Eighteen Layers of Hell. She laughed. "I wouldn't recommend it for bedtime reading."

"Thank you."

"You may not want to thank me when you've read it. I'm afraid it's a hard read. A couple of the Chinese dissidents I know who are featured in it mentioned that there wasn't much humor, but some of their humor is so black that I didn't dare include it."

I glanced at the back of the book. The cover read, "How does it feel to be so lonely that the lice infesting your body provide relief from your solitude? How does it feel to be so hungry that you chew at the leather of your shoes until within days there is nothing left?"

I felt a profound desire to burst into tears just reading the back cover. "I don't understand, Kate. Why isn't anyone doing anything to prevent this?"

"We have Western governments that are supporting the regime. There are a lot of people around the world who don't really understand how China operates, and there is very little political will to understand. But at TIN we don't want to see China as an enemy, and we always strive to be as balanced and as fair as we possibly can be. We attempt to analyze and understand. It's important to look beyond the propaganda being put out by both sides."

"Good grief. I feel as if I need to go back to university for ten years."

"Me, too."

Somehow, despite the coffee and Kate's laugh and her positive smile, I was beginning to feel that I'd had another long explanation of why nothing could be done. This wasn't what I wanted.

"So what can the individual do, Kate?"

"What you are doing fits very well in Buddhist philosophy."

"What I'm doing? I've done nothing."

"Not so. You are concentrating on what is called 'right action.' All the great teachers teach the doctrine of right action. You watch your motivation, and you examine what you are doing."

"So what is 'right action' where Tibet is concerned?"

She smiled. "As I said. You need to change the mind-set of the Chinese in China."

I looked at her dryly. "And how do I do that?"

She laughed. "Write some letters?" I laughed, too, until peals of laughter impaled themselves on the cactus with the pink hat.

HEAD IN THE SAND

I can remember a book making me cry a tear or two. A romantic turn of phrase, a description that's particularly moving or sensitive. But I was totally unprepared for the effect wrought on me by *Eighteen Layers of Hell*. I started to read, and I would have to get up and walk in the garden before I could continue. As I progressed I began to cry and then to sob until my chest heaved and my head spun. Nothing in the book was graphic, and the descriptions by prisoners of the tortures that they had endured and others they had witnessed were spoken with clarity and calm.

In myself I felt such a capacity for tenderness and yet here were my fellow human beings committing institutionalized brutality on a scale that I had not imagined. Of course I have read history books. I knew that this had happened before. I knew of the Holocaust and of labor camps and of the torture there. But somehow I had always protected my consciousness from the knowledge of torture today. I had never joined Amnesty International. Of course I had justifications: "I'm a member of Oxfam and of Greenpeace," "There has to be a limit," "No one can do everything." But as I examined my reaction to the various leaflets I've seen created by Amnesty International over the years, I found there were other reasons I'd done nothing. It was as if I'd found the subject of torture somehow distasteful. Unpleasant. I preferred to live in my ivory tower and think about ecology and the planet and simply deny that these things were happening. I could go to the Imperial War Museum and look at exhibitions on the Holocaust and think how terrible it was that such things ever happened and . . . and . . . well, isn't the point to vow that they should never happen again? And yet they were happening, and the world was doing nothing. Even my reading-glasses case said "Made in China." This very item may have come from a forced-labor camp. Why hadn't I been made to know about this? I forced myself to keep reading.

Then I would put the book down again, make some trendy herbal drink to calm myself down, and sip it like a yogi. I'd breathe deeply and remind myself that there were also people of miraculous goodness in the world. And then I'd start to read again . . .

Suspension by the hands and feet is also common in the labour camps. The "hanging aeroplane" involves suspending prisoners by the arms with their hands tied together behind their back so that the arms are contorted when the prisoners are suspended, causing extreme pain. Suspension can severely damage the muscles and nerves and if prolonged causes dislocation of the arms from the shoulder sockets. On other occasions the guards would grab the prisoners from behind, force their wrists together at the back and yank their arms back and up towards the head, so that the prisoners fall on their knees, as the arms nearly break loose from their sockets. For variation, the wrists could be forced together in front, the arms jerked up over the head and then back in the torture known as the "chicken claws."

You could be forgiven for thinking that I have scanned the book for the most graphic passage. But I have merely opened it at random. This is what we don't want to know. Glancing at the opposite page, I read:

Electric batons are some of the most frequently used torture instruments in Chinese prisons, and they are purchased from trade fairs—sometimes made by European or American companies. . . . At a touch, a shock is released through two prongs at the nozzle of the baton, often emitting a crackling blue light. The batons are shaped in such a way that they can be inserted inside the body, and there is evidence that they have been applied to the soles of the feet, inside the mouth, on the genitals, or inside the vagina or ears of victims.

This may be more information than you want. But I thought that if people were suffering these things (for such heinous crimes as being a monk and shouting "Long live the Dalai Lama") and Kate was going to have the courage to write such a book, then the least I could do was read it. All 241 pages of it.

At one point, still sobbing, I rang her.

"Kate . . . your book . . ."

"Oh, Isabel," she said, "what have I done to you? It's bleak, isn't it?"

"How many people have read this?" I asked.

"It isn't exactly a best-seller." She made me laugh. I suppose if the men who were featured in the book could find humor to help them stay alive, then it was OK for me to smile.

"I think you have two problems with this book as regards people reading it."

"Mmm?"

"Well, there's the title—*Eighteen Layers of Hell*. And the content."

"Ah yes. The content."

Even this truth was black. Hardly anyone had read Kate's book.

"Are there any hopeful conclusions to your research?"

"In the afterword you may find something."

I wasn't going to skip to the end. I read on. When I finally reached it, I read: "China is more open than ever before, but it is still impossible for the Chinese to be free in a society which imprisons, tortures and executes those who stand against it."

The following morning I picked up the phone and rang the Free Tibet Campaign.

THE FREE TIBET CAMPAIGN

CAN WE CALL YOU BACK?

I assumed an important-sounding voice. I had high hopes of them, and I wanted them to have high hopes of me.

"My name is Isabel Losada. I'm a writer and journalist, and I also work for the BBC" (well, once a month). "I wonder if I could speak to your managing director?"

"No, I'm afraid she's in a meeting at the moment. Can I take your number and get her to return your call?"

"Certainly."

I waited patiently. Three days went by.

I tried again, assuming a voice of huge importance and significance. "Hello, I rang a couple of days ago and left a message for your managing director . . ."

"I'm so sorry. I'll get her to ring you."

Two more days went by.

I may have sounded slightly irritated the third time. "I'm calling from the BBC"—totally untrue—"and I'd like to speak with your managing director."

"I'm so sorry. She isn't here today. Can I take your number?"

Sigh.

I was glad for them that I was only myself. I could have been someone who could have been offering them something—a documentary-film opportunity about the struggles of a small direct-action group. Or—damn it—I could have been writing a book.

I persisted. I wanted to support these people. I was even happy to work for them for six months unpaid. You'd think they could return my phone call.

When I finally got my appointment, my heart fell as I entered the office. The first thing I noticed was that no one looked up. No one smiled. This struck me as very odd. I went to wash my hands and found the sink blocked. A bowl full of unwashed mugs was floating in a thick brown souplike substance. I wasn't sure about saying yes to a drink.

I was handed a very hot cup of coffee in a mug with the handle broken off.

Somewhere a voice was saying: "I'm Alison Reynolds. I'm sorry it's taken me so long to get back to you . . ." But I was thinking of other things you could do with a cup with no handle. Grow plants out of it? Store pens in it? Use it for a still-life sketch? Break it up and make a mosaic?

She took me into her office. "This year the European Union had a chance to table a motion on China at the United Nations human-rights commission . . ." I really wanted to listen to her. Fingertips singeing, I looked around helplessly for a surface that was not covered in books, papers, and telephones.

"And they just didn't do anything about it. The EU waited for the U.S. to do something, and the U.S. expected the EU to act. Some of the most serious human-rights abuses in the world are simply ignored, and this has gone on since 1997."

She chatted on effusively. She was obviously a very experienced campaigner.

"So we and many other campaigning organizations went to Geneva, and we were prevented from making any statements."

No. I could not hold the boiling-hot mug any longer.

"Where would you like me to put this down? I'd like to take some notes about what you are saying . . ."

Finally she realized my dilemma. Not the lack of handle or the fragrant smell of burning flesh but purely that all the surfaces were covered.

"Oh, I'm so sorry." She cleared a space, and I put down the mug. I was left wondering why I hadn't simply said, "Alison, I can't hold this mug. You've just filled it to the very top with boiling water, and it doesn't have a handle." Why hadn't I said that? Or even: "Have you considered throwing this mug away?" I tried to listen to what she was saying.

"The EU hasn't sponsored a resolution on China because it's afraid it would result in political reprisals from China. So you have one of the worst human-rights violators in the world going completely unchallenged. Which makes us wonder why we have a United Nations Commission for Human Rights in the first place. Trying to get them to do anything seems to be a total waste of our time."

Gradually my head cleared. I knew I wasn't interested in things that were a waste of time. "So what's next?" I asked simply. "How can I help?"

"There is the BP [British Petroleum] annual general meeting." She pulled out a leaflet. "The Tibetan government-in-exile has asked BP to withdraw the $578 million that they have invested in the Chinese oil company PetroChina because they are building a pipeline through Tibet, using Tibet's natural gas, and it all helps the Chinese consolidate their control over the region."

"So BP is giving the Chinese government exactly what it wants and ignoring the wishes of the Dalai Lama? Why would they do that when they know what has been done to Tibet?" I often ask stupid questions.

"For shareholder profit."

"So none of the shareholders voted against?"

"Shareholders representing 627.5 million shares voted against it last year. That was a market value of £3.8 billion. But it wasn't enough. This year the World Wildlife Fund is attempting to get BP to file a resolution asking them to be transparent about their drilling in environmentally and culturally sensitive areas. Places like the Alaskan Arctic National Wildlife Refuge. They won't stand a chance."

The overwhelming desire for profit. It's astounding. Ignore the environment. Ignore human rights. It was the illogicality of it that I couldn't get my head around. Anything we could do felt so insignificant compared to the power of these multinationals. "So what are you hoping to do?"

"Be there. Raise the issue. Embarrass them a little. That's all we can hope to do, I'm afraid."

"How do you plan to do that?"

ARE YOU BUSY THURSDAY MORNING?

My friends are used to strange phone calls, but this was more odd than most.

"What do you want me to do?"

"Dress up in a Chinese soldier's uniform and come to the BP AGM at the Royal Festival Hall."

"Does this involve getting arrested?"

"Oh, I'd love that. But no, I don't think there is the least chance."

"You would like to get arrested?"

"Yes, definitely. But this is all quite peaceful. In fact we are going to applaud. Rather loudly."

"Dressed as the Chinese military?"

"Exactly. You see, the Chinese army represents the Chinese government, and as BP is doing exactly what the Chinese government wants, we thought we'd go and applaud. It's rather tongue-in-cheek, but the irony will not be lost on the directors."

He chuckled. "And whose idea was this?"

"Not mine. I'm supporting this action by the Free Tibet Campaign . . . I told them I'll do anything that isn't aggressive. I rather like this."

Adrian (an architect, size very tall) and I arrived at the campaign office at a rather impressive 8 a.m. to find a group of about ten people of varying sizes and shapes trying on uniforms. They were dark green khaki. Someone had bought German uniforms from an army-surplus store and done some brilliant work with yellow ribbons, cut-out red felt stars, and gold spray-on buttons.

"Will they let us in dressed like this?" someone said nervously. But Alison had a plan.

"We all have proxy voting forms because there are BP shareholders who support Tibet who have given us their votes. So all our names are on the official list. We will go in and register in normal clothes and then leave the meeting and change into our uniforms. Besides, if people are shareholders or proxies, they have to let them in whatever they are wearing. Last year there were people from the Arctic Preservation Society dressed as polar bears."

We dressed and undressed. Then a beautiful young Tibetan girl arrived in traditional Tibetan dress, and we remembered why we were all there. She was not going to change and was simply going as herself. Alison briefed us. "We are not there to be aggressive to anyone but simply to raise the issue. Alongside yourselves we have those who will go to the mike and ask serious questions. We will probably be ignored, but we will ask them anyway."

"And do we react to you when you are asking questions?" asked a young lieutenant from the rear defense line.

"Yes, you can make loud tutting noises if you like."

We all changed back into civvies and piled into cabs. Some people were nervous and expressed doubts about the effectiveness of the action. "Won't they just think that we are troublemakers?" I pondered the question. "We are not going to be disruptive at all. Quite the reverse. We are going to applaud." It was clever.

We arrived at the Royal Festival Hall to find an incredible number of police cars and what were evidently plainclothes policemen standing around. We gathered in our little group. "Are you the anti-BP lot? The main entrance is up those stairs." I thought the policemen were supposed to make things harder for us. "Why would you help us?" I asked the helpful policeman.

"Why not?" he said.

We headed with our proxy cards for the voting tables. The place was already packed. I spotted an actress I knew, an old friend, wearing an outfit in blue and green that said BP. She walked up to me, smiling. "Hello, Isabel. What are you doing here?" I was still wearing my expensive navy suit at this stage. I winked at her. "I don't think you want to ask that question, Carol." She looked bemused. "Yes I do."

"No. Trust me. You don't."

"What?"

"You'll see me later."

Someone came running up from the registration desk. "They don't have any of our names. None of us are registered."

We looked at each other, bemused. Could the office have made a mistake? Should we all just go home now as we evidently weren't going to get in? The girl who had spent the previous week creating ten Chinese uniforms looked crestfallen. We walked out of the Festival Hall despondently to speak to Alison.

"We can't get in. They don't have any of our names."

Alison looked appalled. "What? It's not possible. I saw the registration confirmed on the screen with my own eyes."

"They've blocked it somehow," said the uniform-stitcher disconsolately.

"It didn't say Free Tibet Campaign on the email address, did it?" I asked Alison, thinking myself very amusing.

"No. It didn't. Maybe they just blocked them because it was a large group. But I did see 'Registration Confirmed.' OK. Round two. Change of plan. How many of you are genuine shareholders?"

Alison and the Tibetan girl had their own shares, donated by supportive BP shareholders. Apart from that, only one man raised his hand. "OK. Well, you're in, then, and you are allowed one guest. Who do you want to take in with you?"

"I'll take Isabel."

"OK. Isabel, you're in. The rest of you will just have to march up and down outside and give leaflets to as many people as possible and talk to everyone about why you're dressed as Chinese military."

It was a beautiful sunny morning. We started to get changed. So I just dropped my trousers there and then, to the amusement of the assembled policemen. Cameras snapped. Campaigners whistled. "OK, guys," I said. "These are legs, OK?"

The other "soldier" was a mousy-looking man. A devout Buddhist. The kind of man that looked as if he wouldn't hurt a rat if it was gnawing away at his foot. Alison and the Tibetan were going in wearing normal clothes so that they could speak at the mike. Suddenly I realized I was on my own. My Buddhist friend would support me, but any risks would have to be taken by me.

We walked back into the crowded hall, and heads turned and looked horrified as we passed. It appeared that my friend Carol suddenly didn't know me anymore. At any rate her glance seemed acutely focused away from me. People glowered. I smiled. "Good morning!" All eyes turned as we entered the main hall and took our seats under the nervous eyes of the security guards.

It was strange to see the Royal Festival Hall like this. The last time I'd been here was to hear the Buena Vista Social Club. The vibrant Cuban music transformed even the stuffy English, and people had left their seats to dance in the aisles. They played to a full house—just as BP was going to today.

Onto the stage walked a large group of well-fed men in expensive suits. I could see one woman. Only two people were to speak: Peter Sutherland and Lord Browne. As the meeting got going, my heart began to race. I seemed to be on my own. I wanted to please Alison by choosing my moment well, to satisfy my own desire to make the point but not to be dismissed by the entire audience as a troublemaker. I sat still for the first hour (or was it two hours?). No one in the audience had said anything or done anything. Peter Sutherland droned on about how wonderful the year had been, then

Lord Browne did the same, then Peter Sutherland gave a second and third perspective on the same theme. Then Lord Browne stood up again and began a long prepared speech; glancing down at his notes, he started to list the various investments that BP had made in a list of countries. He said "and China." I had my moment: I leapt to my feet as did my fellow soldier, and we applauded very loudly. Rather, in fact, as you would expect a Chinese soldier to do at a mere mention of the great Motherland.

People looked around, wondering why I was disturbing the speech. I ignored them and continued to clap. Security guards glanced at each other, wondering what to do. They had no reason to evict us as I appeared to be supporting Lord Browne. I kept clapping for just too long, and then took my seat again, smiling amiably at everyone.

Lord Browne looked perplexed but returned to his speech. He continued to drone on in a rather uninterested way about BP's international achievements: "Seventy percent of our capital employed is in the OECD. The rest in a limited number of selected opportunities beyond that, including areas of rapid growth such as China."

I leapt to my feet and applauded again. Lord Browne looked up at me. I was just on his eye level. I didn't smile at him but gave him a look of appreciation appropriate for the Chinese military. He waited. I applauded some more. He knew exactly what I was doing and looked embarrassed. He must have struggled with asking security to remove me. But how could he do that? Many of the shareholders would be totally perplexed if he removed what appeared to be enthusiasm, and he would certainly not be prepared to explain. Questions would be asked by the press, and he would have to tell them why I was applauding despite being from Free Tibet. No, he certainly didn't want to draw attention to me. Better just to wait. So wait he did. I went on clapping. He stared at me, and I kept clapping just until I thought the security guards would lose patience, and then I sat down quietly, and my fellow soldier sat beside me. "That was fun," he whispered in my ear. "Yes. I hope he mentions China again. I think his speech is prewritten and available for anyone to see, so he can't skip mention of China. It's very funny."

I sat rapt with attention. I don't think anyone else in the room could possibly have been interested.

"The business model also involves a continuous program to high-grade the asset base . . ."

People glazed over. The audience did look rather as if they'd come to London mainly for the free glass of wine and wished they could get to it sooner.

". . . As I go around our different business activities, in Egypt, in . . ."—he winced—". . . China . . ."

And we were up! This time I decided to add a bit of character acting for the benefit of the assembled crowd: "Good, good!" I shouted in my best Chinese accent. "*Hen hao!*" (Chinese for "Very good!"), shouted my companion, who had earnestly studied these two words for the day. We clapped wildly for a long time.

Lord Browne sighed and looked at his nonexecutive chairman imploringly. The nonexecutive chairman looked at me. I smiled and clapped. He glanced at a security guard, who moved instantly towards us. We sat down instantly. There was more fun to be had later, and we didn't want to get thrown out.

The next part of the meeting was when shareholders were allowed to ask questions. Alison had worked her way to the front of the queue.

Peter Sutherland stood up. "Yes, and can we take the first question?"

Alison stepped forward. "So far BP has been silent in addressing the concerns of the many supporters of Tibet that were expressed at last year's AGM. BP continues to hold $578 million of shares in PetroChina, the company that is implementing China's ambitious political plans for Tibet as well as stealing Tibet's natural resources. Have you, rather than jeopardize your commercial interests, quietly forgotten your human-rights policy and your commitment to shareholder concerns?"

Suddenly I admired her more than anyone in the world. I was fascinated to hear his response.

He said, "And are there any more questions on the Tibet issue because I'd like to deal with them all at once?"

The young Tibetan girl in her national costume stepped to the mike. "I speak as a Tibetan on behalf of my people. The Tibetan government-in-exile has requested that oil and gas projects in Tibetan areas be stopped and specifically requested that BP disinvest from PetroChina. This was because BP has supported them when other responsible companies chose not to because of human-rights concerns. A representative of His Holiness is present in today's meeting. What is your reply to the Dalai Lama and the people of Tibet?"

"Any more?"

Another shareholder from Free Tibet who had managed to get in stepped forward. "At last year's AGM, shareholders representing 627.5 million shares voted in favor of your disinvestment from PetroChina on the grounds of the impact of their activities on the people of Tibet. Did you convey these concerns to the Chinese authorities? If so, please tell us what their reaction was, and if not, could you please explain why not?"

I was impressed by the clarity and simplicity of these questions.

Peter Sutherland was not. In two minutes he read his prepared reply on the "Tibet issue," claiming that BP was a supporter of human rights. He said that none of BP's ventures with PetroChina had a connection with Tibet and that "therefore the use of this AGM to make a political point that may or may not have legitimacy is not appropriate. It is not appropriate for us to cause all of the shareholders of BP to have a major debate on a political event or situation that has no part of the activities of BP as a company . . . and that is the end of that particular issue as far as I am concerned."

He had not answered any of the specific questions that had been prepared. Alison stepped up to the mike.

"No. You may not speak!" he shouted at her. And that was it. Seeing an opportunity I leapt to my feet and applauded. "Dalai Lama terrorist!" I shouted. It has always amused me that the Chinese government says this. Anyone that looked less like a terrorist than the Dalai Lama I couldn't imagine.

The young Tibetan girl stepped up to the mike. "We'll have no more questions about Tibet," he said. We leapt to our feet again. "Separatist!" we shouted. "Splittist!" She looked as though she was about to burst into tears and looked genuinely amazed by the way her appeal for her land had been dismissed and the specific questions remained unanswered. The audience had woken up and looked considerably less bored.

"I will now take questions on any issue except Tibet." Our last opportunity to applaud—so we relished it. Then a softly spoken man came to the mike and started to speak in Spanish. Again the directors looked agitated. The translation began: "I am here to represent 200 of my fellow homeless farmers from Colombia . . ."

They recounted their story, but Peter Sutherland dismissed the claims that were made as lies.

"Why would anyone come halfway across the world to tell lies?" whispered my Buddhist friend in my ear. Mr. Sutherland was beginning to lose his smile.

"Are there any questions not relating to Tibet or Colombia?" he asked the room, not without some passion. A hand was raised. "Yes?"

An elderly gentlemen, looking rather as if he may have just popped out of the House of Lords to attend the meeting, stepped forward.

"Was Lord Browne's pay raise of 58 percent to 4.3 million dollars a year really necessary?"

Yes, according to Peter Sutherland, it was. And furthermore, as it was performance-related, it was "entirely justified." This wasn't about China, but I couldn't resist it. I leapt to my feet anyway and applauded briefly. A lady in front of me laughed. Well, obviously he needed that much. How can anyone live on less?

Solitary shareholders raised hugely important questions: Why was the board all self-appointing? Why had various members been there for as long as fifteen years? Each question was swept aside, and I began to understand why people loathe these huge global companies with the power to do exactly as they wish.

"We are a business, not a charity or an aid agency," Lord Browne had said. They obviously couldn't allow anything to come between them and their profits. I decided I'd see if I could get to a mike. Despite my Chinese military uniform, they couldn't forbid me to ask a question.

"Mr. Chairman, Lord Browne, members of the board . . ." I began in my most appreciative voice. "May I congratulate BP on their excellent yearly figures?"

Evidently I could.

"And may I congratulate them for not allowing terrorists to disrupt their profit margins?"

Was I talking about September 11 and its repercussions? I went on: "Terrorists like the Dalai Lama. And on behalf of the Chinese government may I thank BP for their continued support of our government's policies . . ."

The microphone went dead. Funny that. It seemed to work again for the next questioner.

I strolled off to join Alison and the others as we collected our free lunches. "So how was that?" I asked.

"I've filed an official complaint that he didn't answer our questions . . ."

She looked rather glum. Not me, though. I had an irritatingly huge smile. "It's been good fun. I've had a very enjoyable morning, if nothing else. If looks could kill, then Lord Browne would have finished us off several times this morning."

We emerged into the sunshine to find Adrian and the others still giving out leaflets and chatting to shareholders about PetroChina.

It was a wonderful sunny morning, and most people were smiling. Except the Colombians.

"We had hoped they would answer our questions, not call us liars." They sat in a circle.

"We thought you spoke with conviction and integrity."

"Thank you. But it seems they didn't think so."

Alison stood and talked to a woman from a Chinese newspaper. I went to join them, and when they'd finished I asked the reporter, "Don't you have to be very careful what you say?"

"I simply record the facts: 'A group of pro-Tibet demonstrators attended the BP AGM.'"

"I see."

"I don't make comments."

Back at the Free Tibet office, people were ringing the press, who had all been sent press releases. Phones rang, and computers buzzed.

All the papers mentioned the demonstrators "in faux Chinese military uniforms," along with the Colombians and the failed World Wildlife Fund resolution. So Tibet was mentioned. Our action had kept the issue on the agenda at least. But we could not compete with the most newsworthy item from the day: Lord Browne's pay raise.

ACHIEVABLE TARGETS?

Days went by while I pondered my teasing question: "courage to change the things I can." Maybe courage is required to believe that the smallest action matters. Courage not necessarily to take huge actions but to continue to take small ones and not to give up, feeling that the actions are worthless. I stared at the booklets and felt a weight of depression upon me. I could go to see the BP representatives, I could write letters, but it seemed hopeless. I could imagine the conversations in the boardroom: "Of course these people mean

well"—nods of sympathy and approval—"but they have no understanding of business."

There was the might of the international corporations and the
banks, and there was the straggly hair of my eccentric friend Simon
Gould. Why was it that the people who stood outside looked like
Simon, while the best minds of the generation were inside? Arguments and counterarguments buzzed around in my head. Anything
I could do was less than a drop in an ocean. At least a drop made a
difference.

Weeks went by, and my photos from Tibet stared at me from my
wall. Stark and beautiful landscapes. Beautiful and tragic faces.
People who had been too afraid to speak or to ask for a photo of
the man who for them symbolized hope. I felt a weight of self-
judgment as I looked at them. "Isabel, you said you were going to
do something!" Then silence and a voice inside me replying, "But
what can you do?" I wasn't interested in symbolic protest. Maybe
the vigil outside the embassy makes a difference, maybe the Free
Tibet Campaign's actions force the multinational companies and
banks to keep Tibet on the agenda. But it wasn't enough for me.

I had further lunches with Alison Reynolds, offering my services
in any way that would be useful, but she had no suggestions of
ways in which I could help her. It was hugely frustrating. I couldn't
tell whether she herself didn't know what she was aiming at or
whether she just didn't feel she should talk to me. She was always
in a rush and always tired. To me she looked like a woman who
needed support, but for some reason she didn't want any, even
when it was well qualified and free of charge.

One day I rang her and said, "Can you give me a list of your organizations' targets? Those that you feel can be achieved?"

"I'll have to ask the executive committee if I can do that. I'll get
back to you."

Why would a campaigning organization not want everyone to
know what their targets are?

"Could I come and work for you?"

Apparently not. "Isabel, we'd love to have you work for us. But don't you think that it's important that you remain independent?"

Maybe she was right. Maybe she wasn't. Maybe she was just being nice and the truth was that she just didn't want me interfering. I felt more confused than the day I had gotten off the plane from Nepal.

I remembered a famous line attributed to Napoleon: "Don't bring me problems. Bring me solutions."

I asked everyone I knew. I said, "May I ask some advice?" and then I'd launch into a five-minute summary of the history of China and Tibet and then I'd ask, "What would you do?"

"What about doing your very own Live Aid?" suggested one friend. "Have a huge concert for Tibet? That's what I'd do."

I didn't see myself as Bob Geldof, nor did I have his contacts. But I thought it would certainly be a challenge. I was ready for a challenge, the huger the better. I suddenly felt all enthusiastic about it. I visualized the Tibetan flag flying over the Royal Albert Hall and thousands of people dancing. I imagined long articles in the papers, huge profits flowing into the coffers of the Free Tibet Campaign. I thought that maybe Alison would share my enthusiasm and want to get started on the idea right away.

So I calmed myself down and rang her. I floated the idea as if it were purely a passing thought but threw in details like "the Albert Hall?" and "Sting?" There was a long pause.

"What is it?" I asked a little sheepishly.

"I don't like to discourage you, Isabel, but . . ."

"But?"

"But please, Isabel . . . please, whatever else you do, don't go down that path. Last year it was going to happen—there was a special organization set up to create this concert—it was ready to go— the Beastie Boys, Robbie Williams—it was huge. Many people worked on it for months. Anyway, some of the acts pulled out, and it never happened. Huge amounts of time and money were wasted, and all the organizations set up to create concerts for Tibet have folded."

I attempted a positive stance on this.

"So does that mean that some valuable lessons were learned and everyone would know what not to do this time?"

"No, it doesn't. We have to weigh up any likely benefit of such an evening. It takes months to prepare and costs a fortune. We don't have the resources, and even if you were to create an organization to do this for us . . . frankly, it's not worth it. People have a good night out and see some pictures of Tibet, and some of the Tibetans who live in the UK get a chance to speak and tell their story. But what is changed? People come to hear the singers not the politics. You said your desire was to support us. I'm begging you. Don't create a concert."

She seemed fairly clear on this point.

"So you aren't interested in my organizing a concert, then?"

"You can do it if you want to, but it would be against my advice and my experience. You wouldn't be able to do anything until next year because the acts have to be booked that far in advance. It would cost a fortune, even if you could find someone to underpin that level of financial risk, and frankly . . ."

"Yes?"

"It's been done before."

It was true. All that could be raised was money. It would be a huge gamble. If I could raise the money and find the people to support me, which perhaps I could if I really put my mind to it, the way things stood I wasn't sure that even if I had a million pounds to give to the Free Tibet Campaign . . . I wasn't convinced that they'd know how best to spend it.

"Alison, if you had a million pounds, what would you do with it?"

"Go on holiday?"

"I think I meant if the Free Tibet Campaign had a million pounds, what would they do with it?"

"That isn't a problem that we've ever had to deal with." She laughed. "I'd be able to give our fund-raising manager a holiday anyway."

"Seriously?"

"Seriously? I don't know. I'll get back to you on that one."

"OK, I'm sorry to disturb you. No more calls today."

So that was the end of the "huge concert" idea. Six months or a year of my life drifted back into my calendar. Had I been too easily discouraged?

So I sat down and wrote some notes of what I thought were great and positive ideas, phoned, and made a lunch appointment with Alison for the next week. I thought that they could increase the membership if more people read the Dalai Lama's autobiography and the history of Tibet. No one, I felt, could learn the story and not be moved to action. I had an easy idea on how this could be achieved.

The following week we sat in a trendy veggie restaurant around the corner from the Free Tibet Campaign offices while I offered her my various ideas in the hope at least one of them would ignite her enthusiasm.

"Could you run a bookstore gift certificate scheme and ask everyone to buy a copy of *Freedom in Exile* and give it to the most influential person that they know? As it's a really first-rate autobiography I'm sure people would read it and be moved to action. Your members who don't feel that they know anyone or feel uncomfortable giving a gift in that way could send in book tokens to you and you could buy copies for members of Parliament and Euro MPs. We could even get some lovely photos of the Dalai Lama from Tibet House and give those as a gift to MPs, too."

I felt very pleased with my idea. "I could speak to the publishers of the Dalai Lama's autobiography and ask if you could buy copies at a discounted price."

Alison looked at me and wrote it down.

"What do you think?" I asked hopefully.

"It's not our role to promote the Dalai Lama. We are not the Tibetan government-in-exile."

I stared at the floor. So—no ideas based on the Dalai Lama, then?

I skipped the next two ideas on my page and went on with a smile.

"Or I thought that maybe you could have a Chinese-friend scheme. Not for members to badger the Chinese but to learn from them. To listen to their point of view. For an exchange of views. I mean I know that when people appear to hold views that are opposed it sometimes seems hopeless, when people become locked into their position, but I do believe that people listen and are influenced in some way."

She looked at me and wrote it down.

"And then if there were letters that needed writing about the treatment of prisoners, then perhaps the Chinese friends could be asked to translate. I'm sure many Chinese would be horrified to learn about the conditions in Drapchi prison."

She looked at me and wrote it down.

"And I've given some thought to how consumer power could help Tibet. I heard of this girl who has started a range of shampoos and is giving a percentage of the profits to help Tibetan charities. I know it's not much, but I thought that if all your members could really get behind her and help get the products into more supermarkets . . ."

I waited hopefully for some flicker of enthusiasm to match my own. She didn't say anything at all. I had thought that these were good ideas. I started to feel stupid. I didn't want to read her any more ideas. I glanced at them on the page. I didn't need a degree in nonverbal communication to know that she wasn't interested.

I looked up. I tried to work out how I could assist her and be her friend. Perhaps she was under enormous pressures from her board or something, but my efforts to support her were getting me nowhere. I'd asked if we could meet up one evening and I could buy her dinner and we could spend some real time together and be girls and work out a plan she'd be happy with. She'd refused.

A journalist friend had said that it was simple; I needed to "shadow" her for three weeks. Go with her everywhere, to every meeting, until I understood what her difficulties were. Write about how she was fobbed off by the United Nations or by the Home Office. I wanted so much to write a really supportive piece. But she said no. "My staff wouldn't like that."

It was a mystery to me. She had read things I had written in the past. My passion for Tibet was obviously genuine, as was my desire to support her organization, whatever the problems. In her position I would have longed for the kind of support that I was offering.

She stood up. "I've got to go now." None of the ideas I'd suggested were discussed.

Eventually I realized my mistake. Some doors we knock on and they fly open and we are greeted with joy. Some doors we knock on and they don't open. I hadn't been just knocking on this one. I had been banging my head against it, and even from the first phone call, no door had opened. I couldn't be so paranoid as to take it personally. At that time the Free Tibet Campaign hadn't even met me.

Everything I suggested, Alison didn't like. And for the most part the things that they did I wasn't convinced were helpful or producing results. Maybe most of her time was spent not as she would no doubt like, in helping Tibet, but in paying her office costs and looking after her staff. Maybe by helping her I wouldn't be helping Tibet at all, but I'd just be supporting a campaigning organization. I'd noticed that most of the appeals to local groups of the Free Tibet Campaign were about raising funds. Maybe when the local groups sent money, it had to go to paying the rent. And maybe none of that mattered. That's the way most charities and campaigning organizations have to work. But it wasn't enough for me. I would keep up my membership of Free Tibet, but it was time to move on.

"Grant me the serenity to accept the things I cannot change." I had thought that would mean problems with China, not with a campaigning group that I'd wanted to support. But I was getting nowhere, helping little, and changing nothing. Where wisdom to know the difference was concerned, I was a very slow learner. I bought Alison a bunch of flowers, promised to keep in touch and go on seeking her advice, asked her to ring me if there was ever anything I could do for her, and left. Back to the drawing board.

WHAT NEXT?

HAVE YOU WRITTEN TO YOUR
MEMBER OF PARLIAMENT?

The following morning my phone rang. It was the office of my local member of Parliament. I had left a message asking if I could come and meet him. "The surgery* is next Saturday at Safeway. Bring any evidence on paper of what your problem is . . ."

I'd never been to see my MP before, and I had no clue of how to use the democratic process to attempt to bring about change. I needed some advice about what exactly I wanted to ask about, so I rang the Tibet Society. This is a small organization that works with Parliament to attempt to persuade the government to act in "putting pressure on China." What was the process that they used?

I learned that one of the methods used to influence Parliament is called an *Early Day Motion.* This is a formal procedure in which any member of Parliament who wants to raise an issue can write out a concern, and if two hundred or more MPs agree and add their name to it, then Parliament may end up discussing it. I wasn't sure I liked the word *may,* but I was learning.

---

* When members of the British parliament meet their constituents, it's called a "surgery." Don't ask me why. It is a bit like going to see the doctor. You got sick of waiting for peace, didn't you?

So I asked for an example of an Early Day Motion on the Tibetan issue that I could ask my MP to sign. The one that they sent me read:

> That this house notes with concern that over one million Tibetans have perished as a result of occupation and repression by China, and that access to Tibet by international organisations is denied; also notes that the Dalai Lama has steadfastly refused to resort to violence in the struggle for freedom; expresses deep concern that the Chinese Government is actively seeking to prevent Her Majesty's Government from supporting discussion of the Tibet issue at the UN Human Rights Commission; and calls on Her Majesty's Government to support the restoration of human rights in Tibet being discussed at the UN Human Rights Commission as a matter of urgency.*

It looked to me like something that deserved to be signed. I asked them, "How many signatures does it have?"

"Seventy-eight."

"You're joking! But I don't understand . . . surely there are thousands of supporters of Tibet in the UK? Isn't it simple to speak with your MP?" I phoned Tibet House in London, which said, "It's very difficult to get more MPs to sign the EDMs."

I read about the workings of Parliament and found myself, only two days later, phoning Alison Reynolds to ask her about what the Tibet Society was doing. When I mentioned the EDM, she said, "But the UN Human Rights Commission is passed. It has happened already, and the British government did nothing. It was a scandal. Anyway, we are no longer asking people to sign that."

"But I don't understand. The Tibet Society and the Office of Tibet are still asking for signatures . . . and doesn't the UN Commission happen every year?"

---

* This EDM was placed by the MP George Stevenson.

"Yes, but this EDM relates to the one that is passed. If it's for next year, then it needs amending, and it's far too soon for that."

I rang back the Tibet Society. "Alison at the Free Tibet Campaign says that it needs amending, so she isn't asking anyone to sign it anymore . . . and the Office of Tibet, like you, is still asking for signatures. Can you sort this out for me so I know what you'd like me to ask?"

I felt totally exasperated. As if Tibet didn't have enough problems with the Chinese without the organizations that are supposed to be supporting it failing to communicate effectively with one another.

"And could we have an EDM about that young boy who the Dalai Lama identified as the eleventh Panchen Lama and who has been under house arrest since he was six?"

"Yes, I don't see why not. There's been one on the books before."

"Can't it just stay on the books and gather signatures?"

"Yes it can. I'll mention it to one of our friendly MPs, and ask him to put one on the books for us."

"OK. Meanwhile, I'll go and see my MP anyway and ask his advice."

The surgeries of Martin Linton, the MP for Battersea, take place regularly at a local supermarket. This could be a good reason to force myself to go food shopping. I turned up the following Saturday morning with my tins of cat food and other exciting purchases. A queue had formed that was exclusively female. Some very worried-looking women were filling in forms that demanded names and addresses as well as the nature of the problem. I hesitated and then outlined my problem as "The Chinese Government Policy on Tibet." He was reading the card and looked up with a smile when I walked in.

"This is different . . ."

"Yes. Well, I thought a little variety would be good."

"What can I do for you?"

"I'm here to ask your advice really. It may be outside your area of concern . . ."

"Not at all. You are a constituent of mine, so your concerns are my concerns."

Spoken like a true politician. But he was very warm and friendly.

"Can you sign Early Day Motions?"

"No, I'm afraid I can't."

"Why's that?"

"I'm what's called a parliamentary private secretary, a member of the government. EDMs are motions calling on the government to do something, so PPSs, which is what we are called, can't sign those as it would be me calling on myself to act."

"I see." I felt a complete idiot. I could have found this out before my visit.

"But I can help, though. If you write me an official letter about this, then I will forward it to the minister for foreign affairs, and he will be obliged to reply as the letter will be from me. I'll forward his reply to you."

"That's lovely. Thank you. Also I understand that there are cross-party groups in Parliament for various special-interest causes."

"Yes."

"Are you a member of many?"

He smiled. "There is a requirement that if you want to start a group for a good cause you have to have a certain number of members. Many MPs join lots of groups to make up the numbers so that the few real enthusiasts for whatever the cause is can start a group. We all belong to many groups, but we don't necessarily go to the meetings. I'm a member of about thirty groups."

"I imagine that you are ridiculously busy all the time."

"Yes."

It had been suggested to me that I ask him to join the cross-party group for Tibet, but I wasn't going to. I could see that he was in enough groups already. And if he had no particular interest in Tibet, why should he?

"I've brought a present for you." His eyes lit up like a little boy's. I opened an envelope and produced a beautiful photograph of the Dalai Lama looking straight at the camera with the tips of his fingers touching. He looked at it with a smile. "It's for you to look at on days when you are feeling stressed," I said.

"That will be every day, then."

"And did you know that the photo is illegal? Don't take it with you if you go to China."

"I didn't know that."

"He is the spiritual leader of the Tibetan people, as you know, and once a photo of him was the centerpiece of every Tibetan house and monastery, but now it is a criminal offense to own one. Many monks carry empty photo frames as an objection, and apparently even that can get them locked up."

He sighed and looked at the photo. "Send me your letter, won't you?"

"I'll write it this week."

I shook his hand, and the lady at the door showed in a very distressed woman with a baby who burst into tears as she entered the room. Strange, I thought, how all these roles had become blurred. Priest, doctor, politician . . . or maybe Martin Linton was unusual. I couldn't imagine anyone going to a surgery with Thatcher and bursting into tears.

I cycled home immediately, switched on my computer, and wrote my letter to my MP.

Dear Mr. Linton,

It was very good to meet you at your surgery on Saturday. I hope the illegal photo that I left with you is making you smile.

I would be most grateful if you could inform me of the government's intentions regarding the case of a young boy, Gedun Choekyi Nyima . . .

A Chinese official was visiting London that very month. I asked if they had plans to ask for a delegation to be allowed to establish that the boy is alive and being well treated. Surely, I argued, this was an opportunity for the Chinese to receive some good press by demonstrating to the world that their human-rights record is as good as they say it is.

I then asked that if the government did not have plans to ask about this boy, then what steps he would suggest needed to be taken in order for this to happen. I posted my letter.

One month later I received two identical postcards from the House of Commons. They both said, "Thank you for your communication which will receive attention." Six weeks later I received a letter:

Thank you for your recent letter concerning the case of Gedun Choekyi Nyima. I'm afraid this is not a case I am familiar with and I thank you for bringing it to my attention. I have written to the Foreign and Commonwealth Office to express your concerns about this matter and will be in touch as soon as I receive a reply.

My original letter had been timed to coincide with the visit of Li Ruihan, a member of the Chinese government who had been on an official visit to Britain. Ten weeks after writing the original letter, still awaiting a reply, I decided that while engaging in the democratic process was obviously part of what I was going to do, it wasn't going to satisfy me.

No one from the Tibet Society ever rang me back about the placing of the EDM. I rang and inquired several times. "Has the EDM been placed yet?" I stressed how important it was. Eventually, some two months later, I received a reply. "We're very sorry but the MP who had offered to do it never got around to it."

Over two months later I received a reply from the foreign and commonwealth minister. I had expected him to say that the government was "concerned" about human rights in Tibet, that the Chinese government had reassured him that Gedun Choekyi Nyima was leading a "normal and happy life" (as one does when in detention by the Chinese government), and that they resented "outside interference."

Dear Martin Linton MP,

Thank you for your letter enclosing one from your constituent Isabel Losada of Battersea Park Road about Gedun Choekyi Nyima.

Like your constituent we are concerned about the case of Gedun Choekyi Nyima, the Dalai Lama's choice as the 11th Panchen Lama. We raise his case regularly with the Chinese Government, including during our biannual high-level Human Rights Dialogue with them.

We raised his case again in the context of the most recent round of the Dialogue in Beijing. The Chinese side responded that he was in good health, leading a "normal and happy life" with his parents and receiving a good education. They added that his parents did not want their and their son's life subject to outside interference.

The letter went on to express the government's "concern" about other human-rights issues in Tibet. It ended:

We will continue to press for positive changes in Tibet in our critical dialogue with the Chinese authorities. The Chinese Government can be in no doubt about the strength of our views on human-rights violations.

I am returning your constituent's letter.

Yours sincerely

So this was the democratic process in action. Maybe the Chinese government was in no doubt about the strength of the British government's views on human rights, but I was. I pondered the amusing line after that: "I am returning your constituent's letter." Interesting touch.

It's easy to see why activists and people who want to change things resort to extreme measures. Of course I would never support the use of violence. But say there is a beautiful and ancient forest near you, a sanctuary for birds and wildlife and a place enjoyed by the public, and you hear that it is to be sold to developers. Imagine that you decide to do something. I now understand why people resort to living in the trees. It may not be comfortable, but it creates publicity, and the developers may be shamed into saving a tree or two.

If on the other hand you were to go and see your MP about it, you might get a response from him or her. Eventually. But if she is seen to be anti "new housing" or "new business," it won't serve her very well. MPs have their careers to consider. And they are very busy people with many demands on their time. Are they really going to risk speaking up for a bunch of "local environmentalists" (you will of course have been labeled a lunatic by now)? So what the hell? May as well make a home in the trees. More fun than waiting for the slow wheels of the democratic process to turn.

Heaven help the person who decides to work solely with this method. I think the democratic path to seeking change on any issue not in the public eye or in the government's best interests could be looked upon as a profound spiritual exercise in patience. Or developing serenity to accept the things you cannot change. I lifted the phone and noted the details of my MP's next surgery. One month away. I would go and see him again. At least this time he would know who Gedun Choekyi Nyima is. At least this time I could go armed with the Foreign Office's letter. He would know who I was. I could discuss the problem with him rather than explaining it to him.

And maybe I'd even take along *Freedom in Exile* to give him as a gift.

The second time I went I asked him his views about supporting nonviolence as an imperative part of the war against terrorism, and he offered to write to the Secretary of State for me and copy me in on the letter. I locked eyes with Martin Linton.

"If the Dalai Lama dies having made a stand for the path of nonviolence that led to him being ignored all his life, what message does that send into history?"

I attempted to imply that the story of the rest of the Dalai Lama's life was directly dependent on his acting. And who knows, maybe it is. I found out that there are only 650 MPs in the United Kingdom, and as individuals in a democracy, thank God, we all have the direct power to influence Parliament by talking with one of them.* So this plan would have to go on a website. But this would not be the only route that I would be taking.

TITS FOR TIBET?

So what next? I woke up the next morning, made a very large coffee, and staggered to my desk. A copy of the *National Geographic* had arrived, and in it there was an article about Tibet; it said that it is "one of the great moral dilemmas of our time . . . either to side with the Chinese behemoth or to support a tiny group of impoverished people in their struggle to regain independence."

Next to this on the table was a list of some of the objectives of the Free Tibet Campaign, which they had finally sent me in response to my repeated requests.

Get 100,000 postcards/letters sent on behalf of Gedun Choekyi Nyima (and a million world-wide). Get China to grant access to him.

Get the EU to appoint a Special Co-ordinator for Tibet. (The US have already done this.) Possibly first have a senior lead member for the EU/China Dialogue.

Develop a new strategy to interest Tony Blair and Gordon Brown in the Tibet issue.

I looked at the last item and smiled to myself. Well, if Tibet is an issue of nonviolent resistance to oppression, how about, to pick a "strategy" entirely at random, an international war on terrorism?

---

* In the United States, you have 435 representatives and 100 senators. Apparently, it's a little harder to get to meet them, but you have a democratic right to do so. Enjoy!

Maybe if such a thing were to happen, some of the world govern-
ments would think, "Oops, not sure this is the way we want to go.
Is there anyone in the world not being violent? Ah yes, the Dalai
Lama. Maybe we could consider meeting him, then?"

Did you know that not a single world leader will meet the Dalai
Lama in his political role as the leader of his country? And now that
the Tibetan government-in-exile has a democratically elected leader
(Samdhong Rinpoche is the head of the Tibetan government-in-
exile, not the Dalai Lama), no government will meet him either?
"But why not?" you ask. Or maybe, like me, you know the answer
by now. China is big, and everyone wants to sell pizzas there.

I started to doodle artistically on a blank piece of paper until a
strange tapping sound interrupted my surge of creativity.

It was Steve, my builder. In a determined attempt to feel that I
was making progress of some kind on something, I had decided to
have my house painted. It's a girl thing. New white walls would
make me feel better, anyway.

"Mornin'." He clocked the look of gloom and despair on my face.
"Oh, dear. I see you have a face like a smacked arse this mornin'?"

I forced a smile from my smacked arse.

"What's up, mate?" He pottered around in the kitchen, making
tea and pouring sugar into it, and then pulled up a seat at my desk
to offer his support.

I wondered where to start. The face of a little boy stared at me
from a postcard.

"Well, to take one small part of the problem, er, challenge . . .
there is this boy."

"Yeah . . ."

"He's a teenager, and he's been under house arrest since he was
six."

"What's 'house arrest'?"

"More or less the same as prison, but with more than one room.
It means that he and his family are watched 24/7, as my daughter
would say."

"What's he done?"

"Nothing."

"Nothing? He must have done something wrong."

"No. He was six when they took him and his family and put them, well, how can I put this neutrally? Into government protection."

"Has his family done something wrong?"

I decided not to go into the question of the identification of the lineage of reincarnate Panchen Lamas and the political importance of his previous incarnations.

"He's . . . er . . . important spiritually speaking. The Dalai Lama identified him as a central figure in Tibetan Buddhism, so the Chinese locked him up."

"Why did the Dalai Lama do that?"

"It's complex. He had to or the Chinese may have said it was someone else. It was a gamble. He had hoped they would leave the little boy alone. But his gesture of goodwill and trust in the Chinese better nature didn't pay off. Now no one knows where the boy is, and he probably doesn't know who he is."

"That's terrible." He picked up the postcard. It was addressed to:

President Jiang Zemin
Guojia Zhuxi
Beijing-shi
People's Republic of China

"What's this, then?" He looked at the card where I had signed my name to it.

"It's a postcard that the Free Tibet Campaign produces. They want to send 100,000 of them. As you see, it is asking for his "immediate and unconditional release," but they have their work cut out."

"So who is this Seamin bloke? Does he care about this boy?"

"No, Steve. Not only does he not care. He loathes the whole issue. The boy for him is a threat to the peace and stability of

China. He has probably told the boy in the post room to bin all such cards."

"So why do they want to send 100,000 cards to someone who doesn't care? Why don't they send them to someone who does care?"

He waited for an answer. I didn't have one. "You've got me there."

"And shouldn't they be in Chinese? I mean if they are going to China?"

I was forced to smile. "You're not wrong, Steve."

He looked at my list. "Develop a new strategy to interest Tony Blair and Gordon Brown in the Tibet issue? Oh, yeah?" He smiled. "And how are they going to do that, then?"

"I don't think they know. Neither do I know. No one in any of the Tibetan organizations seems to know. They've been doing all the right things since 1954, and no one is listening, you see."

"Well, if they want this boy out, then they have to raise his profile, don't they? The government isn't going to do anything unless there is pressure on them."

"Yes. And how would you raise his profile?"

"Me?" he said, lighting up his third fag thoughtfully. "I'd get this picture blown up to twelve feet high and put it on the back of a truck with thirty topless women around it. I think the photographers would come, don't you?" He laughed. "I'd call it 'Tits for Tibet.'"

I looked at the gentle face of the celibate Dalai Lama smiling at me from the front of a book. I thought of the meek humility of many of the Tibetans I'd met. Of the way that they do not assert themselves and are not pushy or aggressive or . . . naked. It was a horrendously inappropriate idea.

"Steve, you may have the answer."

"I'll drive the truck for you." And off he went to dig up the concrete floor in my daughter's room where a pipe was leaking.

I sat and thought about this. Rock bands have been used for political ends, to raise money for Amnesty International and for every
other good cause imaginable. But have breasts ever been used?
How fantastic it would be to combine men's desire to see women's
bodies with political campaigning. Of course "Tits for Tibet" was
hugely offensive. The association of the word *tits* with Tibet is so
sharp a contrast that it could not help but offend. It even offended
me. But something radical was called for.

I decided I'd pursue it and see what sort of reactions I would get.
The way to go was obviously to do such a thing on my own so that
the Free Tibet Campaign and all the other organizations that I'd
been in contact with could disown me immediately. They could say,
"Never heard of her . . ." if a journalist rang. So I rang friends and
muttered the words "campaign," "publicity stunt," and "Tits for
Tibet" in one phone call. A gasp would come down the phone . . .
followed by a long silence.

"You don't like the idea, then?" I'd enthuse. "I think it's rather
brilliant. It's also a comment on the British media, isn't it? I mean
it's like saying, 'What do we have to do to get this boy's case publicized? We have to show our breasts? Well, OK. So now do we get
his photo in the paper?'"

"But if that is a comment against the media, then aren't you at
the same time depending on the goodwill of that same media to
publicize your stunt?"

"I guess so."

"Will you show yours?"

"Of course. I couldn't ask other women to show theirs and not
be prepared to show my own, could I? I think if I'm to be a leader,
I'd have to lead. It's only fair."

"And would you do the press call topless?"

I hesitated for a second. "I suppose I'd have to. I thought that I
would organize it with the police that the demo would be in bikinis
so that it would be legal and we could get police permission to park

the van by the green at the Houses of Parliament. And then we'd tip off the press that for the photo call the tops would actually come off. What do you think?"

A stony silence would repeat itself. I'd say, "I see. Well, I still think it's a good idea."

I think the thing about doing research is that you start with a point that you would like to prove and then you ask enough people until someone agrees with you. I phoned a couple of PR companies. One girl at a top London company was very specific in the information she asked me. "Have you ever done anything like this before?"

"No."

"How do you feel about showing your breasts to the world?"

"I wish that they were a little larger. To speak frankly, I'm afraid that I may give some tabloid journalist the chance to run a title line of 'Titless for Tibet.'"

She said, "Well, I'd join you but mine are far too large." Then she paused. "This is the most surreal conversation I have ever had . . ."

"I'd thought that I could use models. I don't think that I'd have any difficulty persuading women who are used to showing their breasts for money that it would be good to show them on behalf of a young political prisoner. But that leaves me still with the problem of whether I show my own."

It was certainly bizarre. But the greatest worry remained, Was it in such bad taste that it just wouldn't work? I went to see a woman who ran a PR agency and who, until this time, had been an admirer of my work. She listened with a smile on her face and then recommended several other agencies. Then she said, "Have you told your agent about this idea?"

I had to confess I had not. Some sneaking suspicion about what his response might be had kept me from calling him. I rang him and asked if I could visit, casually mentioning the name of the plan in the conversation.

"Tips for Tibet?" he shouted into the mobile. "That was a *p,* wasn't it? I thought, for one ghastly moment, that you said 'Tits for Tibet.'" He laughed reassuringly.

"Actually, yes . . . 'Tits' . . . that is what I said."

Another of those long silences. I waited.

"What time are you coming to see me?"

I decided I was not going to be put off the plan by his being negative. I had underestimated the strength of his feelings.

"Have you gone mad? It's cheap. It's crass. It's vulgar."

"It's also funny, isn't it?"

"You can see women's breasts in the tabloids every day of the week. It's hardly new."

"What about if I find ten women who have never shown their breasts in public before?"

"Who did you have in mind?"

"I'm really confident that I could find women with a sense of humor and breasts that they like who will be prepared to do it. I have one girlfriend whose email address is 'beautifulbountiful-breasts.' I think she'd be glad of a chance to flaunt them for political ends—and if it's shocking, so much the better. If I can get people talking about the little boy, that's what matters."

"But they won't talk about him; they'll talk about the breasts."

I started to feel very cross and six years old. "I don't know why I came here if you are just going to be negative."

"You came to ask my opinion, didn't you?"

"No, I didn't. I just came to tell you what I'm doing."

"You are my client. I have a right to an opinion. I have your reputation to look after."

"What reputation? I don't have a reputation!"

"That may be, but at least you're not known as 'the tit girl.'"

I hadn't even mentioned the problem of my lack of attributes for the job.

"My opinion," he went on, "whether you've asked for it or not, is that it's a very bad idea."

I huffed and puffed and stamped my feet. "I'll wait for you to come up with something better, then."

"That's not my job, darling. My job is just to take money that you earn for me."

I could not call him a liar.

I took the bus home, discouraged but still determined to go ahead.

The following day brought no letters from anyone in reply to anything. So I thought I'd ring some of the stunt agencies that had been suggested to me. I gave them all the details, and they went away to confer. Later they rang me with the verdict. "Bad idea."

"Why?"

"Too cheap. The important thing is the kid, so we thought you should go down the kid line. What about finding a boy between the ages of 6 and 13 for every day that he has been in prison and staging a demo with them? That would be a lot of boys."

I tried to imagine organizing that.

"But wouldn't it be manipulative of the children? How can children and demonstrations go together? The kids don't fully grasp the issues and they are being manipulated by the adults around them."

"You may be right there. But still, no one here liked the tits idea. Sorry."

I was on some kind of learning curve. I just couldn't work out where the curve was leading. Maybe I should ring the papers directly and ask them.

I found a copy of the *Daily Mirror* that Steve had bought that morning. I knew that they had recently taken on more campaigns, and I thought the story of a little boy might appeal to them. I rang and asked the advice of the editor's secretary. I asked her how they choose what to run appeals on and what not to.

"You need to go to the features editor," she advised, "and if he likes it, he'll bring it to the editor."

Assuming my "great story" voice, I stood up and rang the features editor.

"If I were to tell you about a little boy of thirteen who is in prison and has been there since he was six despite the fact that everyone including those who have imprisoned him know that he has done nothing wrong . . . would you want to run the story?"

I was thinking, "Brilliant, Isabel. How can he say no?" But there was another of those long pauses. Then he said, "What country is this in? Not England, right?"

"Well, er, no . . . but he's still a little boy . . ."

"We must be talking China, right? A lama of some kind or something?"

"He's not a lama as such, no . . ."

"But we are talking Chinese government?"

I couldn't deny it. "Yes."

"We're not interested, sorry. I know it's terribly sad, all these little lamas and such like, but we really like the stories to have an English connection . . ."

"But you do run campaigns about other countries, don't you? You are running one at the moment, I see, about a famine . . ."

"Yes, but that's about a continent of little boys who are starving. Why should we give up space for one boy when there are so many good causes? We are not the good-cause paper, but we do what we can. If it were an English story . . ."

"What about if there were a group of crazy English people organizing a stunt to raise his profile? Then it would be an English story . . ."

"No stunts, please. We loathe stunts. In fact we are stunt phobics. Don't waste your time on organizing stunts. We hate them. We won't come. No one will come. Stunts are a thing of the past. Every week we get someone ringing us about some stupid stunt. What were you thinking of doing?"

Best not tell him at this stage perhaps. I also noticed that the *Daily Mirror* was amazingly lacking in breasts.

"So do you have any suggestions for me? Positive advice, I mean. You are telling me what not to do, but I don't hear any thoughts on what I could do to publicize this boy's plight."

"All I can say is don't do stunts."

He seemed fairly decided on this matter.

As he was very friendly as well as totally discouraging, I thought I'd ask.

"So what would you do if you wanted to raise the profile of this boy? What's your advice?"

"My advice is, 'Don't listen to me.'"

So that was it. A stunt, then.

GETTING ORGANIZED

PRINCESS SMARTY-PANTS

I seemed to have been working on this "Do something" project for several lifetimes and had made no progress whatsoever. All I knew was what I thought didn't work and what wasn't effective. I could have given a short three-hour lecture on the subject. I needed help. This was the one thing I hadn't even tried to do. Create support around me. I was trying to do it all alone. And then, just as I started to flick through my address book despondently, the phone rang. Miraculously it was Isabel Kelly, formerly of Amnesty International. Someone who actually knew something about what I was trying to do and why. Oh, joy!

"Hello, Isabel! How was Tibet? Did you get altitude sickness?"

"Yes. And Tibet was . . . well, you know. My reaction was . . . a kind of rage. Now I'm back I want to do something. I was wondering how you've been getting on?"

I delivered my three-hour speech.

Then she said, "You'll have to start your own organization."

Something inside me went "clunk." That was not what I wanted to do.

"But there are so many organizations out there already."

"But none of them are effective, are they? You want to do something effective, don't you?"

"That was the original plan."

Then my brain had a rare moment of clarity. "What about you, Isabel? What are you doing with all your Tibetan expertise?"

"I don't know. I was thinking of possibly working in PR."

"Really? Are you interested in meeting a PR company? I can introduce you to one. I've arranged a meeting there on Monday. I'd love it if you'd come along. They are called Cunning Stunts."

She laughed.

"What?"

"Don't say that after two glasses of wine."

I'm so innocent. It hadn't even crossed my mind.

"So what do you think?"

"I'd like to come along."

Rachael at Cunning Stunts was positive, well informed, and friendly. If I'd had a million pounds I'd have gone to her company based on my first phone call to her. And she isn't even the boss.

And that was how it was that we got to sit around a table at a fabulous PR company with pictures of a little boy. Isabel Kelly corrected me on details: "You can't say that he has been put in prison. You can say that he has been 'detained.'"

"I see."

I remembered my friend's jibe about removing me from the steps of the embassy.

"They've removed him. He's Chinese take-out."

Rachael looked at us, attempting to be businesslike. "What do you want to do?"

"We want to raise the profile of this boy. The tabloids ideally, not the broadsheets."

"That's a good policy. The broadsheets are fairly useless in this way. They just nod their heads and say, 'That's the kind of thing that the Chinese do . . .'"

"We want everyone to know about him."

"How about finding a Chinese boy and suspending him in a cage in Chinatown?" suggested Guy, one of the staff with a smile and an idea a minute.

"Gedun isn't Chinese; he's Tibetan."

"Do we know any Tibetan boys that we don't like?"

"How about putting one in the window of Harvey Nichols? They have an art-installation window there, don't they?"

"Is there an international missing-persons list?"

"Are there any celebrities with sons of the same age who may want to help?"

"Are there any famous Chinese people?"

"Or famous fourteen-year-olds?"

Ideas whizzed around the table.

"Who is famous and fourteen?"

"Maybe we could get J. K. Rowling to write a story for him?"

"Or Sophie Dahl?"

I had a nasty feeling that everyone in the world who wants to publicize anything probably tries to get in touch with J. K. Rowling.

"What about a huge kung-fu event in the park with fourteen-year-olds?"

"But kung fu isn't Tibetan. It isn't even Chinese, is it?"

"What about doing something in Trafalgar Square?"

"What, like dropping a huge poster of him from the top of Nelson's Column?"

I began to feel rather hysterical.

"Actually I know some climbers who would be happy to do that," smiled Rachael the positive.

"Isn't it illegal?" I asked tentatively.

"Of course, and dangerous, too. Would you like me to ask them?"

"Absolutely." Two bells rang in unison.

OK, then. So it was decided. We were going to do something ridiculous and climb Nelson's Column. But of course we weren't allowed to tell anyone about it. Isabel Kelly and I left the amazing Rachael with smiles on our faces and heads buzzing.

We set off at a brisk pace to look for a coffee shop. Obviously all great plans have to start with large amounts of toxic drinks and muffins.

"We need to start our own organization to deal with all this," she said.

"Only we don't want it to be an organization, do we?"

"What does that mean?"

"We don't want a committee . . ."

"Or a board of directors."

"Or an office." Suddenly all this new venture started to feel fun.

"So what do we want? Do we want a website?" I asked.

But neither of us had a clue how to build a website. I opened a notebook and wrote: "Find a friend who knows how to build websites." Then crossed it out and wrote: "Learn how to build websites." Then I wondered, "Won't we need to form a company so that if people want to donate £10 to help get our climbers out of prison, then we'll have a fund to be able to do that?"

"Yes. We'll need to form a company."

"But no directors?"

"We will be the directors."

"I see. So this is a board meeting, then?"

"Oh, absolutely. Another muffin?"

"Isabel, I have a problem with your name. May I call you Kelly?"

"Absolutely not. Call me PS. For Princess Smarty-Pants."

"You're not serious?"

"Absolutely."

"It's not very flattering, is it?"

"Well PS is quick to write."

And my new friend Isabel Kelly, whom I'd known for exactly a week, became PS.

"Just one question." I had a thought forming.

"Yes?"

"Who will pay us for doing all this?"

"We'll be a not-for-profit organization, won't we?"

"But I wasn't thinking so much of profit, more of a basic wage. I mean £4 an hour to learn how to create and maintain a website would be good."

"The total lack of income is certainly a problem."

"Can we ask people to make donations for website maintenance?"

"I always find it really annoying if I go to a website and the first thing you see is 'If you would like to make a donation press *here.*'"

"Maybe we are working out why so many websites say that."

"We don't want to ask for a membership fee, do we?"

"No. We don't want to become directors of a membership organization—we want to do something new."

"The trouble with so many membership organizations is that the members are passive and those at the 'top' do the organization and come up with the ideas. Then they try to interest the membership in their ideas, and the membership often doesn't respond."

"We want something that isn't top-down. Somehow."

"We could have some kind of criteria for evaluating effectiveness."

"Maybe we could have some kind of effectiveness form and put it on the website?"

"And then people could post their action evaluations for others to read."

"Then people could copy the best actions, those that are seen to get results."

It all sounded so simple. Build a website, persuade someone to climb Nelson's Column. . . . But there was still the problem of how to get paid for all this. It felt, rather illogically, that if we were doing something exciting and innovative, then the money should just come rolling in to pay the phone bill.

There was another pause. We were both thinking the same thing.

"How are we going to pay the bills?" she asked.

"You know . . ."

"What?"

"I was just thinking that."

Another pause. I ate muffins. PS ordered a second cup of coffee for both of us.

I drank it and then, inspired perhaps by the aroma, asked, "Do you think we could ask Rachael to see if she could persuade her boss to let her help us for free? We'll have to have everything for free somehow. No money. Yes, this is a huge problem, but are we going to do it anyway?"

She laughed. "OK."

SO YOU WANT TO FORM A COMPANY?

I don't know if you have ever tried running a home with a teenager in it, starting a company, launching a website, and planning an illegal stunt at the same time. It doesn't leave much time for going to Safeway.

PS was on the phone first thing.

"In order to make progress on the event, we are going to have to have access to some kind of funds just to cover costs . . ." It was logical but ridiculously complicated.

In order to receive even a donation of £20, which one friend had volunteered to give us, we had to have a bank account. In order to open a bank account, we had to become a legal company. In order to become a company, we had to have an accountant. An accountant would want to know whether we wanted to be a limited company, a company limited by guarantee, a not-for-profit "organization," a charity, or a formal partnership. Understanding the implications of this choice seemed to require a PhD. When we'd done this, we'd need to register at Companies House and acquire a certificate. We had to have this piece of paper before we could arrange a meeting with a bank manager. All this so that we could accept £20.

I like to keep life simple, and suddenly I was sitting in front of an accountant who was threatening to put legally binding documents in front of me. He talked to me for a long time until I signed a piece of paper. A month later, with all the documentation finally in our hands, PS and I set off for a meeting at the bank.

Someone behind a counter referred to us as "those two girls." Not only did we feel like amateurs but we evidently looked like them as well. Even though we explained at great length that we were "not-for-profit" and that we didn't want a loan or any kind of overdraft facility, we were still put through a polite version of the Spanish Inquisition.

The business manager at my local branch was obviously far too busy to be concerned over matters like new accounts. He puffed up his chest and looked at us over his spectacles.

"And how long have you been involved in work of this kind? Miss Kelly?"

"About twelve years."

"Miss Losada?"

"About two weeks."

We filled in some more forms. Then some more forms.

"Your age, Miss Losada?"

"Is that strictly necessary?"

What exactly did my age have to do with anything? We didn't even want to borrow money. We had agreed to put in £250 each to get the whole thing rolling, and then before that ran out we would have to find a way to bring in some financial support. It was ambitious, but we were going to have a shot.

"Very well, then, sign here . . ." He sighed again as if it really were all far too much trouble. "You need to read through all this first, and this, and this."

"Can I pay in my friend's £20 now?" I asked hopefully.

"You cannot." He spoke quite clearly. "It will take a number of weeks for all this information to be processed."

"Yes, of course." PS glowered at me. "Can you desist from playing the fool for a couple more minutes?"

I sat compliant and businesslike. "Thank you so much. It has been a pleasure, filling in forms today." I smiled in a docile manner and shook his hand.

"We'll phone you when things are ready."

He swept out with a mixture of deep anxiety and theatrical bravado.

"That was quite an interview." PS watched his exit with admiration. "At least he didn't say, 'Don't call us.'"

THE IMPORTANCE OF BEING WEBWISE

Surely some things have been achieved in the past without websites? Empires have been made and lost. The seven wonders of the world were constructed. But no longer—gotta build a website first.

I went out and bought one of those big computer books. *HTML 4 for the World Wide Web*. And then I read it. It taught me all I needed to know. If we were going to have a website, then we were going to need someone to do it for us.

To have a professional site created for no money was going to require the advice of a genius. My address book offered not a single suggestion. Networking is an interesting idea, but it has always been a mystery to me. People who "network" have cars and business cards and invitations to important events. I had nothing of this kind. My friends were an assorted collection of actors or people who enjoyed weird weekends doing things that the majority of the population would consider dubious or theologically inadvisable. Nowhere in my address book was someone with a computer skill.

I asked people who I thought might know other people who might know someone who might know about building websites. "What you are asking," I was helpfully informed, "costs about £10,000 if it is done well. That is one huge favor to ask of someone who doesn't even know you."

This was now my morning meditation. Something for nothing. No—it just didn't work for me—even if it was in a good cause. There were no circumstances in which it was justifiable. Unless . . . unless there were some benefit to the person who was doing you the huge favor. Suppose, I pondered, the website builder had just left website-building college and was looking for a challenging project with which to enhance his or her resume? Suppose I could find such a person who also had an interest in Tibet? Perhaps I could even find a young Tibetan? I rang my young Tibetan contact who knew the entire second-generation Tibetan community. "No, I don't know any techies," he replied. "Certainly not any Tibetans anyway. None of them are into that sort of thing."

So much for that idea.

I went home inspired to start working on website content. I had to devise something. This needed a link to page 3 and page 3 needed an explanation that perhaps needed to be page 3a or should that be page 4? And did I then want the cyber browser to go back to page 3 or go to page 1? What order should they view the site in? How could I explain Tibetan history in a paragraph? I sat with circles of bits of paper spread out all over the floor.

It wasn't that I had any idea of how to construct a website, but I imagined that the first step would be to have some idea of how it would look. A couple of days later I had what I thought might resemble in some way the beginning of page 1. I emailed it to PS expectantly. She emailed it back with a long list of questions, alterations, corrections, and changes. It wasn't going to be easy, page 1.

Everything seemed to be so hard. At night I dreamt those dreams in which walking forward is impossible, and I woke to find I felt the same. It wasn't so much that I felt it was useless, but I questioned every day whether I had made any progress. I had been involved in my attempt to do something for what felt like a lifetime, and what did I have to show for it? An idea for an action with no money to pay for it and lots of pieces of paper on my living room floor.

Then one rainy morning an email came. I had sent off chatty and informal letters to the heads of some web companies, asking if I could meet them. And here was an email saying yes. I rang PS excitedly. "Where are you? Will you come and have a drink with us?" We had been summoned to a meeting with a cyber genius.

When we arrived at a pub that we had chosen for his convenience, we looked at him optimistically, and he looked at us skeptically. Finally he asked a question. "Why are you two doing this, then?" PS gave a speech about Drapchi prison in Tibet, about personal friends of hers who had been tortured there, about men and women who she knew were still being tortured there . . . "as we speak." She detailed some of the things that are done to them and ended, "That's why I'm doing this."

He turned to me. "And you, Isabel? Why are you doing this?"

"My answer would be somewhat different," I said.

"So?"

"I'm doing it because I believe that the Dalai Lama is the world's leading spiritual teacher today and deserves to be listened to. Because the world is involved in fighting violence with violence and no one seems to be listening to the only voice of peace. Because if we don't listen to this now, then Mahatma Gandhi lived and died for nothing. If we want to avoid war, we have to study and support peace in ourselves, in our families and streets, and the Dalai Lama speaks about that, too. Because I think we are witnessing the destruction of the last of the world's cultures that is dedicated to peace and nonviolence. I don't see any alternative but to support him and his government. Who else is there alive today that is worth listening to?"

There was a silence while he drank his beer.

"OK," he said. "I'll help. Here's what you need to do." He pulled a piece of paper out of a notebook and wrote:

1. Write down everything you want to put in the site, in bullet points, in order of priority.

2. Collate all the copy to back up these bullet points.

3. Collate all images, photos, etc., that you'd like to see.

4. Collate a list of people that should have testimonials or interviews presented.

5. List organizations that you would like to be linked or affiliated with.

6. Work out when you'd like to see things happen for real.

He handed it to PS. She handed it to me.

I suppressed a desire to jump up and down with joy, managed to say "Thank you" politely instead, and bought a large bottle of wine.

ABANDONMENT ISSUES

Now I was beginning to feel really hopeful, happy, and positive. The pieces of paper on my floor were now in a pretty pattern, and www.actfortibet.com seemed to be a great way to run a nonorganization while getting on with our lives. Maybe we could even do something significant with this opportunity. The sky was slowly going all blue and shiny. Then PS phoned.

"I've been offered a great job, Isabel."

"That's fantastic news."

"In Dublin."

I paused. I knew somewhere that the word *congratulations* was lodged in my brain and needed to be articulated by my vocal cords. But the sinking feeling in my heart went down into my shoes. I took a deep breath. There was a long, long pause while she waited.

"I should say congratulations, shouldn't I?"

"I have to live and pay the rent, Isabel. It's a really good job. Be happy for me."

The walls of my new blue, shiny world crumpled.

"I'd hoped that we'd raise some funds and be able to pay ourselves for what we are doing."

"I know but I it's not happening and I have to get paid."

"I can't do all this without you."

"Yes, you can. You're good at it. It'll work out. You'll see."

I put down the phone and burst into tears. My pieces of paper on the floor stared back at me. How was I going to do it all on my own? Approach sponsors? I had no clue about fund-raising. Write press releases? I had never written a press release in my life. I wallowed in self-pity. I had no one but myself to complain to if things went wrong or to congratulate me if things went well. I couldn't do it all alone. I felt pathetic.

And then I lost my personal assistant, too. My daughter had taken to saying "Isabel Losada's office" in an impressive professional manner when answering the phone. It made us both laugh, anyway. We liked to imagine that an occasional caller would be more polite after my "secretary" had "put them through." Emily, or Mez as she calls herself, had finally reached "gap year," that wonderful excuse given to the young to go off and experience their first year of freedom since they started school. She had floated the idea of not taking a gap year and going straight on to university. I wouldn't hear of it.

"Of course you must take a gap year! Are you mad? For heaven's sake, go and enjoy yourself. Where do you want to go?"

"I've been offered a job in South America."

"Then go, for heaven's sake."

"OK. It will be an opportunity for you, Mother."

"What?"

"With Isabel Kelly going to Dublin and me going to Quito, you'll be able to see how well you've worked through your abandonment issues."

JUMPING FOR MONEY

CHANGING CAREERS AGAIN

And so I wrote a list of all the people who were involved in some way or another—and counting all these people as my blessings like a good old-fashioned Christian girl, I felt happy all over again. I turned to my jobs list.

Create website. Ah yes. Items one and two required thought. Solution: move immediately to item three, "collate images." There is a fantastic little picture library called Tibet Images in London with one of the most lovely men that I've ever met working there. He is usually hugely busy and yet always finds time to be helpful. His name is Ian Cumming, and in my eyes he became semidivine. I made an appointment to see him.

"You have to ask yourself why you want to use pictures at all," he told me.

"To make the site look visually attractive?"

"Yes, but it has to be more than that, doesn't it? What do you want the images to say?"

So many Tibetan sites have the same pictures. Colorful prayer flags and smiling faces of exiled Tibetan children. But what do the images tell us? For the younger generation to see your fellow Tibetans constantly portrayed as nomads and beggar exiles must be somewhat irritating if you are just finishing a PhD in medicine in your third language. But I still wanted faces.

"OK, so let's look at faces."

But pictures were the easier part.

The content of the website just wasn't happening. For some inexplicable reason, the cyber-genius company seemed to put all the paying clients first. "We have an international site going live next week." I'd try again a week later, but my phone calls didn't get returned. I was trying to learn about courage, and all I kept receiving were lessons in patience.

I thought up ways to turn the endless delays to our advantage. I wrote letters to people whom I thought might like to help. I wrote to celebs whom I knew had an interest in Tibet—Richard Gere, Pierce Brosnan, Trudie Styler. I wrote to Bob Geldof just in case he would see me. I thought that even if Sir Bob wouldn't help, then he could have a good laugh hearing about what I was trying to do. Richard Gere has a foundation that gives grants to people like us, but they wouldn't even consider us unless we had charity status. I rang the accountant and asked how long it takes to become a registered charity. "About a year, and the paperwork is endless, and there are lots of things that you can't do." Things like slightly illegal stunts no doubt.

I began to feel that I couldn't do any fund-raising until we had the website up and live. Or was this just an excuse? I didn't want to do fund-raising. Even if it was a worthy cause, I still didn't want to ask for money. Why do so many people, myself included it seemed, have such resistance to asking for money?

I met a lady called Tess Burrows who ran her own action group called Climb for Tibet. Small groups of them climbed mountains and collected sponsorship. Sounds simple enough. They had raised £35,000. I spoke to her and listened with horror to the advice she gave me. "I ask everyone all the time. . . . I always have sponsorship forms with me." I read about what she had done and learned that she did quite literally approach everyone. She would sit on a plane and talk to the captive victim next to her about what they were doing. When the innocent soul expressed some encouragement for her climb with a phrase like "Good for you," she would instantly produce a sponsor form and put it in his or her hand. "You need a form," she would say. I cringed. Obviously I was going to have to change my attitudes to all this completely.

PS was no help at all. "I'm not a fund-raiser, and I never will be," she announced. "I know people who do this, and they are very good at it. But I'm not one of them."

"Well, that's not very helpful," I'd whine. "I'm not one of them either, but we still need funds so someone is going to have to raise them."

"I'm a campaigner, not a fund-raiser."

"Haven't you heard of transferable skills? Surely fund-raising is a skill that we are going to have to learn if we are going to make any progress at all. I thought we were going to find a way to make this pay us?"

"I can't help anyway. I've got to live."

"But we haven't tried. We haven't written to ten major sponsors. We haven't met anyone about fund-raising. We haven't even identified the people that we can approach."

There was a pause. I laughed. It was obviously going to be up to me.

She laughed, too. Then she said, "So are you changing careers again?"

GRANDFATHER CLOCKS AND ANGEL CAKE

So this is the next inevitable lesson: Whatever you aim to do to change the world, eventually you will come up against fund-raising. There are professional money raisers out there, and it is a vocation, no doubt, requiring skill, perseverance, and determination. Those who do it for a living know exactly who they can approach, for what, and why. Which left me seriously in the . . . er, in a mess.

I only wanted to raise £5,000, which seemed a piffling amount. It was a challenge, I attempted to reason with myself. A task into which I could throw myself with enthusiasm, determined to use the learning for my advantage. After all, knowing how to find money has to be a useful skill in life.

I climbed onto my trusty two-wheeler and cycled to my local library. *The Directory of Grant-Making Trusts* informed me that there are nine thousand organizations in Britain that exist for the sole purpose of giving away cash. Now, there's an encouraging fact. So it had to just be a question of doing the homework and writing the letters. At least, I figured, I would need to write ten fairly impressive letters to ten major trust funds. With a sum as small as £5,000 to raise, I only needed one good success.

If only it were that simple. The first thing that immediately became apparent was the negative side of not having spent an extra nine months becoming a charity. It seems that many major foundations are set up . . . well, let's be charitable and say, to provide tax breaks. It is only if you give money to a charity that you can claim it as a taxable expense. So the first question many people ask is, "Are you a charity?" If you say, "No, we are a not-for-profit company," then you hear a very polite voice saying, "I'm *so* sorry then, we won't even be able to consider an application from you." There is also a strange new tone of voice as if someone is thinking, This idiot doesn't know what she's doing.

You could spend weeks reading *The Directory of Grant-Making Trusts*. You may like to know that there is a charitable trust called the Swinfen Broun Trust, but they give money only to Lichfield. So if you are reading in Lichfield, go and look them up. Last year they gave a grant of £1,298 to the Friary Grange Cricket Club for new equipment. Now, that is what my ex-husband would consider an excellent use of funds.

And listen to this one. The Bryant Trust gives money within a ten-mile radius of Birmingham city center but only east of the M6. Seriously, I'm not making this up. So how does this happen? Does some excellent elderly person lie on their deathbed and say, "I want to create a trust fund [cough, wheeze], but I don't want to give anything to that lot on the other side of the M6"?

Then there are purely practical considerations. Like what do you do when you find a trust that is interested in doing international work and has a commitment to human rights, but then adds, in bold typeface: "**The trust states that it does not respond to unsolicited applications.**" So how, I wonder, am I supposed to inform such organizations of what we are trying to do?

All this would have been so much easier if I'd had the fortune to have been born a "Freeman of the Haberdashers' Company of the City of London." Then there would have been piles of cash just waiting for me.

If you are the daughter of a cobbler or a blacksmith and only have one leg and want to set up a leper colony in Bognor, then you will be sure to find the very foundation that was created to help you. But be careful not to apply in any month that has an *r* in it or make the mistake of writing on a Tuesday or phoning on a Wednesday, or your application will be instantly disallowed.

I was determined to find ten letters I could write. The librarian wanted to help.

"The Community Fund now has an International Section," she said. "You may like to apply to them."

The operators of the Community Fund, as the Lottery fund is for some reason called, have come up with a perfect plan for putting people off: the guide to the program is 38 pages long; the form is 36 pages long; and the guide to filling in the form is a mere 17 pages long. Obviously anyone who can get through that lot deserves a grant. It must work every time.

I sat in the library for three hours until my list met my self-imposed criteria, and then I committed to writing my ten letters to various trust funds to see how much progress I could make. Each time I dropped a complete fund-raising letter in the mailbox, I sustained my illusion that I was achieving something. But no money was coming in, and I was still no closer to being able to have our stunt for the Panchen Lama.

I rang Tess Burrows for encouragement and ideas. "Do wacky things," she said. "Wacky?" I sighed deeply. Did I now have to train for the London Marathon and then run it dressed as a chicken? Suddenly I was filled with admiration for those wonderful souls who do such things and raise thousands for charity. But wacky?

It happened that a few weeks later I paid a visit to my one and only remaining uncle, who was now nearly seventy-five and in poor health. He had a pacemaker fitted some years back and now walks with a limp. As he lives alone, I occasionally take the train down to Haslemere in Hampshire to spend a day with him. Thinking of him as "elderly," I enjoy cups of tea and stories of his childhood, which occasionally include references to my late mother. An old grandfather clock ticks and tocks, and with that gentle and reassuring sound, time itself seems to slow down.

"I'm thinking of doing a parachute jump," he said as he served me tea.

"A what? You're joking?"

"Care for some angel cake? I was in the Parachute Regiment when I was a lad. Of course I haven't done a jump for over twenty years now. But I thought I'd like to."

"But, but I thought you weren't fit? You've got a pacemaker, haven't you? And I thought you had a bad leg?" Was this me talking? Ms. Nauseatingly Positive?

"Bad leg? Oh no, this old knee gets a bit stiff if I sit for too long, but jumping doesn't involve sitting."

"And the pacemaker?"

"Of course I don't know what the doctor will say, and I think I have to have a doctor's checkup as I'm over forty. But if the doctor will let me, I'm going to do it."

Suddenly my brain came alive. "Who are you jumping for? Any particular charity?"

"I haven't decided yet."

"Would you consider jumping for us? We've got this little not-for-profit thing. It's about taking action for Tibet."

"Yes, I'd support that."

"Fantastic!" I poured more tea with a big smile. Then as I drank it the color drained from my face. A thought had formed. If he can jump . . .

This has always been my greatest fear. The idea of jumping out of a moving object and plunging downwards at nearly 200 miles an hour like a stone towards the earth. Nope, this was not anywhere near my "Things I'd like to do one day" list. Why would anyone want to do this unless the plane was on fire?

"Is anyone going to jump with you?" I asked, desperately hoping it was a "former regiment" day out or something.

"Oh no. It was just an idea I had. I don't have a date fixed or anything."

"So no one is supporting you?"

"No."

"OK, Uncle. If you'll jump for us, then I'll jump with you."

"Oh. That's jolly kind of you." Yes, he really does speak like this. "Are you sure?"

"Sure? Yes!" I was sure I didn't want to do it.

He laughed. "It's not everyone's cup of tea. Aren't you scared?"

"Scared, Uncle? No. I'm terrified. When are we going to do this?"

"Whenever you like."

"OK, I'll arrange it."

So much for a visit to my elderly uncle. I couldn't quite believe what I'd agreed to. I wondered if I was ready to die. I rang Tess. "I'm thinking of throwing myself out of a plane at 12,000 feet."

"Fantastic. Have you got sponsor forms?"

So this was it, then. Fund-raising for beginners. Go to those poor souls known as "friends" and ask them for money. I didn't like this as a system, but at least I was doing . . . er, "something wacky."

HASN'T EVERYONE DONE THAT?

Skydiving divides people into definite groups. Those that were the most impressed by my latest venture into apparent insanity were the group that were unable to stand on chairs and that instantly went into a kind of terror when I even spoke of what I was intending to do. One old friend asked if I would be prepared to add up all the money I'd raise and then she would pay me more than that not to jump. "I want you to be safe." And she meant it, too.

Then there is a group of people who admire the idea but admit that there is no amount of money under heaven that would induce them to do the same. This is the "Gosh, I'm so impressed!" group.

Then there is a small and, to my mind, insane group that says, "That's fantastic! Can I come?" Suddenly I had others wanting to join us.

And finally there is the group of people who have already done it themselves and think it all very easy. There was I, gearing myself up for what I considered to be the most courageous thing I had ever done, and one acquaintance actually said, and I quote, "Oh. Hasn't everybody done that?"

I felt the size of a small worm. "Have you?"

"Of course. But all my friends have done it. There's nothing to it."

I wasn't going to go on and ask this person for sponsor money. I just crawled back into my hole to recover.

One response was a complete delight. A lady that I'd met once who worked for the Tibet Society said, "I'd love to jump with you. I'm doing a sponsored swim to raise funds for the Tibet Society, and I'm not really looking forward to it. This sounds much more fun." I was amazed that anyone was crazy enough to want to jump from a plane. But this was exactly what I wanted to do with Act for Tibet—different people jumping together, each for his or her own organization.

"That's a great idea. You jump for the Tibet Society, and we'll jump for Act for Tibet. That's what I'd love." Suddenly things were moving. I managed to find the name of a parachute school and was much surprised, when I rang them, to find them alive.

"Hello, London Parachute School, I'm Jo," said the voice of a friendly young girl. "Did you want to do a jump?"

"Not really," I replied. "Do you often get killed?"

"Me personally, not so far." Deeply reassuringly. "The only thing is, the season ends in two weeks. We don't jump in the winter."

"Two weeks? What about the weather? Surely it's too cloudy?"

"Cloud isn't a problem as you jump from above the clouds."

Are you feeling faint?

"Even rain isn't a problem, only wind. But the weather looks good."

"So could we look at the last weekend, then? The Friday and if the weather is poor we'll come back on the Sunday, allowing Saturday for the weather to change?"

"The weather on the Friday should be OK. But I'll pencil in Sunday as well just in case."

I went to look at my calendar. Weird. That Friday was my uncle's actual seventy-fifth birthday, and I hadn't known. I don't know about coincidence, but this was definitely what the Tibetans call "an auspicious sign."

I took a deep breath, said prayers to all the gods that I could think of, and sent my deposit.

MONEY RAISING FOR THE WARY

Sponsorship forms brought the subject of money close to home. The dreaded word had to be mentioned to friends. Money? What a heavy word it is and can be. We all seem to have so many issues about it. People believe that one can't have money and have a spiritual outlook on life. The Scripture is often misquoted: "Money is the root of all evil" is not what Timothy says in the New Testament. He says, "The love of money is the root of all evil."

Robert Kiyosaki writes in his best-selling book *Rich Dad, Poor Dad* that so many people claim that they have no interest in making money and yet spend their whole lives as a slave to it. He points out that very few of us have any positive financial education, which makes us vulnerable to all kinds of traps.

I lived in New York for a year in 1996, and I was horrified at how many people I met who lived their lives with huge credit-card bills and thousands of dollars of debt mounting into sums that they could never hope to be free from. Yet now, in London, I know more and more people who regularly spend money that they don't have. Offers of credit cards started to drop through the door for my daughter on her eighteenth birthday, along with other inviting loan deals.

Few things make me mad, but this does. I would like to start a little campaign in which all offers to people to run up debt would be torn up and returned to the sender in the prepaid envelope. And another thing, while I'm having a little rant: A friend of mine who works for a small charity, on a low wage, recently went to see an "independent" financial adviser. This service, as we know, is free. She came away from this meeting very happy. She had been persuaded to "consolidate her debts" and extend the period of her mortgage, thus reducing her payments. Of course they hadn't fully explained that they are on commission for advising her to do this and that she would now be paying thousands more to a mortgage company. It's quite depressing. Kiyosaki asks why anyone goes to a "financial adviser" when these people are not themselves rich. Why, he asks, do we not ask people who are rich for their advice? Why don't we learn about money? His book was like a wake-up call. I don't have much money. But I try to view money as opportunity and the lack of money as a challenge to action and to feel positive about it as a form of energy. What other way is there to feel about something that plays such a large part in all of our lives?

But now I needed the stuff, not for myself but to proceed with what I was doing. It brought to mind the only phrase of Margaret Thatcher's that I had committed to memory: "No one would remember the story of the Good Samaritan if he'd only had good intentions. He had money as well."

If you ever want to see a new side to your friends and acquaintances, try a sponsored skydive to raise money for your favorite charity (or not-for-profit organization). It brings both delightful surprises and nasty shocks. With some friends that I'd known for years, the subject of money had never really been part of the conversation.

The day after I'd sent off my deposit, an old friend rang. A man that I may have seen five times in the last ten years. He asked me what I was up to.

"I'm gearing myself up to jump out of an airplane in a couple of weeks."

"Goodness. Are you looking for sponsorship?"

"Yes, actually, I am."

"I think it's very brave to jump. I wouldn't have the guts. I'll give you one hundred pounds."

I was staggered. I hadn't even asked him.

"Well, thank you, John. That's very generous."

Most people offered £20. I felt that this was very kind. And I thought that this is what I would have given. Perhaps it depends on the event. I'd recently been contacted to contribute to a sponsored walk for treatment for a friend with cancer, and I'd given £50. But goodness what a thorny subject this is. It even seems inappropriate to write about it. In an age where there are so few taboo subjects, this is one of them.

"Ah? You have a job, do you? And what do you earn?" Try that at a dinner party.

As pledges of money started to come in, I was delighted by the response. One day I had an email from someone whom I'd not even met who wanted to contribute £25. It was all very strange. But it was still painfully slow progress. Then I had the opposite experience.

I asked one of my best girlfriends who had recently admitted that she "owed me, big time." I had offered her a job that she had worked in for over a year and then introduced her to a potential business partner. Together the two of them had made thousands of pounds. Admittedly my role here had only been the introduction, but I still felt I had played one. I asked her if she would sponsor me. Perhaps she believed that raising money was easy for me. "Yes, I'll sponsor you," she said. "Fantastic!" I replied, so appreciative of her support.

"Ten pounds," she added. There was an awkward silence as I wondered how to respond. I wondered if she was joking with me. I tried to make light of it—"That's not enough"—voicing my honest response. I laughed. "I'm laying my life on the line here."

She said, "Try to be gracious."

"OK." I mustered all the honest enthusiasm I could. "That's lovely. Thank you very much."

We said our good-byes, and I put the phone down. What was I doing? Putting a value on the friendship? Thinking that the amount she offered was an indication of how much she valued me? This was obviously not the case. And yet I felt slighted. It was as if this were all I was worth to her. Ten pounds? I sat back in my chair, shocked at my reaction.

I could just have said, "Thank you very much. It all adds up." I could have been positive, but I knew that by those few words I had done harm to our relationship. Of course I had not done anything in the past in the hope of being "paid back," but now that I needed support I felt robbed of the spontaneous generosity I had expected from her. I had thought she was someone who would delight in giving money away, even if she didn't have much or any at all to spare.

And all this from a simple question about money. If she had said, "I'll give you twenty pounds, and I'm sorry it can't be more. I'm really broke at the moment," I'd have said, "OK, I understand. Thank you." Of course other friends had offered £5 or £2, and I'd been delighted. But £10 from this friend seemed like the least that she could possibly offer, and some child in me wanted to tell her to keep her £10.

I was learning a lot from asking friends for money—because I suppose that is what sponsorship is, or what it feels like. I didn't like it at all. And I wouldn't make that mistake again. In future I would be gracious even if offered £1 by someone whose life I had saved. I wondered about a friend who had emailed me recently, asking for sponsorship for a round-the-world trip and, involved in raising money myself, I hadn't replied at all. I decided I'd ring her that day and explain why I hadn't rung. It was because I was raising money myself and not enjoying the experience much.

My uncle was having similar problems. "People are offering the same as when I shaved off my beard last year to raise money for the local donkey farm," he said. "One pound? Of course I say, 'Thank you, kindly.'" He is a wiser man than I am.

I was doing better with jumpers. A seventeen-year-old son of a friend had spotted an opportunity for a day off school and offered to join us. Catherine at the Tibet Society acquired another jumper, and two Tibetans were also lined up to jump with us for their own trust fund, Tibet Dreams. A joint activity was beyond even what I'd hoped for. The Meridian Trust, a small charity that takes care of archive film materials of Tibet and films on Buddhism, also produced a jumper. I was thrilled. I rang the Free Tibet Campaign and invited them to jump with us, but they had their own jumping event happening next year, so they declined. But it was still a joint event.

Then checks started to arrive. Before the jump. Obviously some people were more confident than I was that I was going to come down alive. Every day I added up the pledges like a child: £245, £250, £275, £310, £340. It was slow progress. I asked my agent, who sent me £120 of his personal money by return of post: £460. . . . It was creeping up, but it was only going to reach £2,000, maybe £2,500. I needed to raise £5,000.

I have one very wealthy friend. An American. I can't imagine what it must be like to be that well-off, but I imagine it must bring hazards. Hazards such as people asking you for money (to pick an example entirely at random). I had never wanted to be one of those, but I figured that the money wasn't for me. Americans, on the whole, are much better informed about what has happened in Tibet than the English are. After all, there was a war on, and I was attempting to support the great man of peace.

Fortune appeared to be smiling on me. My friend would be in London a number of days before the jump, and we would be having dinner together.

"So, how are you?" he asked. I prattled on about the project, how challenging it was, the new website, all the little successes. Then I told him about the jump and about the eleventh Panchen Lama. And about what I wanted to do to raise his profile.

"The thing is," I said, "that when I've raised all the money I've collected in sponsorship, I'll still only have about two thousand pounds. And I need five thousand pounds."

"Just ask for what you want, Isabel," he said. "I have so many sycophants around me."

"Well, OK . . . I was wondering if you would make up the difference for me? Or match what I've made?"

"No. I won't do that." It was a direct answer if nothing else.

"You won't? Oh. Why's that?"

"I don't care about Tibet."

"I'm sorry?"

"If you'd been doing it for AIDS victims or for a hospital or a school, I'd have said yes, but I don't care about Tibet."

I argued the case. "But this is for a little boy who is the world's youngest political prisoner. He is the future of Tibetan Buddhism . . . for heaven's sake . . . you live in New York. There is a war on terror going on. Don't you think that those who have refused to fight violence with violence should be rewarded? Don't you think that the Dalai Lama's message of peace is one of the most important voices in the world to be supported? That . . ."

"Listen, Isabel. I think Bush is doing a damn good job. I met him before 9/11, and I met him afterwards, and he has come forward as a great leader."

"Mmm," I said, "this salmon is really beautifully cooked."

I savored the taste while I adjusted my reality. I wasn't going to argue with him. At least his answer was an honest one.

"Never mind," I said. "It'll be a greater challenge without your support."

I had one other wealthy friend who also said no. And a third who gave £500. I had learned a lot about raising money, and it was exactly what Tess had told me. The large donations would have been lovely. They would have made it easy. But there was a lot in the power of the many.

DO THEY THINK I'M CRAZY?

Everyone seems to assume that, because I'm jumping out of an airplane, that means that I want to jump out of an airplane. Do they think I'm crazy? Just because I smile and laugh and say, "Well, I won't be bored that morning, will I?" can anyone honestly believe that I'm looking forward to it?

I give talks about "comfort zones" and how important it is to expand your comfort zone. I've always used "jump out of an airplane" as an example of the one action I can think of that is furthest from my comfort zone. I know, in theory, that it's good to leap out. But at 12,000 feet? Who taught me these stupid ideas in the first place? What's wrong with being comfortable in my comfort zone?

The truth is, while I am terrified, other people keep coming forward, all smiles. Even Steve has offered to abandon his paint pots and lay his life on the line: "Can I come? I'd love to jump." It's totally bewildering.

I'm bound to die. My will is out of date. It's all about who should bring up my daughter, who was two when I wrote it, in the event of my death. And the person who is supposed to be executor to the will, my daughter's godfather, has become a reclusive hermit living in the northernmost reaches of Scotland, communing with the sea. My sudden demise would be most inconvenient for him.

But there is one reason that I think I'll live. It's only a short diversion, and it's a true story, I promise you.

Last year I met a Japanese saint. She is what they call in Buddhism a bodhisattva and has total recall of all eighteen of her previous lives. This is all true. She is called Reverend Ryugen Tanaka, and she lives near Hiroshima in the Ryugen-in Monastery that her followers have built for her. She stunned me by mentioning my exact age without hesitation and then my daughter's age. At the end of the interview, I said to her, "I see that you are aware of things and see things that most people do not see. Is that so?"

"It is."

"Well, then, I don't want to know anything that would be negative or damaging, but if you see anything in my future that you think it would be helpful for me to know, then I would be grateful to know it."

"You will recognize your life partner when you are forty-five," she said, quite simply. "He is in your life already, but you haven't recognized him yet."

My mind went into a whirl as I mentally flicked through my Filofax and wondered if perhaps she could provide his address.

"He is very kind to you," she added.

These few phrases have had an interesting effect on my life. Of course I've tried to ignore them. On the one hand they were encouraging; at least she had said that I will have a life partner. On the other hand there seems to be little point in meeting new and interesting men since it seems that I know the most important one already. "He is kind to you" created an interesting subsection of my acquaintance. Had she said, "He loves you," it would have been different. Many people may say that they love us but are never there when we need help, encouragement, or support. But kindness? Well, that's an action, isn't it? People who are kind do things. I did a calculation among the men I knew and narrowed it down to two. We'll see.

But the encouragement I gained from this prediction is that I would be doing something—anything—at the age of forty-five. The parachute school also seemed to think that we would all survive. After all, it's "only" a skydive. It's only my greatest fear.

Maybe there really are some people out there who are not scared the first time they do something like this. But maybe they are just very stupid or lack imagination. One friend had phrased it rather positively in an email: "Good luck on your journey into pure exhilaration." *Exhilaration?* I suppose that's one word. *Terror* would be another. The best thing will definitely be getting in the car afterwards. Yes, that's the bit I'm looking forward to. Putting my bum on the car seat for the journey home.

On a tandem skydive, you are strapped to another person. There is a total stranger out there somewhere in the universe, into whose hands I am going to commit my life. So once I have agreed to jump and I'm in the plane, I can't change my mind, no matter how terrified I am. I won't have to pluck up the courage to jump. He'll jump, and I'll go along whether I like it or not. The cheerful man at the parachute school said on the phone, "Once the plane takes off, there is only one way down, and it's not by plane."

Then there I'll be, descending towards the earth at 200 miles an hour, with the wind lashing my face so hard it'll hurt. (Wonder which moisturizer I should use? Now, there is an advertisement opportunity. Forget studio models; try skydivers.) So I'll be falling and falling and actually have time to think, "I really don't like this feeling, this pure undiluted panic. No, I'm not happy." But then eventually a parachute opens. And maybe, just maybe, there will be two or three minutes of floating down like Winnie the Pooh holding on to his balloon, that will be enjoyable. That is how I imagine it will be. But I'm attempting to concentrate on the unlikely possibility that I may enjoy the whole experience.

NOT FALLING, BUT FLYING

On the morning of the jump a check for £8 arrived from a poverty-stricken friend who had previously offered £5. I was hugely touched. And even though it was all part of my determination to raise the profile of a young Tibetan boy, today it was the feeling that one more person was supporting us that mattered. I was no longer the fund-raiser who was disappointed by the offer of £10; now I was one who was moved by the offer of £8. Of course it's not the money.

We'd picked up my "elderly" uncle the night before, and we all bundled into cars for a little convoy up to the Royal Air Force base. To add to the excitement, the doctor, who had only been able to see my uncle the previous day, had refused to sign the medical clearance until he'd spoken to the parachute school about the effect of the air pressure on the pacemaker. So here we were, trying to get through to a National Health doctor on the telephone. "I'm sorry, the doctor is in surgery until twelve," said a voice.

"Yes, we know, but we need to be put through now . . ." Sometimes being bossy is the only way. The parachute school called: "I can't let him jump unless I've seen a doctor's signature. We have to have it for the insurance. If he dies it will ruin us otherwise."

"Uncle," I turned around in the car to shout instructions. "The London Parachute School says that you are not to die . . ."

He didn't look reassured.

"Will the signature be OK by fax?" This was madness of all kinds.

"Yes. How is he anyway?"

"Uncle?" I shouted. "They want to know how you are . . ."

"Oh, splendid. Jolly good fun."

"He's fine. And could you ask how I am? I'm terrified!"

He just chuckled. "Get the doctor to fax the form. There is no problem with air pressure."

So our little convoy arrived. What a strange collection we were.

Alex was still at school and my uncle way past retirement, two members of the Tibet Society, one from the Meridian Trust, Steve the smiling builder, who drove us, two members of the Tibetan community in Britain jumping for Tibet Dreams, and a nervous wreck—me. Just another day's work to the tandem guys.

An instructor greeted us. "My name's Tommo, and I'm a legend." These were the exact words he used.

The sky had turned an inexplicable shade of blue, light fluffy white clouds dotted it, and there was very little wind.

"Will we be able to jump?" Alex, our heroic seventeen-year-old, asked enthusiastically.

"Perfect jumping weather. If you could all sit on the floor, we'll give you the training."

We sat down nervously. The Tibetans may have been worried, but they wore huge smiles. Everyone was smiling. I wondered if I could make a dash for the parking lot.

"It takes twenty minutes for the plane to get up, and about five minutes for you to get down again." This was humor. "Now, if you could lie down on your stomachs on the floor and cross your legs over?"

We obliged.

"Yes, very good. That is the position you take when you jump from the plane. Remember to get your legs under the plane as you jump. This is very important."

What was I doing here?

"Now your arms. You cross those over as you jump, and then when we tap you on the shoulder, you open your arms to the open 'skydiving' position. Like this."

We copied him. "Very good. Let's go, then. Oh, any questions before we leave?"

We were stunned into silence. That was the training. Two minutes.

"If you could all put these jumpsuits on?" They were thin cotton.

"These aren't going to keep us warm," I said to Migmar, the smiling Tibetan. "What purpose can they serve?"

"If the parachute doesn't open and you hit the ground, they must help to keep all your body together. Make it easier to scrape you up."

"Of course." Obvious, really.

We strapped on our parachutes and headed for the plane. A little Twin Otter plane stood waiting to take all eight of us up at once. We smiled nervously for each other's cameras and clambered in. It was easy to clamber as the plane seemed to have a wall missing. It just had a piece of transparent plastic on one side that slid up so that we could . . . I didn't like to think about it.

Ah, well, I was thinking to myself, if I'm going to die, life has been OK, all things considered, and I'd really rather die like this than of cancer. In my more Christian days I'd have seen all this as an exercise in trusting God. Just jump and trust that He will hold you. But in the last year all this Tibetan Buddhist influence has offered no such easy promise of a loving God, just the certainty that I was not properly prepared for death, had probably accrued much bad karma in this lifetime, and might come back very shortly as a mosquito or some such sentient being.

"If I die and you don't, tell my daughter I love her," I shouted to Steve as they started up the engines.

I looked around at my uncle. He had an absurd smile on his face. Honestly, you'd think the older generation could be relied on to set an example and be appropriately nervous.

The plane started up, and suddenly we were off the ground. Oh God, this was it. No way back now. I was going to do what??? The little plane climbed steeply. We put on silly pointed hats and adjusted our goggles. I chatted to the skydiver who was taking a video of my uncle: "Well, this is not as bad as I thought it was going to be so far." He didn't tell me that the video had no sound.

Tommo the Legend was strapped to my uncle, who had asked to be first out of the plane. "Looking forward to it, Uncle?" I shouted above the roar of the engines. "Yes," he mouthed back. "You?"

"Oh, absolutely . . ."

We sat for a while, watching the houses get smaller and smaller, and then finally they disappeared totally as we climbed above the clouds. It was deceptively warm and cozy in the plane, comforting, peaceful. How many times had I been in planes and looked at the cotton candy clouds and thought how magical it would be to jump out into them. It's easy to think that when you aren't strapped to a man who's just about to dive out.

Then Tommo the Legend opened the hatch, and he and my uncle shuffled forward. "Ready?" he shouted. My uncle nodded. The pacemaker presumably kept doing its job. And then they weren't there anymore.

I thought, "Now I know that I really, really do not want to do this. Oh, fuck." The plastic flapped above a gaping hole in the aircraft. The freezing air rushed in, and the man behind me shuffled forward. I was strapped to him in several places. I had no option but to shuffle. I was glad he wasn't a legend. He was lovely.

"I'm not sure I want to do this, Leigh!" I shouted.

"Legs under the aircraft, remember?"

"Yes."

And then there I was. Flying. Not falling. Suspended in midair with wind rushing by. It was fantastic. A tap came on my shoulder, and I uncrossed my arms and legs and just hung there. No sensation of falling. I was flying. So peaceful. So beautiful. I thought, "This is a wonder . . . I love this . . ."

Then there was a lurch, and suddenly my legs were beneath me and I was surrounded by straps.

"We're going to spin the parachute through that cloud," said a calm voice behind me. "You may find this a little disorienting." And then I seemed to be on my side and then facing heaven knows where. The cloud was cold. No cotton wool anywhere. I suddenly felt sick as if I were on some fairground ride that I couldn't get off. Then the houses appeared, but we weren't floating down to them gently as I'd imagined. No "Pooh Bear holding balloon" experience. This was more like Tigger holding on to a kite with a hole in it.

"Are you OK?" said the voice behind me.

"I feel sick," I said. And for a moment I wondered if I was actually going to be sick in midair and in exactly what direction any projectile would travel under these circumstances.

"Lift your legs up in front of you so that I can take the landing," said the voice.

Ah, so that's why you don't break your ankle doing a tandem jump. You don't even have to land; even that is done for you. He landed, we bumped along a bit as he grabbed the parachute in, and then I put my feet down and then my bum and sat on the grass in a state of amazement. This was the ground, and I was sitting on it.

My uncle came jogging up to pull me to my feet. "Marvelous," I heard him saying. "I want to do it again when I'm eighty."

ASKING WHY

TEA WITH THE AMBASSADOR

So gradually money came in. My wealthy American friend made a contribution, after all. "I'm doing this to support you, not to support Tibet," he said.

I sighed. "That's what T. S. Eliot called 'the right deed for the wrong reason.'"

"Say again?"

"Never mind. Just write the check out to 'Act for Tibet' please and not to me."

"Of course."

So, with all this, one response to my letters from the library that brought a £500 donation, and all the small amounts from other sponsors, we had enough to proceed with the stunt. The website was clicking into life, and meanwhile I was still reading about Tibet and gaining some small knowledge of the greater picture.

There was one thing nagging away at me. I had only listened to one side.

I wanted to find out what the Chinese thought about all this—what they really thought—to establish whether I was being fed propaganda by the London organizations. I wanted to talk to the Chinese government, or as close as I could get. Perhaps I could speak with someone at the embassy? Maybe I could meet the ambassador himself? After all, his job was to be an ambassador. There was nothing to stop me from finding out if he would do this job for me.

I rang up and left several messages that were not returned. I tried different lines; eventually I reached the ambassador's secretary. He was quite affable, and so I asked his advice. "You will need to send us a letter and a resume along with details of your project and why you wish to interview the ambassador."

"Certainly. I would be delighted."

I brushed up my details along with an adapted version of what the project was about. I explained at great length how difficult it was to obtain the Chinese perspective on Tibet in London and how I wanted to gain a correct understanding of China's viewpoint.

Then I waited. A week later I telephoned. "Ah yes, Ms. Losada? Could you possibly submit the information that you sent to us, again?"

I could. And I did. Then I waited. Two days later a phone call came, seemingly the voice of very young girl. "Hello. This is the Chinese embassy. We have read your letter, and we would like to invite you to meet the press secretary . . ."

"Ah. I see. Is this as well as the ambassador or instead of him?"

"We would like to establish why you want to speak with the ambassador."

Best not to argue with them. "OK, I'd be delighted to meet whomever you'd like me to."

So I dressed up in my poshest suit and walked the familiar route down Portland Place. I smiled at the policeman on the step, rang the doorbell, gave my name, and was invited inside. A step up from the step.

A deferential young woman, who looked as if she might be in her twenties, greeted me. Her card informed me that she was the "third secretary."

"Come this way, please."

She showed me into an elegant room and brought China tea. We sat and chatted for a while. "Have you been posted here for long?" I asked.

"A couple of months." Her English was, of course, perfect.

"Do you live near here?"

"In the official quarters that are provided by the government."

"Ah, I see."

A tall attractive man with an intelligent look about him walked towards us with a warm smile on his face. He must have been in his late thirties or early forties and had a fresh and positive energy about him. "Welcome to the Chinese embassy." He held out his hand. I shook it warmly. "Have you been here before?"

"No, I haven't." Best not to add that I've stood outside a couple of times.

"So, please, take a seat. You have had some tea? Ah yes, I see you have." He sat down and poured himself a cup. "So, please, tell us about what you are doing."

I chatted on about my examination of "the Tibetan question."

"Have you been to Tibet?" He smiled at me.

"I have, yes."

"And what were your impressions?"

I spoke at great length about the beauty of the scenery. He was no fool.

"And apart from the landscape?"

I spoke at great length about the beauty of the monasteries, the confusing panoply of Tibetan Buddhist deities. "I find Tibetan Buddhism very bewildering. I think I am more naturally drawn towards Zen Buddhism. That seems more simple to me. But that may be because I know nothing about it." I chatted on, keeping the conversation completely off politics.

"How long were you there for?"

"Oh, about ten days. I wish it could have been longer. I suffered quite badly from altitude sickness on the road from Nepal." I chatted about altitude sickness.

He recognized all my evasions. "So how can we help you?"

"Well, I once lived with a professor from Shanghai. Professor Yibin Ni." An unexpected fact of my past that had come to help me. "He taught linguistics at the School of African and Oriental Studies in London." They could verify this fact if they chose to.

They nodded politely.

"He was born and raised in Shanghai, and he and I lived together for eighteen months."

They probably wondered why they were learning about my private life.

"From him I learned about the anti-Chinese bias in the Western media. He couldn't believe the way that we in Britain see things only from our point of view. He bought me a Chinese map of the world, which, as you know, has China in the center. I looked at Britain, a tiny island out towards the edge somewhere, barely visible. I noticed that the whole of Europe appeared utterly insignificant, and I began to understand his frustration with our perspective."

"Yes?"

"I promised him that I would not reflect the bias of the West. That having lived with him I would not be so narrow-minded, even if I have not traveled to China myself. We are so limited in our outlook, in our refusal to learn other languages. If the main international language were Chinese, we wouldn't stand a chance. You are so much better educated than we are. You can't deny this, can you?"

"We learn English in school," was his diplomatic reply.

"So in exploring the subject of Tibet . . . Well, to speak frankly . . ." I had his attention. "I'm very aware that I am only hearing one side of the argument all the time. There is complete freedom of information on one side, and I'm not happy with that."

I sipped my China tea delicately.

"I want to give the ambassador a chance to be an ambassador for his people. I was told by one of the Tibet organizations in London that there would be no point in seeing him as he would purely speak the party line. I want to know if this is true."

"It is not true," said my charming host. "During the Cultural Revolution people were afraid to say anything that parted from the party line, but that was a long time ago."

"I thought that this was the case. So that's one question, for example, that I'd like to ask him. If his personal view is different from his government's view on any issue, and, if so, would he feel free to express that?"

"And what would you like to ask him about Tibet?"

"I'd like to ask him what his views are. Has he traveled there, do you know?"

"He has, yes."

"So then I would like to ask him what his impressions were."

We talked on and on. The third secretary poured more tea. I chatted in my usual friendly way, and they seemed to be enjoying the entertainment. "I think there is a lot of misunderstanding about China in Britain." They would certainly agree on this point. "I can't believe that I lived with a Chinese professor and I missed the chance to learn so much from him. He cooked fantastic Chinese food for me; I remember he had a way of making chicken in peanut-butter sauce that was simply sublime, and I never asked him to show me how. And I had the chance to travel around China with him, and I didn't take it. What a fool I am! Wouldn't you agree?"

Politeness required that they agree with me, but they could not call me a fool.

They laughed. Not a formal diplomatic laugh but genuine open laughter. What a charming (and good-looking) man he was. I liked him enormously. He was obviously genuinely concerned about the misconceptions about his beloved China that are everywhere in the West. We passed to family matters. "Is your family here?" I asked.

"My wife is here, yes. And I have one daughter. She is nineteen."

"I also have a daughter of nineteen. Isn't it a wonderful age? What is yours doing? Is she interested in the diplomatic service?"

"No. She hates it." Yes, I bet she does. "She is studying English at university."

"You just have the one daughter, then?"

"Yes." Oh heavens, of course he only has one daughter, you idiot, Isabel. Haven't you heard of the "one-child" policy? He was too polite to point this out to me.

"Well, I won't keep you any longer." I had been waiting for them to end the meeting, but it seemed they weren't going to. I looked at my watch. We had been together for over two hours. It had been a lovely meeting. Warm, friendly, and informal.

"I have really enjoyed meeting you," I said. Quite sincerely.

"Yes, we have also enjoyed it." We all shook hands.

"I will see what I can arrange with the ambassador." He showed me out. As we stood at the door, we could see the Falun Gong protesters on the pavement opposite. They had fixed up a huge sign: "Falun Gong killed in custody: 517."

Two people sat silently meditating. It was their peaceful protest. Someone was there seven days a week from dawn till dusk and often overnight.

"These people . . ." I dared to say, "whether you agree with them or not, you have to admire them, don't you?"

He did not reply.

A week later the phone rang. It was the charming and delicate voice of my young friend, the third secretary.

"The ambassador can see you on Monday at three o'clock. He is most sorry, but he has only half an hour. Would that be suitable for you?"

"Yes. Please tell the ambassador I'll be delighted."

I was delighted, but half an hour posed a serious problem. Where to start? What not to include?

I sent out a couple of emails. I emailed Michael Buckley, the author of *Heartlands* and the *Bradt Travel Guide to Tibet*: "What would you like to ask the Chinese ambassador?" He replied, "Why zero progress has been made on negotiations in the last forty years." I emailed another author who had been dealing with China for years: "I'd ask how it is that an atheist government now knows more about reincarnation than Tibetan Buddhists." I emailed Kate Saunders: "I'd ask about the destruction of Serthar Buddhist Institute and show him photographic evidence. There is a provision in the Chinese constitution about religious freedom, and we have more evidence of what's happening there than on any other issue of religious freedom in Tibetan areas. You could even print out photos from the TIN website to show him." I spoke to Isabel Kelly: "I'd ask him about the treatment of prisoners in Drapchi prison." Then I had a second email from Kate: "I'd also ask for a definition of 'an offence against state security.'" Why does a nun making a solitary peaceful protest in Lhasa constitute a threat to stability? What do they mean by 'stability' in this context?"

I sat and looked at all these questions. I wrote them all down and numbered them. I added some of my own: Does the ambassador consider Tibetan Buddhism to be a medieval superstition or a product of thousands of years of spiritual growth that needs to be protected? What, in his opinion, is the impact, if any, of Western campaigning organizations on Chinese government policy? Taking the other side's point of view for a moment, what advice would he have for them?

And the question that I'd warned them about: Would he be prepared to express an opinion that differed from the party line? And the history question: Were they really going to say that Tibet has always been a part of China because of a marriage of a king in some ancient dynasty? Did they really spout this stuff?

Then there were the central questions—about Tibetan autonomy, the Panchen Lama, and the case of two Tibetans who were under sentence of death in Tibet. The Free Tibet Campaign had been running an urgent appeal that asked people to write letters and to contact the Chinese embassy on behalf of these men. They had been found guilty of planting a bomb. The appeal was going through, and if it did not succeed (apparently they rarely did), then these two men would be put to death. I had a chance to do more than write. I could appeal to the ambassador directly.

My head swam as I stared at the questions. Such an opportunity but so little time.

So I could do any number of interviews. Kate's interview would be one. Isabel Kelly's another. But what about my interview, I wondered. These were the things others would ask. What did I want to ask? What approach did I want to take? What is unique about me? And then I remembered. I am Miss Nauseatingly Positive. OK, so how could I do an interview that would be 100 percent positive?

I thought about it. I deleted all the questions that would put him on the defensive. That was most of my prepared material. I started again. Perhaps, just perhaps, I could catch his imagination? Perhaps I could place an image in his mind. Maybe I could find a chink of visionary in him. I could try to create the possibility of a possibility in his head. I could try to weave a little magic. I might fail, but I'd have done my best.

I would appeal to his love of China and ask his advice. What could I do? What could he do? I prepared my questions with care.

This time I was shown upstairs in the embassy to a large and very splendid room. I had arrived a little early and was again served Chinese tea while I waited. I sat and sipped my tea, wondering what I should do when the ambassador walked in. Oh heavens, do you bow in China? How do I address him? Good afternoon, Ambassador? I would have to hope that a winning smile would work.

Suddenly a gray-haired man appeared at the end of the room. He was in his late fifties or early sixties with an air of huge importance about him. He walked towards me with a scowl. I smiled broadly and held out my hand. "Hello." I tried the simple and direct approach. "I'm Isabel."

He shook my hand in silence. No reply. No presentation of a

card. Nothing. I waited for him to introduce himself or to say, "What can I do for you?" He said nothing.

The press minister walked in behind him, smiling at me. "Ah, hello!" I said.

Goodness, was I pleased to see him. I turned back to the ambassador.

"Thank you so much for agreeing to meet me. I would like to ask you some questions about Tibet. I understand that you visited there last year?" I smiled warmly and took a seat.

"That is correct. How long were you there for?"

"For two weeks."

"Where did you visit?"

"I saw Nyalam, Lhatse, Shigatse, and Gyantse, and I had the pleasure of spending eight days in Lhasa."

"Unfortunately I was not able to be there for so long. We visited a number of small towns and a chemical factory."

"Yes, I imagine it was mainly work for you? Do you ever wish, like the princes in the old fairy stories, that you could just abandon your official clothes and put on something casual and go and be with the people?" Was there a man in there somewhere who would love to shake off his role?

"The ambassador does not always travel in a suit," my press friend interjected.

"No. When we went to Tibet I was dressed casually, and we visited the homes of several Tibetan families."

I see. So that's an end of that attempt at empathy. Better pass to my one firm plan for the interview. How to approach this?

"You will be pleased to know that I am not going to ask you your views about the war on terror . . ."

He stared at me impassively.

"But personally I am not happy to be associated with aggression, and I'm sure that you'll agree with me when I say that there is far too much violence in the world at the moment?"

He nodded.

"I think it is terrible to see the escalation of violence that is happening."

He nodded again. He could hardly disagree with me so far.

"Did you see the fall of the Berlin Wall on television?" I asked. Possibly not the most tactful example for a Communist, but it was the joy of the moment that I wanted him to recall. "Wasn't it amazing? Do you remember the excitement in the world? The hope that was engendered? The feeling of celebration?"

"Yes." He was obviously wondering where this was leading.

"Well, can you imagine switching on your television and seeing the Dalai Lama and millions of Tibetans returning to the Motherland? Wouldn't the celebrations in China be wonderful? Everyone would be so happy. Can you imagine the pictures and the joy that would result?"

This was less of an interview and more of a speech by me.

"It seems to me that at a time when America is seen as an aggressor, China has an opportunity to take the moral lead in the world by demonstrating that nonviolence and diplomacy pay. Could you even measure the positive outcome if negotiations with the Dalai Lama were successful and this were to occur? The world would come to a halt for a week. Millions would celebrate. The nonviolent path would be seen to be the wise one, not the path of aggression."

I watched him for a flicker of enthusiasm. I didn't spot one. I waited for him to speak.

"Yes." He was wordy, the ambassador.

"Well, I would be interested in switching on my television and seeing this in my lifetime. I am interested in doing whatever I can, in some minute way, to help bring about this joyful day. What advice do you have for me in my desire to see this take place?"

"This is up to the Dalai Lama. China is always open to negotiate. But the Dalai Lama is a separatist who seeks to break up the Motherland, and he insists on telling lies. Tibet has always been an inalienable part of China, since ancient times, and he has never made a public statement to say that this is so. He refuses to do this. Also he claims that Taiwan is not a part of China. While he insists on his separatist activity, no progress can be made."

"But surely if we consider the international impact of the opening of talks and the huge good that it would do to the perception of China in the world . . . surely if some of China's best minds were to come around the table, something could be agreed on that would be acceptable to both parties? After all, the Dalai Lama is no longer asking for independence but for autonomy, and autonomy is written into your constitution. It's even in the name of the Tibetan Autonomous Region."

"The Dalai Lama wants independence. He is a separatist."

What?

"I beg your pardon, sir, but it is my understanding that he ceased to ask for independence in 1988, when he put forward a five-point peace plan and officially gave up requesting independence."

"No, he is seeking independence. You hear it everywhere. He instigates riots in Lhasa. He has never ceased his illegal separatist activities. You have only to come here on a Wednesday evening and listen to the people and hear what they shout."

I was more familiar with what they shouted than he imagined. I knew the words by heart. "Free Tibet! China out!" So, they did listen, then.

"But the Dalai Lama doesn't control these people."

"His government is responsible for these separatist activities."

"No, sir. I assure you the opposite is true. His government seeks autonomy, having given up on their hope of independence."

Was it possible that the activities of the Vigil were sending a message that was counterproductive to the embassy? That while the Tibetan government-in-exile worked away diplomatically to convince the Chinese that they were genuine in seeking only autonomy, the "supporters" of Tibet in London sent the opposite message? I wondered if he really believed that the Tibetan government was behind these actions.

"The Dalai Lama can't control the actions of these Western organizations that act entirely independently of him. I think you overestimate his power."

Couldn't resist that one. He was furious.

"No. We do not say he is powerful. He is nothing."

"So if he is not so important . . ." I tried to turn the conversation back to the positive, "then why does it matter what he says? He is only one man. Surely the Chinese and Tibetan politicians can argue about history? So many wars are fought because of history, whereas it seems to me that China is a powerful nation and wants peace and that millions of Tibetans in exile want the same thing. It's not as if he is hiding nuclear weapons, after all."

"He is not so nonviolent. Tibet was peacefully liberated, and his army attacked the Chinese forces. Even now, he has an army in India."

The Dalai Lama has his own army in India? I tried not to chuckle out loud. I wouldn't discuss this. I wasn't even going to whisper the phrase "Nobel Peace Prize."

"And he is trying to split up China. You need to read between the lines of his speeches. He speaks of 'greater autonomy' or 'high-level autonomy,' and Tibet will always be governed by China."

I wanted to reach him in a personal way. It wasn't going too well.

"Tell me," I backtracked. "My image of all Tibetans returning and the international moral status of China being affected because of this . . . is this something that you would like to see? You, personally, I mean?"

"It is up to the Dalai Lama. He must admit that Tibet and Taiwan have always been a part of China."

I didn't see that Taiwan was any of the Dalai Lama's business, but I wasn't going to debate this one either.

I tried to move back to the positive again. "There has been great hope raised among Tibetans as a result of the recent invitation from Beijing for a group of the Dalai Lama's representatives to visit Tibet."

"Have you spoken to any of the representatives who visited?"

"Not personally. But I heard that they were very happy with the visit, that they were warmly received, and that everything in this visit went well."

"Yes. This is a sign of how open Beijing is."

"Do you think that, as a result of this, there may be more talks about the possibility of negotiations taking place?"

"This, again, is up to the Dalai Lama. He must stop asking for independence and stop inciting splittist activities."

So the Dalai Lama was on the phone to the Tibet Vigil in London: "And I'd like you to paint a banner, stand outside the Royal Institute of British Architects, and shout abuse at the embassy." I couldn't see it somehow. Anyway, I was getting nowhere with this. Try something new.

"I wanted to ask about the boy that the Tibetans believe to be the eleventh Panchen Lama."

His face went from a scowl to thinly disguised rage.

"There are many in the West who think that China has killed him . . ."

"This is nonsense."

"Yes." My method of finding things that we agreed on had some small merit. "I'm quite certain that it is nonsense. China is a great and civilized nation. The greatest and most civilized nation." Was I groveling a little now?

His face returned from rage to a scowl.

"And I am quite certain that you have not killed him and that he is living happily with his family and going to school. Also I understand that his family does not want him to be disturbed . . ."

"That is correct."

"But surely, again when you consider the international importance of this boy to so many people, surely his parents could be persuaded to allow a small UN delegation to confirm that he is alive and well?" I had said the wrong thing again.

"What has this got to do with the United Nations?"

"Well, anyone from the West?"

"What has it got to do with the West?"

"If China cares at all about world opinion, then surely it is in your interest to prove that he is alive and well?"

"We must respect the wishes of the parents."

"If you will pardon my saying so—if I thought that international perception of China was affected by this case, then I would say 'tough' to the parents."

I was of course already assuming, for the ambassador's benefit, that the Chinese government knew the real wishes of the Tibetan parents who might still, in the silence of their hearts, be loyal to the Dalai Lama.

The ambassador looked at me. "He is just a little boy." For the first time he smiled. But it was not a warm smile. It was a smile of disdain.

I had a sinking feeling of helplessness. I glanced down at my questions. I certainly wasn't going to attempt to ask him if he felt free to disagree with his government. Hopeless to mention Serthar. I had one question that was a matter of life and death. Maybe I could seize this moment to appeal on behalf of the two men who were about to be executed. I knew that the Free Tibet Campaign and others had been writing to the embassy to ask for the repeal of the death sentence. As far as I knew, hundreds of letters had been sent.

"I wanted to ask your advice as to the best way to appeal for mercy on behalf of the two men who have recently been sentenced to death in Tibet."

They both looked at me with genuine bewilderment. "Who is this?"

"The Rinpoche and his relative, in the Sichuan province."

The ambassador turned to his press assistant. "Do you know anything about this?"

"Who are they?" the press officer asked me.

"One is called Tenzin Delek Rinpoche. He is a reincarnate lama in the Sichuan region, and the other man is his cousin. I believe he is also known by his lay name, Ngawang Tashi."

They both looked at me blankly. I kept going. "Anyway, apparently they are accused of planting a bomb and have been sentenced to death. The case is with the appeal court now."

"I have not heard of this case." He hadn't even heard of them? So much for the "high-profile campaign." What had happened to the letters that had been written, the faxes, the emails? They didn't look to me as if they were bluffing. He was certainly genuine about this. Neither of them had heard of these men.

"Well, I could get you more details of exactly where they are." I struggled on. "But my question is—I don't want to discuss whether they are guilty or not—obviously I have no idea—but I wanted to ask, on behalf of people in the West . . ."

"Do you speak on behalf of people in the West?" the ambassador interrupted. "There are five million people in London."

"I suppose not, then. But on behalf of some of them, then, all those who don't agree with the death penalty, which I think is the majority . . . I wanted to ask if you could appeal on their behalf? If you could ask your government for mercy on behalf of these men?"

If seemed a reasonable enough request to me. Apparently not.

"It is nothing to do with us," he said simply. "You must understand that China is a country with a rule of law. The law is the law."

"Yes, of course. But you have read Shakespeare, no doubt, sir?" I ventured to pay him this compliment. "'The quality of mercy is not strain'd; It droppeth as the gentle rain from heaven Upon the place beneath.' There has always been the law, and there has always been mercy. Even if the law requires that they be put to death, one may still ask for mercy. Is that not so? Even if the request is ignored? One may still ask? So, may I ask you to appeal for clemency for them?"

The press man spoke to me. "You don't understand. It is not the ambassador's place to appeal in matters of the law. It is only for the courts to show mercy. If the men show the proper levels of repentance and show that they are sorry for what they have done, then the court will be merciful to them."

Oh God. The scales fell from my eyes. So the film *Red Corner*, in which a man has to plead guilty to a crime he has not committed, really was relevant to the Tibetan situation. If the men pleaded guilty, confessed, and showed repentance, they would be shown mercy. But only if they pleaded guilty. This was also the case if they happened to be innocent. If they were innocent and their vows as monks forbade them to lie and they insisted on declaring their innocence, then they could not "repent," and there was no hope for them.

I stared at the carpet for a second. "As an individual I would still like to ask for mercy for them. So who would be the best person for me to write to?"

The press man looked at me. "You would have to write to the courts."

The ambassador looked at his watch. "I have another appointment now."

"Yes." I stood up. "Well, thank you very much, Ambassador, for taking the time to see me." I didn't know whether that was the correct form of address, but he hadn't told me any other. I had a gift, but not for him.

"I have a gift for your secretary. I have an antique mah-jongg set, but I don't play. I don't like to have objects in my house that are not used."

He glanced at the set with a moment's curiosity.

"I was going to offer it to you, but your secretary tells me that you don't play—but he does. I would like someone to have this set who will enjoy it."

"You give it to him." An order was issued to the press man. He turned to me dismissively. "I don't understand the reason for this meeting. I don't see what the point has been."

For him to speak for his country and his people?

"Oh, I'm sorry. It has been most useful for me. Most informative."

He walked off without bothering to shake my hand. The press officer and I were left looking at each other. I think he may have been as embarrassed as I was. An attendant walked through and filled my cup with more tea.

"If you have five minutes, I have some questions that we did not have time for?" I asked him.

"I'm sorry. I have a minute or two, but not much time, no." I wondered if he would get into trouble for having asked the ambassador to give me time when I had raised so many difficult questions.

"I just wanted to ask about the Western campaigning organizations that, like me, would like to see a solution to the Tibetan problem. I wondered if you see their actions as counterproductive?"

He didn't answer.

"Or whether you have any advice for them?"

"Yes. They need to understand the real situation, and they need to read the history."

"I see. Well, thank you." I stood up. I really liked this man—whatever his views. "The ambassador was not pleased with my interview, I'm afraid. I hope this will not reflect badly on you in any way?"

He smiled at my concern. "No. Don't worry about that."

I was sure that it would be impossible to meet him again, so as I shook his hand I said, "You have been most kind." He, at any rate, had been an excellent ambassador for his country. As he showed me out, I noticed that the sign opposite the embassy had been changed. The number of Falun Gong supporters that had died in detention had gone up to 530.

THE DALAI LAMA'S REPRESENTATIVE IN LONDON

Now I didn't want to wait for anything. Alongside all that I was doing I was determined to understand the Tibetan issue from all sides. I typed up the transcript of the interview, sent it to the Dalai

Lama's representative in London, and asked for an appointment immediately.

It seemed a long time since I had walked from St. John's Wood station and lost my way, trying to find Tibet House. This time I knew my way and was very pleased to be having a formal meeting with Kesang Takla. Migyur Dorjee, the representative of the Dalai Lama who had succeeded in weighing me down with unreadable booklets, had now gone from this job, and in his place was a likable and engaging woman.

Mrs. Takla's late husband had been one of the bodyguards to the young Dalai Lama when he escaped from Tibet. She had studied at Cornell University in the United States and had been working for the Tibetan government for forty years. I guess she knew her job. I had met her at a number of Tibetan events and had always been impressed that she listened to me. After all, the exiled Tibetan community is continually besieged by do-good Westerners who understand little or nothing about Tibet and China. It would be perfectly understandable for Tibetans to roll their eyes towards heaven, wearily asking for strength to cope with this new ignoramus. But this is not the approach of Kesang Takla.

She somehow managed to assume that I might have something interesting to say or something useful to contribute. More than that, she is a warm woman with a kind and sympathetic air about her. Perhaps she sees it as her job to represent the Dalai Lama spiritually as well as through her governmental role. It may or may not have been conscious on her part, but as I made my way there I felt that I was going to meet someone special, and I felt privileged to have this appointment.

She smiled warmly as I arrived and ushered me into her office. A large photo of the Dalai Lama looked down on us from the wall. I smiled at him as if he were an old friend. The inevitable tea was served. I was amused to note that they didn't serve Tibetan tea but English tea, which, after the excellent tea at the Chinese embassy, seemed most inferior. But then they also served very classy biscuits.

There had been none of these on offer from the Chinese government.

I felt very relaxed and at home.

"So, you've read about my experiences at the Chinese embassy?"

"Yes. I read the transcript this morning." She allowed a smile to crinkle the corners of her mouth but gave nothing away.

"I'm confused. It seems to me that solving 'the Tibet problem' would not be too hard for the new Chinese leadership. The world would see that they are constructive and forward-looking, and it would be an astute way for them to cement better relations with the West. But the demands that the Chinese government are making on you are completely unreasonable."

"They are asking us to say that black is white."

"Am I correct in thinking that they used to insist that, before talks could take place, the Dalai Lama stop asking for independence?"

"Yes. But since the Dalai Lama did stop asking, they claim that he is not sincere. In 1988 the Chinese government said that they were willing to have talks with His Holiness if the question of independence was not raised. We took that to be a committed statement, and in order to encourage dialogue the government-in-exile has said that they will not raise the question of independence. Even though if you look back historically you will find that Tibet was an independent state, it seems to us that the most important question is the future. Of course agreeing not to raise the question of independence was a huge concession for us. His Holiness has said that what is past is past so let us look forward. We have said this both publicly and privately to the Chinese, so I don't understand why the Chinese authorities still insist that he is not sincere. What more can His Holiness do than to have made this statement all over the world in talks and on paper in official statements?"

I had an answer.

"Well, according to the ambassador there is something more that he can do. As you saw from the interview, he said China believes that your government is responsible for the activities of the Western support organizations that continue to shout 'Free Tibet, China out.' They are saying that His Holiness is responsible for that. Now, I understand that the Western organizations are independent of you . . ."

She nodded.

"However, if your government is sincerely wanting to persuade China that you only want autonomy, is it possible that the activities of the Western support organizations are counterproductive?"

She had obviously had forty years to think about this question. "If you think in a wider sense, first of all the Tibetan government-in-exile is a democracy. In any democracy you have different people with different views. Even in our own community the Tibetan Youth Congress still asks for independence. That is a sign of the fact we practice democracy. If China really wants talks, then they should listen to what the Dalai Lama and the Tibetan government-in-exile is saying."

Fair enough. They are a democracy, but had she answered the question?

"I am coming at this with a fresh perspective and taking the support groups in the UK as an example, although I know that you have support groups all over the world. If this were a war and I was interested in helping both sides get to the table to talk, I would think that, on the Tibetan side, it looks a bit of a mess. To speak frankly, on the one hand your government is asking for autonomy, and then you have all your supporters asking for independence. Now, I've not met the Dalai Lama, but from what I've read he doesn't strike me as a man who makes rash decisions . . ."

She laughed.

"It seems to me that he is a pragmatist. China is not about to walk out of Tibet. He could have spent his whole life preaching independence, and he's chosen not to do so. The job of the Western organizations is to bring attention to the plight of the people. Isn't it more appropriate for them to support the Dalai Lama and ask for what he asks for?"

She listened in a diplomatic silence.

"It reminds me of the Western organizations that used to accuse Nelson Mandela and black organizations in South Africa of not being radical enough. I mean, is it posture politics in these organizations, or are they actually trying to change something?"

I was having a little rant. She did not, as she continued to remind me, have responsibility for any independent Tibet organizations.

"They are not part of the Tibetan administration, and it is not for us to tell them what to do."

I couldn't tell whether she was as frustrated as I was becoming. She was like a Buddha of patience.

"No, you can't tell them. But have you asked them?"

"We have asked the world community. Everyone knows that we are seeking autonomy. It's not something that we have kept away from the ears of support groups. If China is sincere, its government can talk to ours. Are they really going to blame the Dalai Lama for the actions of groups that want to support Tibet?"

Yes. From my limited experience and from everything I'd read in their propaganda, it seemed that they were. So I was determined to persevere with this question.

She went on. "I think the position we have taken is very clear to everybody."

"Your position is not clear to me."

"We state what we want. What supporters do is up to them. And some of them feel very strongly that they want Tibet to be independent. How can you ask us to stop people supporting us in the ways that they consider appropriate?"

"We appear to have evidence, whether or not it is truthful is a different question, but we appear to have evidence that some of the activities of people who wish to support you may not be serving you at all. For example, the Tibet Vigil—there is a group of people who shout 'Free Tibet! China out!'—is seen as evidence that your government is not genuine. They shout in quite an aggressive manner. They sometimes shout 'Bloody murderers out of Tibet' with megaphones. Now, if I give you the number of the woman who currently coordinates the Vigil, would you ask her not to shout this?"

"The last time Professor Samdhong Rinpoche was here, he did ask all the groups not to express support for Tibet in any manner that was aggressive. We did make that request."

It was true. I remembered seeing his email circulated asking this. It caused a little storm of emails, and then everyone went on shouting exactly as they had before.

"We can't gag these people. If you weigh up the problems that prevent negotiations taking place, which is more important? The things that we overlook—the sufferings and persecution of our people, imprisonment with no evidence of crimes—or the fact that a few individuals shout outside the embassy? The government is not responsible for private individuals."

"But what struck me about my meeting with the ambassador is that, no matter how illogical the Chinese stance may seem to me to be, this man believes his own propaganda completely. He believes that the Dalai Lama is an evil, selfish man, hell-bent on separatism, and only pursuing his own selfish motives. I think we all look around in the world to find evidence that our own beliefs are true, and in the case of the Chinese, then we are providing it. It's in their face on a Wednesday evening."

"But the Dalai Lama has nothing to do with this."

"Of course. I know that, but even the head of the press department, who struck me as a very sane man, believes that your government must be paying the Vigil members to stand there."

It was absurd. We poured more tea. I thought about Simon and Paula and how glad they would have been to have been paid even £5 an hour to stand in the cold with flags and banners.

She looked up at me thoughtfully. "If all the support groups listened to us and asked for autonomy, do you think China would then say, 'OK, you are good now so we will talk with you'?"

"No, I don't think that. But at least you would be sending a united message."

She picked up a biscuit. "You know they now have this new requirement before they will enter into talks—that His Holiness make a statement on Taiwan. It's absurd. They want him to make a statement to say that Taiwan was always a province of China. On the one hand they say that he has no right to make any statements about his own people and that he is not sincere or trustworthy. Then, on the other, they ask him to make a statement on Taiwan. It is a ridiculous combination, and all the governments know this. His Holiness, as a monk, cannot tell a lie, so he can't say that Taiwan was always a province of China or that Tibet has always been a part of China. How can he say that history is not true?"

"Why this new requirement for him to make a statement on Taiwan?"

"The absurdness is that, even if the Dalai Lama were to make a statement that Taiwan is a province of China, what difference does that make? Does it make Taiwan a province of China?"

"Maybe they do think he is a living god, after all. He speaks. History and geography change."

We smiled. It would be funny if it weren't absurd.

"I wanted to ask you about Lobsang Dhondrub and this high lama, Tenzin Delek Rinpoche. Is there any news?"

Her face fell, and a look of genuine sadness came over her.

"It is very difficult for us to receive news. We don't know what to believe and what not to believe. Some people say the second trial has not yet taken place. One day we were told that the two men were on a hunger strike. We heard that they had been tortured to ensure the 'confessions.' We don't really know anything for sure because we don't have firsthand information."

"But as far as you know, the two death sentences are still in place? Despite the international appeals? I saw one email circular that used the phrase 'murder for trumped-up terrorism charges.'"

"Yes, despite the international appeals. One really interesting thing has happened. It is not only Tibetan journalists who are shouting about a fair trial; this time it is also Chinese journalists and even Chinese lawyers who are asking questions. We heard that two Chinese lawyers had come forward and offered to represent the monks in a retrial but that the authorities had turned the offer down."

"It's so bizarre that the Chinese authorities are going to put these men to death just at a time when they seemed to be open to the possibility of improved relations with Tibet. I don't get it."

"It's been a problem in the Kardze Prefecture. Tenzin Delek is highly revered by the local populace, and the local government doesn't like it."

"The Chinese embassy in London didn't seem to know anything about him."

"I find that very strange. There was a bomb attack in Chengdu City, and Lobsang Dhondrub, a distant relative of Tenzin Delek's, was accused of planting the bomb. Then Dhondrub 'confessed' that it was Delek who had masterminded it. They arrested the lama, who then 'confessed' to having masterminded six unsolved cases of bomb blasts. We don't like to think of the circumstances that these confessions may have been made under. But if you knew what the Chinese do . . . The head of Nyagchu township has spoken to the populace and actually said . . . Wait a minute, I have it written down here in a report written by a mainland Chinese writer."

She reached into her desk and produced an article. "He told the supporters: 'Whoever speaks in favor of A'an Zhaxi will be treated as guilty as A'an Zhaxi himself.' So of course everyone is afraid."

"What name is that? Isn't that a different name?"

"It's the Chinese version of his Tibetan name. The Chinese often have difficulty with the pronunciation of Tibetan names. They do sound completely different by the time they have translated them."

"So are the authorities capable of putting hundreds in prison?"

"Yes. And of course people have families."

"So what do you think will happen?"

"I don't know, but these cases of what certainly appear to be extorted confessions have raised international demands for a fair trial. Lobsang Dhondrub appears to have been used as a way to arrest the high lama because he was too popular. It's like this with many of the best teachers of Tibetan Buddhism. If a teacher gains too much popularity—many even have devotees that travel from China—then they find a way to get rid of them or simply close down the monastery."

"I suppose someone must have planted the bomb."

"Yes. But the issue is about a free and fair trial. In this case it was a closed trial, and even the Chinese lawyers who wanted to represent these men were not allowed to."

I glanced up at the picture of the Dalai Lama.

"And this system of obtaining forced confessions, I must be naïve, but I find it hard to believe that it still goes on. Especially sitting underneath a photo of His Holiness, who teaches us not to cause suffering even to an insect."

"The practice of compassion is not universal."

Someone tapped at the door. The next appointment had arrived.

"Don't worry." Mrs. Takla smiled. "Was there anything else you wanted to ask?"

How to stop them carrying out the death sentence on these two men? The solution to the illogical Chinese position? Why she thinks Tibetans have suffered so much since 1950? The meaning of suffering? How she has found serenity to accept what she can't change?

"No. You have given me a lot of your time. Thank you so much for all your patience with me."

I was really fond of this tiny Tibetan lady. Kesang Takla stood at least a foot shorter than I was.

I kissed her on the cheek, a touch of affection that the Chinese ambassador had not permitted me, and walked out into a snowy St. John's Wood.

Snowflakes fell, so slowly, so gently, from the sky.

A week later we heard that, hours after these cases had been "re-viewed," Tenzin Delek had been given a two-year suspended death sentence. Lobsang Dhondrub, age twenty-eight, had been executed.

PUBLICIZING THE PANCHEN

So I hope you are wondering, "What about the stunt? I thought this woman was actually going to try and *do* something?" Well, yes, I was. I mean, yes, I am.

One of the things that it had taken me time to work out was that I needed to gather brilliant people about me. Gradually they had appeared. I now had not only the amazing Rachael, formerly of Cunning Stunts, but also her replacement. "Hello, I'm Nicky. I'll be doing your PR." She held out her hand warmly when Rachael suggested that we all go in for a meeting to discuss the piece of civil disobedience that we seemed to be planning. Occasionally even PS was around.

I instantly knew that everything would be OK. Nicky looked like the kind of girl who could have done PR for the maiden trip of the *Titanic* and made it into a success story. Except that if Nicky had been involved, I found myself thinking, it wouldn't have sunk. She would have made sure that someone had checked the maxi-mum speeds and got the engineering right in the first place. And then, just in case anything did go wrong, she would have provided more than an adequate number of lifeboats and stocked them with more blankets and food than was necessary. Everything would have been fine if they'd employed Nicky.

I emerged from my daydream to find that PS already had a note-book out and was deep in conversation with Rachael. "Isabel, we will have to do this on the Panchen Lama's birthday—twenty-fifth of April. OK?"

April? April was about four months after I had hoped to stage this day's madness.

"Do we have to wait that long? I'd rather not," I said forlornly.

"It has to be on the best day for the press to have a reason to run the story," Rachael explained. She was ten years younger than I was and with ten years more experience in PR.

"OK, so what about the Tibetan New Year?" About a month earlier.

"No one has heard of it."

"The Chinese New Year, then? Surely everyone has heard of that?"

"Not sure it's very sporting to have a go at them in the middle of their party, is it?" said PS.

"What about Tibetan Uprising Day? The tenth of March, when the Tibetans commemorate the independence demonstrations?"

"The trouble with these, Isabel, is that they are other stories. You'd have to explain about the uprising as well and why you are talking about the eleventh Panchen Lama on a day that commemorates something different. No, you need the strongest day possible. His birthday." Nicky had spoken.

"OK."

"Great—we have a date, then."

They all got out their diaries and wrote it down. I felt a tremor of fear go through me.

"So have you spoken to the boys?" Nicky turned to Rachael.

"Yes, they've been to look. They say that getting over the plinth is only a level-E maneuver. Easy, apparently. And they can pull someone up."

Now, there was an offer I couldn't say no to. It's not often you are offered a chance to shake Nelson's hand and get a good view down Whitehall.

"I'll go. I'd love to go."

"No, Isabel. We need you on the ground for the EPK."

These professionals spoke a language all their own.

"A what?"

"An electronic press kit. We will have our own press team there, and we will interview you and do the editing and then just give it to the press as a preproduced kit."

"Oh. Is that what you do, then?"

"If you don't want to rely totally on the press coming along, then you employ a freelance camera crew and do it yourself."

"And you'll want to interview me?"

Why did I feel absurdly nervous about this? I had sat in TV studios and talked about tantric sex, but standing under Nelson and explaining Communist party politics and why the police were arresting my friends somehow seemed to be a totally different square of lions.

"What about interviewing PS? She's done these things loads of times for Amnesty International. She'll know how to sound intelligent and serious and full of authority."

"I'll do it if you really don't want to, but I think you should do it. It's your project."

Why were they all nodding and looking at me?

"We'll give you a list of the sort of questions that we'll ask you. Don't fret."

I started a fret that was to go on for months.

"What else do we need to discuss?" I said. Surely there must be something.

"The banner that we are going to drop down," said Rachael. "I'd like you to meet the designer." She beckoned over a very pretty blonde who looked younger than my daughter.

"Hello. My name's Elise. I've just finished the designs today, based on the brief Rachael gave me. The poster is fifteen meters long and five meters wide and will be made out of ripstock, which is what the climbers need because it's very light. And this is what it will look like."

She pulled out two drawings. Both showed the little boy's face as he looked at six years old. Along the top was written "Act for Tibet," and underneath it said "The 11th Panchen Lama" and under his portrait the words "Where is he now?" and then the website address www.actfortibet.org.

"Yes, that's great . . . not sure about the lettering. Can you show us something less stylized?" PS asked immediately.

I was so overwhelmed by the quality of the work that I just wanted to say, "It's brilliant, Elise. Thank you." And buy her ten bunches of flowers. But then as I looked at it, I suddenly noticed that I wasn't happy with it.

PS and Rachael were examining the design carefully. "It's really good that it says 'Act for Tibet' really clearly across the top. Don't you think, Isabel?"

That was the very thing that I was worried about.

"Actually I was thinking that I don't want that there at all. I don't care a hoot if people don't remember Act for Tibet; I'm not promoting Act for Tibet. The point of this is to draw attention to the eleventh Panchen Lama, not to us. I'd be ashamed if I saw this on the front of the newspaper."

"But people need to see who is doing it. Greenpeace always has its name bigger than anything when they make a banner." Rachael looked at PS.

"Yes, and so does Amnesty," PS added.

"But this is different," I said. "We aren't doing this to promote ourselves; we are doing it to promote a boy. It's about him."

"But you need to direct people on where to go if they want to find out more."

"OK." I'd agree on that one. "But can we have the web address at the bottom and just his name at the top, please?"

It was a strange thing, but despite the fact that these people all knew more than I did, I still seemed to have the final say. It made a pleasant change after TV meetings in which I was not the Controller of the BBC.

"I can do that for you. It's no problem. So lose the top line and different lettering. Anything else?" she asked.

"Yes, Elise. I really like it. I love the colors, the shape, everything."

I was so excited by all this. Terrified, but excited.

"Any other items or concerns?" Nicky looked around.

"Yes, I have a concern."

"What, Isabel?"

"The international political situation."

"Oh that. We're ignoring that."

"I did wonder whether it's responsible to be contemplating civil disobedience and wasting police time when they are the very people who are there to protect us from lunatics. It just doesn't seem . . . well . . . appropriate. Even thirty topless women on a truck is safe and funny."

They all looked at the ceiling. PS said, "Isabel, may I remind you that we have already decided against Tits for Tibet?"

I looked at Rachael helplessly.

"I've spoken to the boys about this stunt, and they are fine with it."

"Even if there is a terrorist attack on Britain?"

"We can't plan for that."

The irony is that this boy is supposed to be an incarnation of the quality of wisdom. The world certainly needed a little wisdom.

"Aren't there twice as many cameras in Trafalgar Square as there normally are?"

"Probably. And?"

"So we are going to go on as normal, then?" I looked around the table. Everyone was nodding. "Yup." I'm obviously a coward.

Somehow I seemed to have gotten myself on a path of no return. So we went on planning and talking about a little boy, who, somewhere in China, was approaching his next birthday unaware even of who he was.

And I went on trying to understand the greater picture. I trusted Rachael and Nicky to play their part and went back to wondering why the campaign groups didn't follow the same policy as the Tibetan government-in-exile. I was weary of feeling frustrated. I was a little wiser now than I had been when I'd started, so I wanted to go back. To ask Alison why they did things the way that they did things. To try to understand.

A MUG WITH A HANDLE

My arrival at the Free Tibet office was a little different this time. Most of the faces I knew. Some I'd even been in the Chinese army with. People looked up and smiled. They even said hello.

In the kitchen, piles of dirty mugs stood in the sink, unwashed. So nothing had changed here—except perhaps me. It didn't bother me anymore. I considered pulling two dirty mugs out of the bowl to wash them and make tea, but the hot tap didn't work, so I thought better of it. I took the last two clean mugs out of the cupboard. As I waited for the kettle to boil, I wondered whether I was the mug that didn't have a handle and had got into hot water. I was determined to find a handle on something at least. I grasped the steamy situation and made my way through into Alison's office. There was still nowhere to put anything down.

She cleared two spaces, and I put the tea down and got out my tape recorder. "Where can I put this, Alison?"

She took out a large book, put that on her knees, and balanced the tape recorder on that. Well, if she was OK with that, then so was I.

Here in front of me was the leading voice for Tibet supporters in Britain. All that I was doing outside her organization I would willingly have done within it. I was still confused, and I wanted so much to understand.

We chatted for a while about mutual friends, and then I switched on the recorder for my first question: "Tell me, please, when I came to you with my idea about your giving away copies of *Freedom in Exile* to bring new people into the Tibet movement, you said, 'Why would we do that? We don't support the Dalai Lama' . . ."

"I'm not sure I said it like that."

"Well, I may be wrong. But anyway, if I was mistaken, can I set the record straight by asking you: Does the Free Tibet Campaign support Tibetan independence, or does it support the Dalai Lama and his government in seeking autonomy?"

"We are independent of the Tibetan government-in-exile, but we recognize that, while Tibet is under occupation, the Tibetan government-in-exile and the Dalai Lama are the legitimate representatives of the Tibetan people. We support whatever Tibetans want, and our understanding is that most want independence from China."

But why didn't they choose to work for the same ends that the Tibetan government was working for?

"Please can you read out exactly what it says on the Free Tibet Campaign notepaper, Alison? Your official policy statement?"

"Yes, it says, 'Free Tibet Campaign stands for the Tibetans' right to determine their own future. It campaigns for an end to the Chinese occupation of Tibet and for the Tibetans' fundamental human rights to be respected. It is independent of all governments and is funded by its members and supporters.'"

Well, that seemed logical enough, but there was still something that didn't make sense.

"The thing is that—as I said to Mrs. Takla—the Dalai Lama doesn't seem to be a man who makes rash decisions, so would it not be logical for Western organizations to follow the lead of the Tibetan government?"

"We believe that if we promote the right of the Tibetan people to choose independence and we raise awareness of the fact that Tibet was an independent country, then we put the whole issue of what the Dalai Lama and the Tibetan government is trying to achieve into the proper context."

I gave a big sigh. "It sounds very logical when you say it, Alison. My experience of meeting the Chinese ambassador, who despite being a talking propaganda machine . . ."

"He sounds like a dinosaur."

"Maybe, but to give the man credit I think that he believes his own story. I think he is quite genuine in believing that the Dalai Lama doesn't want autonomy and is just using the principle as a back door to seeking independence, and he sees the activities of all the Western supporters as proof. He says that if the Dalai Lama asked all the Western organizations to drop their demands, then they would do so."

"It's impossible for the Chinese government to see beyond an attempt at control. Their entire system is based upon it."

There was a point that I was going to reach. I decided to reach it.

"Has the Tibetan government asked you to support their stance for autonomy?"

"No. In all my conversations with Samdhong Rinpoche and other officials I've assumed that they are extremely grateful for the existence of Tibet support groups whether they follow the Tibetan government or not. They never attempt to influence our policies other than to ask for nonviolence."

I was wading through treacle, living a cliché of nonprogress.

"OK, Alison, I'm sorry if I'm being very slow, but I'm still trying to get my head around this. At a very basic level, for all those that know nothing about this situation—we have the Dalai Lama and his government saying, 'We want genuine autonomy for Tibet,' and we have Western 'support' groups that don't support the Tibetan government's position."

"We do support them; we just don't follow their policy to the letter."

"You don't think that your position makes everything more entrenched? The Chinese aren't about to leave Tibet, are they?"

Was I making sense at all? I didn't know any longer.

"The point of a campaign is that you ask for what you want. In the course of your campaign you get the other side to move towards you. I believe that the diversity in views within the Tibetan cause is part of its strength. It means that we can reach out to a wider range of people."

This is what the Church of England says. I envied her certainty that she was right.

She went on, "Put the whole issue in the broader context. Tibet should be free, and the ultimate outcome needs to be a negotiated settlement between the Chinese government and the Tibetan government-in-exile. We are not trying to dictate what that outcome should be. We just want that process to take place."

"So you think that, although they don't state it directly, the Tibetan government-in-exile doesn't mind you shouting 'Free Tibet' because it highlights the fact that they are taking a middle way?"

"Yes."

There was a long pause. I looked at her.

Eventually she said, "Isabel, there is something that I've hesitated to tell you with the tape running because it is so easily misunderstood. When I and the leaders of other Tibet support groups met the Dalai Lama, in 1999, he said to us all, 'You must continue.' He took me by the hand and said, 'You must continue.'"

"To do what?"

"Well, he didn't say, did he? If he'd done that, it would have meant that he was trying to control us. He didn't interfere. I imagine he said the same to everyone regardless of their policies. Some Tibet support groups ask specifically for autonomy, not independence."

Aha! Now finally I understood. Now it all became clear. The Dalai Lama was a diplomat as well as a spiritual teacher. Perhaps the Tibetans were not, after all, allowing their cause to be confused by Western organizations that thought they knew better than the Dalai Lama. I shouldn't, I suppose, have been surprised to discover that it was I, the interfering Westerner, who had been lost in this unknown world. As the Dalai Lama had maintained his stance of noninterference and had not specifically asked them to change their policy, it seemed entirely reasonable for Alison and the Free Tibet Campaign to assume that he didn't want them to.

Yup, I was the mug who had been dim all along and not seen

this. I'd only seen things in black and white. Perhaps in real politics it is the shades of gray that give everyone room to maneuver. While little scales fell from my eyes, she went on talking.

"So now do you see? He recognizes that if the more radical Tibetan groups go on demanding what they want, then his case for seeking to resolve the situation through compromise can be shown for what it is: a reasonable and workable way forward. The Free Tibet Campaign's policy was already in place, but I hope this demonstrates the point that I was trying to make that the Tibetan government-in-exile understands that there is benefit to us sticking with the policy we want."

So I just had to hope that all this really was the best policy.

I couldn't forget the ambassador's rage. "But if the Chinese ambassador genuinely represents the views of his government, then . . ."

"I told you, he's a dinosaur, Isabel."

"Yes, but his government is full of dinosaurs, and the dinosaurs are still in charge. If he really believes that the Dalai Lama isn't genuine, then surely the support groups, instead of creating activities that are seen as separatism, might be better plugging away at convincing China that the Dalai Lama is genuine? Is that possible?"

"No, because I believe that we can be more helpful by advocating the Tibetans' right to choose what they want. And I tell you what the Dalai Lama said to me merely as a way of demonstrating that it's not just something that I came up with because it suited me but that it is something that is shared and understood by Tibetan support groups internationally and by the Tibetan people."

"OK, Alison. I hope you're right. I really do."

Outside the office in which we'd been sitting, banners were being put together for a pro-Tibet march through London. It was due to start outside the Chinese embassy. Up to a thousand people shouting, "Free Tibet! China out!" I looked at the banners as I stood up to leave. "Outside the embassy, will the people who are shouting have megaphones?"

"Oh, yes."

• • •

So in case you are as lost as I was: By continuing to shout "Free Tibet! China out!" Tibet support groups all over the world keep the "Tibetan problem" on the agenda of the Chinese government.

The difficulty is that for China, the unity of the Motherland is of supreme importance. When Great Britain handed back Hong Kong, national celebrations were held. The last thing that they want is to give any degree of independence to any "Chinese ethnic group" such as the Tibetans. The government has always considered attempts to influence policy from outside China as interference and from inside Tibet as "separatism." In Chinese politics "separatism" is a crime that they punish as the West punishes terrorism.

Perhaps it would be better for Tibet support groups to lobby quietly behind closed doors, as this is certainly the approach preferred by China. Or maybe this allows China to get away with human rights abuses and believe that Tibetans have given up. That is why there are still people standing outside the Chinese embassy and waving the flag of an independent Tibet.

So, internationally, Tibet support groups have chosen to do both. Some people talk diplomatically behind closed doors while others go on shouting "Free Tibet!" Those shouts can be interpreted by the Chinese government as a demand for independence or can be heard literally as a plea for freedom—freedom to follow Tibetan Buddhism, freedom to live as they choose, and even the seemingly impossible, freedom to elect their own rulers.

DOING SOMETHING

DON'T DILLYDALLY

Meanwhile my own plans were all going tits up even without the tits. The situation in London was going from bad to worse than worse. I knew Cunning Stunts and the climbers said that I had to ignore the international political situation, but it was proving impossible. It was one thing to have the serenity to accept things that I couldn't change but another to pretend that nothing was changing. We had leaflets designed; we had a fantastic banner; we had everything ready to go. There was just one problem. I knew that it wouldn't work.

I had wanted to raise the profile of the Panchen Lama because of who he was and because of what China had done to him. But I imagined what the voice I'd spoken to at the *Mirror* would say when the papers were full of terror. The voice would say, "Who cares?" and there would be nothing I could do to persuade him that Gedun Choekyi Nyima was worth caring about.

His innocent face stared at me from the board behind the desk where I sat. I wondered what his parents must think as they look at him. Unable to explain to him who he is but knowing that, if things had happened differently, people would have traveled across the world for his teachings. How they must wonder what their son would have been, who he would have been if the Chinese hadn't got there first. Perhaps they saw signs of the wisdom that Tibetan Buddhism says is born in him. I would have to leave his story untold.

I rang Nicky. "It isn't going to work, Nicky, is it? Not with the world like this."

She hesitated for a second and then said, "I think you're right."

"I don't want to just go ahead and hope for the best. I don't want to waste everyone's time. I've trained myself to try to work with negative circumstances that come along and not against them. I could keep going if I never watch the news, but I do watch the news, and if I were a journalist, I wouldn't touch the story we are preparing. It's not relevant."

"So what do you want to do?"

"I think there is a more important message. I set out to try to do something to help Tibet. But now there is something that Tibet is saying that the world needs to hear."

"Nonviolent resistance?"

"I'm not specifically advocating that; some people believe in that. I do myself, but we have a message that is valuable for everyone no matter what they believe."

"We do?"

"It works like this. Some people believe that you have to fight dictators, Hitler, Stalin, Saddam Hussein. The Dalai Lama hasn't had an easy time with Mao and the government, but he has never advocated violence."

"But Mandela used violence."

"Eventually. But my point is not which is better to achieve your ends. What I believe is that if we want to fight terror, then world governments should reward the Dalai Lama for the path he has taken. For refusing to resort to violence."

"Reward the great man of peace for sticking to his guns. So to speak."

"Exactly. Why are we fighting terrorists with sticks and not rewarding the lamas with carrots? What message does this send to would-be terrorists all over the world? 'Do it this way. Don't be like the Dalai Lama, or we'll ignore you.'"

"Logical. So what does this mean for us?"

"It means that we do the stunt, but instead of the Panchen Lama we put the Dalai Lama on the banner and proceed as before. Then we will be relevant."

"OK, good—and what's the slogan?"

"Oh shit. I have no idea."

The grim reality of the fact that I would now have to come up with a whole new plan sank in slowly. Nicky wasn't fazed. She was unnervingly blasé. "OK, I'll tell Elise to stop the production of the banner and to wait for a new photo and some new wording. Got to dash now, sorry. I'm in the middle of something." And she was gone.

It was that easy to cancel all our plans. A sense of panic and inadequacy set in about three seconds later. Voices started to shout things in my head like "Oh fuck, what am I going to do now?" and "I need heeeelp." Before I questioned them I found my hand on a telephone.

"Hi? PS, it's Isabel. Can we meet up? I really need to see you, I need your help, you see, and . . ."

"Isabel, I'm going to Dublin tomorrow. I'm sorry. I can't talk now, I'm on a train."

That always makes me laugh. I visualized all the people round her, glaring at her. I couldn't resist it.

"Sorry, I didn't quite hear you. Where did you say you are?"

"I'm on a train!"

I laughed. "And is there one of those signs that says. 'No mobile phones'?"

I could almost see her looking around.

"Yes." Oh the small joys of life. I know it's sad that these things make me laugh. That's what happens when you spend too much time on your own at a computer.

"OK. So when are you coming back from Dublin?"

"In two weeks, I can't talk now."

"Byeeee."

So by the time PS was in England again I would have to have solved this problem. I rang Rachael.

"Hi. Is this an OK time to talk with you?" Better do it right this time.

"No. I'm at work. I'll call you tomorrow, OK?"

"OK." I sighed. So another profession loomed. I'm sure the people who make up lines like "Things taste better with Coke" get paid a fortune. They have groups of people that sit around tables and come up with things together. I was going to have to become a one-person team.

I opened a notebook on a clean sheet and wrote "The Dalai Lama." So I had to come up with something witty. What rhymes with Lama? Banana? Pajama? Very useful. What rhymes with Dalai? The first thing that I thought of was a dubious plural beginning with a *ph* that I couldn't even write here.

OK, forget rhyming. So what did I want to do? I wanted to draw the UK government's attention to the fact that it would be a good idea to reward the Dalai Lama. So "Reward the Dalai Lama" was the message. I looked at it and wrote it down. Then I wrote it so that "Reward" was above "The Dalai Lama," and suddenly I became convinced I was a genius. I could write "Reward" all in red and then a picture of the DL underneath as the Chinese think of him, portrayed as a criminal. So it would look like a police poster, but the meaning would actually be that we should reward the Dalai Lama. This seemed utterly brilliant. I couldn't contain my excitement and found my hand on the phone again.

"Nicky?"

"Yes? You sound as if you've been running?"

"Only to the phone. What do you think of this?" I explained my idea as if it were the publicity campaign of the year.

"Mmm," she said. "Not bad. I see what you are trying to do." She sounded less than ecstatic.

"You don't like it, then?"

"Yes." She was always very polite. "I do. I can't see it catching on. But it's a good start. Why don't you try coming up with nine or ten, and then we'll have a chat? OK?"

"Ah, right. OK, then. Bye for now."

That should keep me off the phone for a week or two. I went back to my piece of paper. And wrote silly lists of words. Dalai: Delay, Dialogue, Dillydally, Delightful. Do something Dalaitful. No. No more harmer—support the Lama. No. What about "Don't dillydally with the Dalai?" It was certainly tabloidy and no mention of a tit of any kind.

My phone rang. Oh joy, it was Rachael.

"Hi, I'm sorry I couldn't talk just now when you called, I was in the middle of something. I still am, really. I'm just phoning to say, call tomorrow at 5 p.m."

"OK. Can I ask you one question?"

"Yes."

"What do you think of 'Don't dillydally with the Dalai'?" I chuckled, thinking myself suitably absurd.

"I hate it."

"Ah—say what you mean, Rachael." I laughed. "Why? I wanted something silly to make people smile."

"It devalues the product. I'll speak to you tomorrow."

Devalues the product. I see. I didn't like to think of the Dalai Lama, still smiling at me from a photo on my desk, as a product, and I certainly didn't want to devalue him. That was the opposite of my intention.

So I needed something silly or catchy without it being disrespectful. It needed, ideally, to be suitable for a giant banner and a T-shirt. Something that the tabloids would love and the Tibetan government-in-exile wouldn't be too offended by.

OK. I rolled up my sleeves and started to scribble seriously. I discovered I needed the communication last so if the meaning was "Reward the Dalai Lama," what could I put before it? I wrote out my list of all the words that rhymed with Lama again. I rather liked *drama* so I wrote, "Rewrite a Chinese Drama, Reward the Dalai Lama." This would have been good if my target audience had been dramatists. But useless for anyone else.

What about *karma?* "Fighting Terror Is Bad Karma, Reward the Dalai Lama."

Not sure *karma* is really a very tabloid word. It's not even a concept that most people who have not met Dr. Roger Woolger (or read about him in my last book) or spent a year involved in Buddhism take seriously. No, I'm afraid *karma* devalues the product, too. I sat and chuckled to myself. I could now make up new shouts for outside the embassy: "Don't let's fight—do what's right!" "Suppression is bad karma—long live the Dalai Lama!" "Stop the killing, stop the war" (a Vigil favorite), followed by "What's the Dalai Lama for?" Not sure they would catch on.

My phone rang again. It was Clive Arrowsmith, the photographer who had heard what we were up to and was keen to help. I explained that we no longer had a banner with the Panchen Lama on it and that we were looking for a new slogan.

"I have the copyright on 'Don't Be Frightened, Get Enlightened'—you can have that if you like it."

Brilliant. It would be great for a T-shirt, but not for the banner. "That's wonderful, Clive. Can I get back to you about that?"

"Sure. When Dave Bowie and I were doing stuff like that we used to take all the words and put them all over the floor. Kind of spread them all out."

"OK." I'd not yet met Clive, but his reputation of being extraordinary went before him.

"I don't really know what I can do to help, but I can take a photo for you."

"Thank you, Clive—that will do nicely." I'd become a slogan machine in an afternoon.

"When you are thinking of this stuff you need to stay calm." I listened, and my mind was thinking, "Be calmer, lama . . ."

"Thank you, Clive."

He rang off. I wrote on my sheet. "Be a Little Calmer, Support the Dalai Lama."

I had no idea what to do with all these half ideas. I emailed Nicky and begged for a meeting. I couldn't make any more phone calls without moving into the area known as "How to lose friends and alienate people." Haven't read that book, but it's a great title. Take a well-known phrase and invert it. There was only one phrase in the Tibet world: "Free Tibet! China out!" Maybe we supporters could take up megaphones and shout, "Free China! Tibet in!" That would confuse the ambassador.

The meeting, when it came, was simple. Just Nicky and myself. She said, "I think just 'Reward the Dalai Lama' is the clearest."

"But it's not funny."

"No, but with the world the way it is, it's difficult to guess what level of humor will be appropriate. So let's just go for the message and rely on the stunt and the jump to give us the publicity opportunity."

"OK, Nicky."

So this was it, then. This would be the "something" that I had wanted to do. I would be suggesting to the government, hopefully with a little help from the press, that they "reward the Dalai Lama" for doing the right thing in a world that seemed to have gone crazy. Suddenly watching the news supported me. It supported all of us. I was hoping to say, with a picture, what was in my humble opinion the most important message in international politics. It was unrelated to any war. Whether people thought it was necessary to topple dictators or whether they thought it was wrong to use force, my message was the same. Don't just fight terrorists, "Reward the Dalai Lama." Maybe fortune would favor the brave. And we were certainly being brave.

FLAMES WON'T BE NECESSARY

The following day I met Gary Connery, a stuntman who would jump from the top of the column for us. The column had been climbed before, but no one had ever jumped from the top. It had been considered too low to be jumped safely, but Gary was special—a tiny, wiry man without an ounce of fat on him. He bounced into my house, all energy and smiles.

"Hello, Gary." I held out my hand.

"Hi."

"So, you're happy to jump for us? That's very good of you."

"Glad to help. I enjoy a challenge."

"You are going to be OK? I mean, you aren't going to kill yourself or anything?" I poured tea.

"No. I've already jumped from a lower height, and I was in flames at the time."

I added milk.

"I was 'an attraction' at the Shrewsbury Flower Festival. I was covered in a mixture of petrol and glue. The cage was about 120 feet, someone set light to me, and when I saw the flames pass my face I jumped. It was an experiment because I didn't really know how the flames would affect the parachute. But it was fine. When I got to the ground, five mates came up and doused me down with fire extinguishers. Oh, I was wearing protective clothing and a silicone mask, by the way."

"Wasn't there a danger that the flames could affect the parachute?"

"That's what some of my friends in the Stunt Register said. But I was convinced that it could be done. Courage and conviction. That's what you need."

I made a note: courage and conviction.

"We won't be needing you in flames."

"No?"

"No. Jumping into the air will be just fine. I understand it's never been jumped before?"

"Not yet. I'm looking forward to it."

I felt a cold sweat of fear break out. Was I going to encourage this man to risk his life?

"Gary—you will be all right, won't you? I mean, you're completely confident?"

"Oh yes. I messed up once. I won't do that again."

"What did you do?"

"I jumped off the Eiffel Tower. I knew it was a bit too windy, but it was a one-off event and I thought I'd risk it. I had a writer and a photographer who were eager to get their story, and I was eager to jump. It was an ego thing, I won't deny that. I knew that it was too windy, but I still jumped. The parachute opened and everything, but I hit the ground so fast I was knocked unconscious immediately. I spent eight days in intensive care in a French hospital. I'm a vegetarian. It wasn't a good experience."

The life of a stuntman.

He looked at my desk. It had about thirty books on Tibet and China in a large pile.

"What do you do for a living?"

"Me?" Ah, that old question again. "In theory I'm now, er, a campaigner, or the managing director of a small not-for-profit action group for Tibetan awareness, or an odd-jobs person, or a writer, or a mother, or something. Do you have a partner, Gary? Kids?"

"Yes, Vivienne is a hot sexy chick. We have two children: Lydia, ten, and Kali, my son aged six. He is nagging me to do his first base jump. So I'm going to let him. He'll do it with me. It'll be a tandem base jump. I believe he'll be the youngest person ever to have done one."

"Why a base jump? Why not a tandem skydive?"

"Because this is safer. We'll do it into water. There are fatalities with skydiving."

I see. Glad I hadn't spoken to Gary a month ago.

"Anyway, you are happy about doing this jump for Act for Tibet?"

"Yes. You are making the most important point that anyone could make. Killing people doesn't solve problems."

"So, what do I need to tell you?"

"Nothing really. Just the date."

We didn't yet have a date, of course.

"Your girlfriend, is not, presumably, of a nervous disposition?"

"No. She enjoys what I do. So do my kids."

I thought about the possibility of creating two orphans. All my old codependent behavior patterns kicked in. I felt as though his life were my personal responsibility.

He saw my crestfallen face.

"Have you been a stuntman for long? I mean, have you always done this?"

"I'm very well qualified. Do you want to know what you have to do to become a professional stuntman?"

"Yes. I think I do. I'm scared, Gary. First it's illegal, and second it's dangerous. I'm not used to either of these."

"It's nothing really. I've been doing this stuff since I was a kid. I had a misspent childhood. Now I get paid to do the things that I used to bunk off school to do."

"But does this involve qualifications of any kind?"

"To be on the professional Stunt Register you need six qualifications in various skills. There are six headings and six subheadings in each section."

In my next lifetime this is the job I'd like.

"There is fighting, falling, strength and agility, cars/bikes/horses, water, and miscellaneous."

"It sounds fantastic."

"And in each of those headings you have subheadings. So in fighting you've got boxing, judo, tai kwon do, aikido, kung fu, etc."

"So you can choose?"

"You have to be qualified to a certain standard as laid down by the governing body of that sport. For example, in the British Judo Association you need the grade one below a black belt—that is acceptable as a qualification. Then you go to the falling category, and within that you've got high-board diving, trampolining, and sky-diving, and again you have to have a qualification. And so on in every other category."

"It just sounds wonderful. I feel a child in me go wide-eyed and think, 'Wow! You get to do all these exciting things and get paid?' I mean for the man that is eternally a boy this is the perfect job, isn't it?"

"Yes, but it takes time, courage, and commitment. I have nine of the necessary qualifications because I didn't want to not get in."

I questioned him for an hour about all his qualifications until he finally said, "Are you really interested in all this?"

"Yes. Definitely. And now you've got all that, are you still learning new stuff?"

"Oh, yes. Since then I do a lot more driving. I live near a military range, so when they are not exercising I take a beaten-up old car up there and practice my rallying skills; same with the motorbike. I do track days on a sports bike. And then there's base jumping, which is a constant ongoing thing."

"When did you qualify?"

"In 1997. And I haven't really looked back since."

"Fantastic."

"At the moment I'm learning to fly a helicopter. Which is great because I'm now able to go solo. You can get away with anything when the instructor isn't there. Does it really go that fast? Can you really bank it that far over?"

I laughed nervously. "Bank it over? That means tip it, right?"

"Yes, and other things that the instructor wouldn't let you do."

His craziness inspired confidence. He was so confident that he could do whatever he wanted. Who was I to disagree with him?

There was a pause. I smiled at him. "You aren't going to die if you do this for us, then?"

"Look, I've died hundreds of times. I died twice in the last film I was in. If you don't need me to die, I won't die. OK?"

"Thank you, Gary," a voice seemed to be saying that sounded like mine. I shook his hand.

Interesting that trust doesn't come into the serenity prayer. This was a new form of courage. The courage to trust. Maybe trusting people sometimes is part of wisdom.

TWENTY-TWO AND CLIMBING

The following two weeks were not easy ones. No matter how much I tried to focus on the positive and put into practice everything that I had learned about serenity, I still had a sick feeling in the pit of my stomach. A man could die, and it would be because of me. I easily forgot the fact that he had offered.

And it wasn't just him. Four men were to go up the column. The first and the best climber was also the youngest. Just twenty-two years old, Simon Westaway looked liked one of my daughter's better choices of boyfriend. This boy was going to climb the column with his bare hands and some rubber climbing shoes. It's called "free climbing." There are no ropes or anything to help you get up, and in this case there were no little holes or indentations to put your feet in and nothing to grab on to either. If you are ever in London and find yourself in Trafalgar Square, just go take a look at the column and imagine climbing that with your strength alone. He had to attach little clips behind the lightning conductor as he went up—"treads" they are called. "I'll have to put the clips in at regular intervals because I don't want to scare the crowd and the police by taking too long a fall."

I took another deep breath.

"Also, if you fall, apparently it can generate ten times your normal body weight, and that might damage the lightning conductor. You don't want to get done for criminal damage."

"Sod the lightning conductor," I said, perhaps lacking the appropriate level of respect for public property. "What about you, Simon? I mean, you're not going to fall, are you?"

"I'll try not to."

"Do you often fall when you climb?"

He smiled at me compassionately.

"Don't worry. My brother Harry has planned this very carefully."

The big brother Harry Westaway had reached the age of twenty-seven.

"OK, Simon."

And then there was Damian Walsh. Sometimes you just meet the most extraordinary people, and I seemed to be meeting a lifetime supply at once. Damian would be our banner and rigging man. The banner of the Dalai Lama was five meters across and fifteen meters long. By some extraordinary miracle it would be unfurled and secured with ropes. This was Damian's department.

We were a mixed bunch now. Rachael was still project manager despite having left Cunning Stunts.

"I know it's a cliché, but I just had to do something with some meaning. I was worn down with sending people into shopping centers dressed as giant bananas, grass turf, squirrels, and mobile phones. I went into advertising because I thought it would be creative, and I just ended up promoting rubbish. There was no way I could do that with my life. So this is a pretty good first project."

She caught me for a moment. The wonder of her words. In the world that I came from, this was a sentiment to be mocked. The ultimate way to kill an idea for a TV show is for it to be "worthy." They actually use the word as an insult. You will hear someone say, "It's an interesting project, but it's a bit worthy." And that will be given as a reason for not making a program or a series. So her words were a touch of magic for me, far more than she knew.

"I wish everyone thought as you do, Rachael."

"What?"

"If everyone who didn't believe in what they were doing stopped doing it and found a way to make money doing something they did believe in, even if it was for less money, think how different the world would be."

"You're a crazy idealist."

"Thank God."

We were sitting in a pub next to the Greenpeace offices. We'd had a call from Richard Watson on the Greenpeace action unit, who had heard what we were planning and had offered to help. Wonderful people were appearing from everywhere.

The boys sloped in one at a time. Simon and Harry, or "the Muppet twins" as everyone called them. They hardly spoke. Simon just looked at everyone with large brown eyes. Many hearts would be broken for this face. Harry, his big brother, always looked surprised due to a large amount of hair that stuck up in the air as if he'd just put his finger in an electrical outlet. He looked lost, too. But when we spoke, he turned out to be one of the least lost people I'd ever spoken to. "I took physics and philosophy at Cambridge, and there are lots of things I could do. But we pick our projects; we climb a lot. We never have any money, but we have a good lifestyle."

Then Richard Watson, who they called "Watty," arrived and brought drinks for everyone.

"Hold on," I said desperately, "I'm buying the drinks."

"It's done now."

So this was another situation where I just sit back and let everyone get on with it.

"So what's the plan? What's the timing? When do we arrive? Who is arriving first?" Rachael took up her role as project manager.

"We thought we'd go in under cover of darkness. That seems to be when it's easiest." Watty was as calm as a millpond.

"And are we going to go and act as a diversion so that you can all get started without the police trying to grab you off?"

"The crucial part is the frieze before we reach the column," Damian explained. "That's the bit where they could take us off. It's Simon to go up first on one side, followed by Harry. I'll go behind

Simon, and then we can winch Gary up. Then, when we are all up to the base of the column, we're OK—they can't reach us then."

"There are security staff on duty in the square. I saw them last week." Rachael had done her homework.

"But they will only go back and phone their superiors." Watty swigged his beer, the old hand who had done this a hundred times. Breaking the law was a regular event in his life.

"Surely with all this terrorist fear, Trafalgar Square is full of security cameras?" My face screwed up into the worried expression that it had become accustomed to.

"Yes, it will take the police about two minutes to get there once they spot us. That's why the first ten minutes is vital."

"In the past we've had a large group of Greenpeace volunteers who form a human chain to stop the police from reaching the climbers." Watty linked arms with Damian to demonstrate the standard procedure.

This sounded far too aggressive for me. I just wanted to tell the police what we were doing and why we were doing it and appeal to their understanding.

"Can't we just write something to give them so that they know what's going on?" I asked.

"That's a very good idea," said Watty.

"So what time do we arrive?" Rachael tried to create order in the chaos.

"Just after 4 a.m." I could tell her something. I'd worked this bit out. "Gary told me that the best time to jump is between six and six-thirty as that is when there is least wind. So if it's going to take you about an hour and a half to get over the plinth and then to make it to the top, I'd like to go just after four when it's still dark."

"Are you guys happy with that?"

The Muppet boys smiled and nodded.

"We can't climb if the column is wet," said Simon.

"And Gary can't jump if it's windy," said Damian.

"And I don't want to do this unless Watty can be there the date we pick," said Rachael.

"And we need to have no commitments for twenty-four hours after the date in case the police decide to hold us," said Harry.

"And there are loads of days that Gary can't do as he's working on a film at the moment," said Rachael.

"So when are we planning to do this?" asked Simon, not unreasonably. He was in his final year at Winchester University. "I have to travel."

They all looked at me.

"I'll start looking at the weather forecasts and ringing you a lot, I suppose."

"OK and where is everyone going to sleep the night before? It would be best if we could have everyone together."

"You can all sleep in the warehouse at Greenpeace if you like," Watty offered immediately.

"That's a great idea. I'll arrange a friend I know who has a van to pick you all up together and get down there for four." Rachael was in organizer mode. "You don't need to sleep on a mattress at Greenpeace, Isabel. You'll need a good night's sleep, and it's unlikely that anyone will get one. It's a good idea for you to stay away from us anyway, and then if there is any trouble you'll still be available for interviews with the press. By the way, has Nicky had a chance to tell you that she's leaving Cunning Stunts?"

My world stopped again.

"No."

"Don't worry. There is a new guy that is taking over her job. I'm sure he'll be fine. We'll go in for a meeting next week."

"So I'm losing Nicky, too, then?"

"Don't be daft. She still wants to be involved with this. She's just leaving Cunning Stunts."

"I see." The cast list was becoming confusing. There was now no one working for the PR company that was supposed to be helping me that knew anything about this project. The energy had been

Rachael and Nicky. What an exercise in serenity this exercise in courage was turning out to be.

But it still seemed to be coming together. We sat and laughed and drank, and Rachael tried to manage the unmanageable. She quietly asked me if I'd gotten the guys to sign anything to say that they were doing this at their own risk, but we both agreed that it would be offensive and inappropriate. I'd asked Damian, and he'd said, "Don't worry about any of that legal stuff. You're not paying us so you are not liable, and none of the guys would sue you anyway. If anything went wrong, they'd take responsibility."

I thought that if I were the mother of Gary's children and he was killed I'd try to get some compensation from someone. "Well, maybe you would," said Damian, "but she won't. She knows the score."

Learning how to trust these people totally was a bit like falling myself—falling into the arms of strangers and knowing that somehow I had managed to surround myself with arms that would catch me. I trusted them all. I knew that Rachael and Nicky would think of all the details. That the guys would work out all the climbing equipment and plan each moment. If there was trouble with the police, I knew that Watty would smile at them and give them my leaflet. I just had to hope that Gary's parachute would open and we would not be on the front pages for the wrong reason.

I just had to relax, drink red wine, and then go home and pray.

VEGETARIANS AND ANARCHISTS

It was the last week of Nicky's job at Cunning Stunts, and she'd wanted to get everyone together around a table to brief her replacement on the entire project.

But the man who was taking over from Nicky and Rachael had none of the enthusiasm of these two women. He sat and looked at the motley bunch of vegetarian-looking women and scruffily dressed anarchists with a look of bemusement or, even, what appeared to be open disdain. Gary was an hour and a half late for the meeting, which didn't help. By the time he arrived, others had already left. These guys hated PR companies and had already refused to work for them on other occasions, even though they'd been offered huge sums of money. Watty bore no resemblance to the version of him that I'd met at the pub. He was monosyllabic and evidently wondered why on earth he was there.

We attempted to enthuse the new PR head about the project, but it seemed that he was very busy and had many more important projects on his mind. Cunning Stunts was pitching for a contract with a well-known furniture company, and that seemed to be very high on the list of priorities. It was certainly way above my pathetic attempt to raise the subject of nonviolence on the international political agenda.

"The main point that I want to get across is that, as we are fighting an international war on terrorism and the Dalai Lama is the world's leading proponent of nonviolence, then it's logical that world governments support him. We want to lead people to our website, where there is a call to individuals to visit their MPs. The idea is to influence Parliament one MP at a time."

"You have to understand, as far as the papers are concerned, it's a story about a man jumping off Nelson's Column."

"Yes, but surely they'll want to know why? I mean, we've got a fifteen-meter banner of His Holiness. Could we discuss how we'll approach this in the press release?"

"Send something through, and I'll have a look at it. I've got to go now." He got up, looking very busy. Maybe he was very uncomfortable with this bunch of dangerous misfits in the nice clean PR company. Maybe he thought the project would be canceled because it was too risky or too ill-conceived. Maybe he cared about the financial position of the company that had just given him a job and therefore didn't want to spend too much time with a project that wasn't paying. Whatever the reason, he hadn't asked any questions, and he had to rush off.

I left this meeting feeling rather unjoyful.

The following morning I drafted a press release and sent it to him. It was a Monday, and I had an email back on Tuesday, saying that he'd look at it and reply on Friday. But Friday came, and no phone call or email came with it. Then Wednesday of the following week I rang and left messages. He was certainly very busy. Every time I called, he was in a meeting or out of the office. Eventually I began to feel I was being a nuisance, so I stopped phoning. Instead I rang the managing director of Cunning Stunts and arranged to meet her.

I'd been taught the principle of win/win, so I thought that if I could catch her imagination, then we could work out how we could get the maximum publicity and benefit her company, too. I arrived full of hope, and I waited.

I remember the actress Stephanie Beacham giving me some advice once upon a time. "Never," she said, "allow anyone to keep you waiting." She went on, "If it's really important, give them ten minutes, and if you haven't had a message, leave."

"She's in a meeting," one of the staff had said as I arrived.

"OK, as long as she knows I'm here I'll wait," I said happily. Punctuality is a matter of courtesy for me. I am very, very rarely late for a meeting, and I sat with Ms. Beacham's words ringing in my ears more than ten years after they were spoken to me. Ten minutes, tick tick, fifteen, tick tick, twenty . . . this was very odd. No message came. No one offered me a drink. At twenty-five minutes I got up and found the girl who had shown me in. "Excuse me, did you tell your boss I'm here? I'm sorry but I don't recall ever being kept waiting this long when I have a specific appointment and have traveled across London specially. I have other things that I have to do this afternoon."

"She knows you're here. Please take a seat."

Perplexed, I returned to my seat. At 2:30 she arrived for my 2 p.m. appointment. "Do you mind if we go out to lunch?" she said as she arrived.

"No. I don't mind, but I've already had lunch. I'm sorry, I had 2 p.m. in my diary. Did I make a mistake?"

"No you didn't, but I got stuck in that meeting, sorry."

We left the office and moved to the pub opposite. "Our new PR head will be coming along so he can talk through the press, OK?"

I thought, "Ah yes, the person with no phone." We went to lunch, and the managing director's husband joined us, too. "Doesn't the Dalai Lama live in Paris?" he asked.

"Er, no—India." What a surreal lunch it was. I evidently bemused them all as much as they bemused me. I picked up some cherry tomatoes that had been discarded off one of the plates—very odd behavior. The new PR head told me that he would give an "exclusive" to the *Mirror,* the *Guardian,* and the *Independent.*

"What about TV crews?" I asked.

"Oh, they won't be interested unless you do it at the weekend. Saturday or Sunday would be the best days for you."

"Nicky had suggested that you may like to make an EPK?"

"Yes." Anna smiled. "We are going to do that." She was friendly and was obviously trying to understand me. "Have you got something in writing in case anything goes wrong? We're not worried for ourselves, we are just thinking of protecting you. Have you written a statement that you can read out to the press in case one of the boys is hurt or killed?"

"I haven't. No. I'm not sure that I think it would be appropriate . . ."

"You must write one. Have you sent them something in writing that states that they are doing this at their own risk? It's a question of liability."

"If you are worried, you don't need to be. I am accepting full responsibility for the planning and the event itself. All I need your help with is the PR. If anything goes wrong, then it won't come back to Cunning Stunts. I'll make sure of that."

"No, no, for your own protection."

It did seem crazy to say that these were just not the kind of people who would sue.

"Perhaps you are right. I'll email them."

"And get them to send a reply so that you can show that they have received it."

"OK. But about the press—you are only going to let three papers know?"

"And the Press Association, and they will send it out."

"I see."

"As it's highly illegal, we won't give the names of the climbers, and we've asked the person doing the EPK not to show their faces."

"Hold on," I said, bemused. "Who says it's highly illegal?"

"You may be damaging public property."

"No. We've put a lot of thought into this. It's what I've called 'slightly illegal.' And I know that something can't be 'slightly illegal,' that it either is illegal or it isn't, but we are not doing any damage to the column whatsoever. It's solid stone. We are not leaving anything on the column, we are explaining in full what we are doing, to the police, in writing . . . and actually I think it would be rather good for Gary's career if we put his name in the press release. He is a member of Equity after all. He may get more work as a result."

"I see."

"But they may be arrested?" Anna asked.

"They will get arrested. But we know that. We have a good solicitor who is coming along."

"Are you expecting them to be fined or go to court?"

"I'm hoping that they will be given a caution and then we can all go to the pub. We just about have enough money left from our fund-raising to replace their climbing equipment if it gets confiscated. It might sound weird to you, but I think that when everyone sees the portrait of His Holiness the Dalai Lama, they will be so impressed that no one will press charges of any kind."

It evidently did sound weird to both of them.

Anna asked some good questions about the follow-up after the stunt and what I was hoping for. But now that I sit to write about this meeting, I realize that I can't remember the head of PR asking any questions about the Dalai Lama at all. I only remember him reassuring me that the *Mirror* would definitely come because he had a good friend there.

I was unsure whether I felt reassured or depressed. It would, of course, be wonderful to be in the *Mirror,* the *Guardian,* and the *Independent*. But in my heart of hearts, if it all worked, I'd been hoping to send a ripple around the world.

RED ALERT

I know I'm always giving out unsolicited advice. But here is another piece: If you ever plan an event that is both dangerous and illegal, at least make sure that it is not dependent on the weather.

Every morning my day would start by logging on to the BBC five-day weather forecast. I began to notice an interesting thing. They might predict five days ahead that there would be no rain and winds would be low, but suddenly, as a day moved position from day five to day three, the whole forecast would change. I had been hoping to see the little sun symbols work their way back from five to one in an orderly fashion, but no such luck. You could have a sun up ahead on days five and four and then suddenly when it got to day three it would become a cloud, and I'd want to scream with exasperation, "Yesterday you said that Monday would be sunny!"

To add to all this, everyone had different advice. One day Harry phoned to say, "I'm just giving you a call as I happened to mention to the PR people at Greenpeace that you were considering a weekend. They say that they never do anything at the weekends as it's such a slow time for news and no one ever watches TV anyway."

I phoned Cunning Stunts and spoke to an assistant in PR and

asked why they had chosen the weekend. "Because we think the press are more likely to come along then . . ."

"And can I ask why you don't have any TV crews on the list?"

"There is no interest in a feature . . ." she hesitated, "of this kind."

"Oh."

I felt myself sinking deeper into confusion. I thought I was making the most important point in international politics, but other people seemed to think that this was not a point that was worth making—even though people were risking their lives to make it.

I couldn't understand their lack of interest. I called them again but was told about the important pitch for the furniture company contract. I was confused, but I just kept trying to think of all the positive support they were giving. When the time came, I was sure they'd help.

Then the time came. I had found a day when, miraculously, all the boys were free. It was a Monday. An innocent Monday morning. On Wednesday of the previous week the BBC assured me that the weather was going to be OK. I rang around all the team, and they all agreed to go up to Greenpeace on the Sunday night. Finally, after all this waiting, we had a date. There was a lot to do. I was still waiting for a reply to the press release that I'd sent three weeks ago. I rang and left a message. "Would the PR boss please ring me, please?"

The following day I had a reply from the man who had something more important to do. "I'm sending over a photocall notice. Make any changes you want, and send it back, please."

"OK," I said cheerfully. "And the press release?"

"We'll get back to you about that."

I opened my email. The first line said, "Act for Tibet. A nonprofit organisation working towards the release of the Dalai Lama."

I was not happy. This man hadn't even read the website or bothered to learn the first thing. Where did he imagine the Dalai Lama was to be released from? Paris perhaps? And this was the person who was talking to the press on my behalf?

I rang immediately. He was out of the office. That afternoon I received a phone call from a girl who was working as his assistant. She had been trying to write out answers for questions such as "Wasn't it dangerous what you did today?" and she had also sent a long statement for me to read out in the event of damage occurring to the column.

This was madness, and I found myself speaking to her in an irritated voice that I very rarely use. Then I caught myself. "I'm sorry, this isn't your fault at all. It seems to me that you are suddenly doing everything, and you can't be expected to know answers to these questions. Is the head of PR there?"

"No, he's not here." I thought, If she mentions that furniture company one more time I'm going to scream. "OK. Is Anna there?"

"No. She's not here, either."

"I see. Well who can I speak to then?"

"I'll put you through to Sarah."

Whatever!

"Hello, Sarah—may I ask what your position is?" I was now steaming.

"I'm a project manager here."

"Sarah, this is probably not your problem, but could you please go out and buy a bunch of flowers for the girl that I was just speaking to and send me the bill. I was short with her, and it isn't fair. I am a nonpaying client of your company, I know. However, Act for Tibet is, we believe, giving your company one of the best stunts— no—*the* best stunt, without a doubt, that your portfolio contains. Weeks of work have gone into the preparation, and the only reason that you have this project at all is because of the quality of two women who no longer work for the company."

Ear-bashing, I think they call it.

"Why has this entire project been put on the desk of a girl who has evidently not been properly briefed? It's not fair on her. She now has two weeks' work to do, in one day, on the most important and dangerous stunt that your company has ever done. I don't want to complain about anyone, I just want to ask what on earth is going on there?!"

She mumbled. "I agree. Yes, I understand. Yes, I'll buy her some flowers. Yes, I'll see if I can help."

I rang Rachael and had a similar rave. She sighed and said, "That used to happen to me. That's one of the reasons that I left."

On the Friday morning I rang back the girl who now had flowers on her desk, and together we worked out the press release and the question-and-answer sheet to go with the EPK. We devised possible answers in case of accident and created a contact sheet of everyone involved in the project. She sent me a list of all the places that the EPK would be sent to. I wrote out the police statement and made sure that she had a copy. We double-checked how a video of the action would get from the edit suite to the computer screen.

The head of PR, who was supposed to be in charge of the project, was out of the office all day on the last day before the stunt. I couldn't quite believe it. At 6 p.m. I called him and he was in the pub. "Give me a call on Monday morning. I'll meet you there about five with the press. OK?" Maybe he thought that the job was done.

At 8:30 p.m. the girl with the flowers was still at her desk, double-checking everything and helping me.

"If you need anything over the weekend, call me," she said.

"Thank you."

And what a weekend. For some reason the VHS tapes for the EPK were sent to me, which gave me time to label them all correctly, write out envelopes for the places they were going to, and deliver them to the edit suite ready for Monday morning. We had to go to the sign shop and collect the banner, all fifteen meters of it, and deliver it to Damian who was at Greenpeace waiting to attach ropes. Someone had to go and buy a piece of climbing equipment for Harry, who had neither the time nor the money.

"It's called a Camalot — not sure if I want a 4.5 or a 5 size."

"Harry, please tell me that your life doesn't depend on your making the right choice. 'Cause I can buy both."

"Too expensive."

"Don't be crazy; we can take back the one that you don't use."

"No. That's OK. I'm pretty sure it's a 4.5 we'll need."

Saturday came and went. My nerves were in a state of high alert. Something in me was flashing "Red—Red—Danger." I spoke calmly to myself. "It's OK, Isabel, by Monday night this will all be over."

The phone began to ring constantly. Rachael called on Sunday to say that she had dreamt that we were all climbing the column, and it went on and on and towered over London. In an attempt to stop herself feeling nervous, she had invited the friends who wanted to come along for dinner the night before. They were then to go on to Greenpeace.

Gary was doing a night shoot on a Harry Potter film and so couldn't be with everyone else. "I'll just meet everyone in the square at four. Don't worry. It'll be fine."

Simon took another day out from his final year at university and traveled to London. Even Steve, my crazy builder friend, turned up to support us.

"I'll be your gofer," he said. "If anything needs going for, send me."

Then finally, the night before, my best friend in the world came over to tell me what to wear. "No, not that jacket." Katrina was firm in her opinions. "Yes, that jacket. And something lighter for later in case you get dragged off to a TV studio." So I was all set. It was 11 p.m., and we had the alarms set for 2:30 a.m.

At 11:30 p.m. the phone rang. I lifted it excitedly to hear Gary's voice. There was a pause, and then he said, "It's too windy."

WHAT'S THE BUNTING?

Of course I knew it wasn't my fault, but phoning everyone hadn't been easy. The following morning I sat staring disconsolately at my morning cup of coffee. I couldn't believe that Monday would come and go and we still wouldn't have been near the column. I switched on the computer to stare at the weather forecast. An entire week of cloud and heavy winds. As if to mock me there was even a gale forecast for Wednesday.

I repeated an old mantra, "Use everything for your learning, upliftment, and growth," and tried to think of ways that I could benefit from the delay. I dusted the house glumly. I thought about asking more questions about days of the week. Why would Saturday be a better day for press than Friday? But all these questions seemed irrelevant now. It was almost impossible to get everyone available on the same day anyway.

The girl with the flowers still on her desk rang. "Are you going to try to go for next weekend?"

"If the weather is OK, possibly."

But Damian couldn't do one day, Watty couldn't do another. I tried to find days when they would all be free if the weather got better. It turned out that a Wednesday two weeks away was the first day.

Then Gary phoned again. "I've spoken to Maggie, the solicitor, and apparently the police will have the right to hold me for twenty-four hours if they want to. I can't do next Wednesday if they do that because I'm working on a film on the following day."

"But couldn't you be booked at short notice for the day after any day?"

"I suppose so but it's unlikely."

"But not impossible."

"No."

"What is a day of your time worth if I book you myself for twenty-four hours?"

"You can't afford me. But anyway I'm not charging you for doing this. It'll happen. Just be patient. Have some serenity."

"OK, Gary."

The days ticked by. Now I had a new addiction, checking weather and wind speeds. I noticed that a week's prediction could change in the middle of the day. Gary needed a wind speed of 0–10. There was nothing under 12 for the foreseeable future.

People tried to be helpful. "I know a site that does a fourteen-day forecast." But when I mentioned this to Gary, he laughed. "The only certain way to know the weather is by looking out of the window. Just relax. Wait for it to change. It will."

Then the BBC World Service phoned and asked if I could write and present a series on angels.

"I can write it for you today." With a sigh of relief in my heart, I sat down and contemplated the possibility of angelic reality. By Monday of the following week I was looking for pieces of music, and as I sat and listened to a flute sonata by Poulenc, I noticed the sunshine streaming through my windows.

I rushed to the five-day forecast. And there it was: Friday of that week; sunshine and a wind speed of 3. Not the best day for press perhaps, but that depended on whom I listened to. If everyone was free, we'd go.

One by one I phoned around: "Yes," "Yes," "Yes," "Difficult . . . I don't know . . . Oh sod it, OK, yes."

I phoned Cunning Stunts' PR. "You'll lose the *Evening Standard* if you go on a Friday, but never mind."

"Why?"

"It's not a good day for them. But, well, if you say you have to go that day, we'll just have to do our best to get you the coverage."

"Thank you. So all systems go for Friday unless the weather changes again, and then I'll ring you."

This time I felt slightly less nervous. I just wanted action. I felt an incredible sense of humility. The freedom of Tibet is a subject that so many people have died for. A recently published book on Tibet had told the story of a man who had set light to himself knowing that his death would get the word *Tibet* on the front page of a newspaper.

And here was I, here were we, with our attempts at making a ripple. I glanced at my desk, at the same image of the Dalai Lama that had been enlarged to fifteen meters and was now crumpled in Damian's rucksack. Somewhere, somehow, I had to believe that his blessing was on us, that the angels were going to come and look after Simon, that Harry's planning would work and that Damian's rigging skills would suspend the Dalai Lama and the boys on their rappels safely above London.

I redated the press release and checked it over:

> *In the early hours of this morning in Trafalgar Square Londoners saw an extraordinary sight; stuntman Gary Connery became the first person to parachute from the top of Nelson's Column. Behind him a fifteen-metre portrait of the Dalai Lama was unfurled with the words "Reward the Dalai Lama." Known as base-jumping, the drop of 120ft had previously been considered too dangerous to attempt. The Dalai Lama's peaceful smile appeared to bless his courage and all who watched the spectacular feat.*

I was writing this before the event. Praying that this would be the right description of the morning. The press release went on:

> *Isabel Losada, founder of "Act for Tibet" who organised the action, said: "If world governments want to fight terrorism they must support peaceful proponents of change. The Dalai Lama has been resisting the Chinese presence in Tibet for more than fifty years whilst insisting that Tibetans do not resort to violence to achieve their freedom. He has been ignored. So what message does that send? If you want attention—bomb someone. The Dalai Lama is nearly seventy. We all know that terror promotes*

*terror and we must do something different. This is it. It is time for re-
warding non-violence with determined and positive action.*

Act for Tibet has set up a website, www.actfortibet.org.

I fretted and worried and double-checked everything. This time
Gary would go and sleep on the floor at Greenpeace, and they
would all arrive together. The weather forecast continued to be
good. I bought sweets to give out to everyone. I called everyone I
knew in London who cared about Tibet. They all wanted to come.
"Don't arrive until 6 a.m.," I said, "and ring me at 5, and I'll let
you know if it's worth getting out of bed."

I couldn't let Mrs. Takla and the Tibetan government office in
London know. As it was illegal, it would have put them in an impossible position, so the first that they would hear about it was
when they saw it in the papers. Alison at Free Tibet gave me loads
of encouragement and support. "Sounds like you've thought of everything. Enjoy it."

Steve arrived again—"I wouldn't miss this for the world"—and
he cycled off to deliver some VHS tapes for me. Angels are everywhere.

Then it was Thursday evening, and it started to get dark. I
watched the darkness fall over London as I've never watched it before. The first suggestion of dusk, the beautiful change in the light
that catches you unawares, and then suddenly, quickly, the night
falls. I looked at the blackness and knew that before it was light
again the adventure would begin.

"What do you suppose I've forgotten?" I asked Steve as he
tucked into fish and chips. "I bet there will be something. Something we've not factored in for. Something we've not imagined."

There was an uneasy silence while he tried to hold back my fear
of the unknown.

"What do you want me to do tomorrow?"

"Well, Katrina is coming along to help Rachael with the police.
You can stand close by in case they have any problems."

"Show me that stuff you've written for the boys in blue, will you?"

It said:

Statement for Police and Security Personnel
Good Morning.
Peace be with you!
We are "Act for Tibet," a small not-for-profit organisation promoting
His Holiness the Dalai Lama's
stance on non-violence.
We are of course non-violent ourselves.
We apologise if our action inconveniences the police or
any security personnel in any way.
Today's action will take three or four hours. Nothing will be
damaged. Please be kind to us.
Four professional climbers are going to climb Nelson's
Column and lower a banner which is a photograph of His Holiness
the Dalai Lama. They will not damage the statue or the plinth in
any way. When the banner has been lowered in order to photograph
it, the climbers will come down
bringing the banner with them. Nothing will be left on
the column and no harm will be done to anyone.
Thank you for your Patience and Understanding.

"Well, that seems to explain everything."

"I hope so, and on the back we have this picture of His Holiness."

"What a beautiful picture."

"Yes, isn't it?"

"I like 'Peace be with you.'"

"Thank you. Anyway I have a bag full of those so that Katrina and Rachael can give them out to all the police. No preferential treatment for senior officers."

"I get it."

"Are you hoping to get some sleep tonight?"

"Oh yes, a couple of hours. I've set my alarm for 2 a.m."

I went to bed at 11 p.m. Every five minutes my phone bleeped, but this time it was just messages. "Good luck," "I'll be thinking of you," "I'll be there." Then the next beep was the alarm and the night was over just like that without even a change of paragraph.

I dressed in five minutes, adding the jacket that Katrina had recommended, and stumbled into a taxi. We arrived at the meeting point, and I saw Katrina and Steve stumbling up the square.

And then there it was, the factor that I had not thought of. A group of men cleaning down the frieze. Water falling on our precious bronze, not from heaven but from the hoses of men.

"Don't panic," said Steve. "They're not doing all four sides."

I said more prayers. Then we noticed a cherry picker, a huge great crane used for cleaning. Which could, of course, also be used to remove anyone who tried to climb the column. It was all too much. I wanted to sit down and cry.

"Let's see what the boys say."

We walked up to the van where they were already parked. "Move away from the van, move away from the van!" said a girl I didn't know.

We moved, fairly sharpish, away from the van and attempted to stroll casually up the street. We sat down on a step, trying to look as if we were waiting for a taxi. My phone rang. "Sorry about that," said the voice I didn't know. "It's just we saw the cherry picker and we thought someone may have blown us out so we are being careful. I'll put Watty on."

Then Watty's voice. "Look Isabel, that washing may be bad news, and the cherry picker is certainly bad news. I'm going to try to have a look. You and your crowd just stay out of the way for a while, OK?"

"OK, Watty."

We waited while a solitary figure got out of a van and ambled across the square. He walked right around the column and then back to the van. Ten minutes later the phone rang again. "It seems to be OK. We're going in. You can just walk across the top and watch from the bus stop."

"OK. Watty." I felt like a child. I wanted to add, "I love you." I loved the fact that this morning I wasn't in charge. For the next ten minutes I could only watch and pray.

Four figures walked across the north side of the square while the cleaning went on over on the south side. We sauntered across to the bus stop to meet Rachael and her friends. "I feel sick," said Rachael. Then, as we watched, one black figure was suddenly halfway up the frieze, then a second, then a third, one still stood on the ground. The semidarkness hid them. We watched a police car drive straight past, then a siren screamed towards us. The fourth figure stepped onto the plinth, and as we held our breath the police car turned into the Mall and screamed away again. We watched; we prayed. As they edged their way slowly up, two community police officers decided to take a morning constitutional through the square. "Look at the pigeon shit on the ground," Rachael suggested to them under her breath . . . but no. One of them had looked up. The cleaners covered for us for a minute or two as the police stopped to ask what was happening. There was a visible shaking of heads, the police spoke into their phones, and a matter of seconds later, every police car in Charing Cross was on the way. One, two, three, four, five, a van. But the boys were on the ledge, they had made it up to the point that they needed to, and no one could reach them. You could see them walking around chatting to each other, bemused policemen looked up and then, as we all watched, Simon started to climb.

One hand movement at a time, one step at a time, he was going up. Red police cars started to arrive. "Who on earth are the red cars?" someone asked. "Something antiterrorist, I think. I mean, that is the South African embassy behind us, and now Gary has his hood up. Well, let's face it, he could be a sniper," Steve observed dryly.

"For goodness sake," I pleaded. "Can't we give out the leaflets so they know what we are up to?"

"Not yet, it's all going well, leave them." Rachael and Katrina had decided to let be for a while. The police were standing watching Simon climb. An ambulance arrived. Obviously they were less confident of his climbing skills than we were. "Will we get charged for that?" I asked Katrina.

"No. We didn't order it, did we?"

"Yes, but what about the cost of bringing out an ambulance?"

"Don't be daft," said Steve, "they were only sitting around playing pool. There is no cost, it's a myth. My brother's a paramedic, so I know this."

"I can't watch. I feel sick," said Rachael without taking her eyes off Simon.

Everyone was watching. This was the most amazing thing to see. One twenty-two-year-old boy free-climbing—it was awe-inspiring. Just two feet somehow using the grooves in the column to grip and two hands holding the weight of his body.

Occasionally you'd see him stop and dip a hand in chalk or shake the tension out of an arm, and then he'd press on. Meanwhile below him, if he stopped to look, there was now a show. The ambulance staff had gotten out to enjoy the performance, and there must have now been thirty policemen for the four men on the plinth. There was much scratching of heads but no megaphones, which is what we'd expected.

Then the cleaners took their cherry picker and went home. We resisted the temptation to cheer. By now it was light, and we were being joined by members of the public, who seemed to be interested in actually getting on the buses that came by. "After you," said a considerate member of the public, walking towards the bus while keeping his eyes glued to Simon.

"Oh no. We're not really waiting for the bus. We're with them." I smiled.

"Shut up, you idiot," Rachael snapped at me. I loved her for being anxious. She was the person here who really cared about it all working, about the boys being safe, about the plight of Tibet, about everything. Everyone had made a contribution, but Rachael was the only one who had been climbing the column in her dreams.

She looked at me guiltily for having snapped at me, and I just radiated even more affection.

"The boys are OK, Rachael."

Then, just when we started to relax, fire engines arrived.

Someone said, "Fucking hell, fire engines—that's it. We're finished. They'll reach them and get them down."

"Get those leaflets in there now!" Steve pulled leaflets out of a bag and gave them to Katrina and Rachael. "Get them in the hands of the police, go! Go!"

I had been forbidden to talk to the police so that I could talk to the press.

"And the firemen, too. Steve, please give them to the firemen."

Watty was over to the fire brigade in a second.

"Don't worry," said a girl who had come along with Watty from Greenpeace. "Watty has a way of handling the fire brigade."

"What will he say?"

"Something like, 'We're not going to see the fire service become the police service this morning, are we, gentlemen?' or 'Would any of you like a cup of tea?'"

Katrina could now be seen throwing her hair around in the vicinity of the man who seemed to be in charge. Uniforms were running backwards and forwards with my picture of the Dalai Lama in their hands. Rachael gave out some more. I strained my eyes to see what was happening. Katrina was now at the center with Rachael beside her, and they were talking to a woman in her early fifties and an Indian man who looked like a sergeant of some kind. I hoped he was a devout Buddhist; at any rate, as an Indian he was in a pretty pickle, in charge of a protest in support of nonviolence in the heart of London, meters from Downing Street. If the spirit of Gandhi was around, he must have been smiling.

Then a van pulled away, and the red cars started to drive off. You could imagine the conversation between the firemen—"Well, I'm not pulling them off; the police will have to do it"—and some policeman replying, "I'm not climbing up that ladder." So they stood and watched. Watty's friends gave the firemen tea and smiled at them. Still Simon was climbing, every eye was on him, and then he reached the top and a cheer went up from the crowd. The firemen drank their tea and left. And it seemed as though the law wasn't going to cause us problems. No doubt bowled over by the personalities of Rachael and Katrina, they had decided to let us do what we wanted. Or maybe it was the picture of the Dalai Lama on the handouts that made the difference.

Except that there was no mention of the base jump on the handouts. Gary had warned us that if the police knew about it, then they might send in a helicopter to create wind so that he couldn't jump. So we were only going to mention the jump at the very last minute. Simon had attached a rope, not to Nelson but to some bolts and brackets that someone had thoughtfully put there to hold the statue in place. Harry was now the second one up, still a difficult climb but with a rope to help him.

About this time the press started to arrive with the PR team from Cunning Stunts.

"Which side is he going to jump from?" said a photographer who was apparently from the *Evening Standard*. "What time will he jump? We are holding the front page."

"He'll jump when he's ready, I'm afraid. I'm not sure what time that will be. They are lowering the banner first." I smiled.

"Oh yeah—Free Tibet."

"No, actually. Are you writing the article? We are not demanding a free or independent Tibet at all. The question we are asking is a simple one, which is . . ." He wandered off. I tried again: "Excuse me, I'm the organizer today. Is there any information I can give you?"

"Yeah, this stuntman Gary Connery, do you know what films he's been in? What town does he live in? Do you know how old he is?"

"Er, no—I'm afraid I never asked him any of those questions."

"Don't worry; we've got his resume here."

"But can I tell you why he's doing this for us?"

"Oh yeah, we'll put in a line about that Free Tibet stuff."

It was incredible. Had he seen a press release, I wondered?

"Actually this is relevant to the international war on terror . . ." I tried to get him to look at me.

Someone passed a phone. "LBC radio wants an interview."

"Oh, OK." And I started to chat until Rachael rushed up.

"These guys are from *London Tonight*. Get your wits about you."

"But I was told there were no broadcast crews coming."

"Katrina rang them," she said. "She called the BBC, too. They're here; word has gotten around. Come on, you've got to do an interview."

We darted up to them, and I blurted out: "So if we are fighting a war on terrorism, then why aren't we supporting the Dalai Lama? What are we saying? If you want attention, bomb someone?"

"Thank you very much," they said. I thought, I hope they don't edit that too tightly, I don't want to be on the ten o'clock news saying, "If you want attention, bomb someone."

Then Anna rushed over, "Can you do the EPK now?"

"But we need them to unfurl the banner first."

"We are running so late. We need your bit now, and then we'll get the banner and the jump on it later."

"OK." I rushed up and gave my message again. It was all so manic. I could hear myself talking in my "strident" voice. "The world is fighting a war on terror . . ."

Something in my head was yelling at me, "It's not what you say, it's . . ." But then another phone was handed to me. Some angry journalist was shouting at me. "Isn't it awfully dangerous what you are doing?"

"The climbers are all fully trained, and the stuntman is very well qualified." I sounded confident . . . and as I spoke I looked around to see Damian and Harry rappelling down the column with ropes, unfurling the banner, and tying it into position. I was stopped in my tracks.

There was the face of the Dalai Lama. Patience, serenity, and gentleness looked down on us all. I was caught by this glance and suddenly so full of pride. I had done this. I had made it possible for the face of His Holiness the fourteenth Dalai Lama of Tibet to look down over London. The portrait was wonderful, a gentle smile and the tips of his fingers touching together gently. I looked around at the crowd all staring up. The banner flapped gently in the breeze, and Damian released a long string of prayer flags that had been made in India by Tibetans who had been imprisoned by the Chinese.

"What's the bunting?" asked Anna cheerfully.

I laughed. "They are prayer flags, Anna, Tibetan prayer flags." I guessed only the Tibetans who saw the pictures would appreciate that detail.

Then Isabel Kelly, PS herself, appeared beside me. "Congratulations. That banner is amazing."

I couldn't take my eyes from the Dalai Lama's face. Damian and Harry had made it secure and were now climbing up the ropes again, making it look like a fun day out.

"You've done it," she said.

"Well, we've done it."

"No. I've done nothing."

"You came along at the right moment and encouraged me to start all this."

"OK, I suppose I did that."

More photographers started to arrive; there must have been thirty of them. I was still standing staring up at his face. For me this would have been enough. But for many he was just the backdrop.

Rachael ran up to me. "Gary's getting ready to jump." I remembered the first time I'd spoken to someone about the base-jumping idea. The advice had been: far, far too dangerous. Suddenly I felt sick.

I looked up again, and there was the man who had inspired such confidence in me when he had sat in my living room. He was checking something in his pack. Damian was now holding up a video camera. I wondered what they were saying up there.

I looked around the square. The moment froze like a video film when you hit "pause." I scanned the faces of the police, the small crowd from Greenpeace, my friends, and the strangers who had made it possible that this banner could fly over London; I noticed Nicky from Cunning Stunts and beside her Kate Saunders from the Tibet Information Network, sitting on a bench with their eyes straining upwards. I looked around again, and Gary walked up to the edge of the cornice. He spent a moment moving his shoulders about as if to loosen them and then, without a second of hesitation, he leapt into the air. A split second later and a parachute opened and, in what seemed to be the same second, he was on the ground. But he was standing. The crowd woke up from the shock and the speed, and an incredible cheer went up. He was alive.

Thank God. He was alive.

SATURDAY SPORT

The police all rushed forward to grab him, but the journalists were ahead of them. Somehow one desk had rung another, and there were now about thirty photographers and journalists around him.

"Was it worth it, Gary?" shouted one.

"Absolutely," said an adrenaline-filled Gary as he pulled his parachute out of the fountain.

"How did you feel, Gary?" said another.

"Scared shitless," Gary mumbled.

Anna, bless her, ran up to me. "Now go in there," she suggested.

So I dived in and kissed Gary, leading to widespread rumors later. Then I was off . . .

"The reason for this stunt today has been to ask the question why, if the world is fighting a war on terrorism, are we not rewarding nonviolence?"

I rambled on a bit in that same horrifying strident voice that a part of my brain hated and then said, "Thank you very much, everyone." Then the police came forward and grabbed Gary and bundled him, with his wet parachute, into the back of the van. I moved over to him. His face looked white. Not the relaxed man I knew, he was in some other place.

He put a piece of paper in my hand. "That's Vivienne's number. Please ring her."

"OK."

Cameras clicked away. He was a stuntman, a hero, a first-rate entertainer of the morning crowd, and a criminal all rolled into one. Then they shut the police-van doors, and he was gone. The TV crews rushed away to meet their deadlines.

There were three more men yet to get safely to the ground. Harry and Damian were rappelling down to untie the banner. It would have been lovely to have left it up, but then we would have been charged for removing it. Better to bring it down and make sure that we took it away with us.

Figures who had just arrived looked up in amazement. "You missed the best bit," I heard someone say.

Kate and Nicky were still sitting on the bench. "Don't say a word," said Nicky, "or I'll burst into tears."

In a matter of minutes the banner was down. Rachael rushed forward to hug the boys. We wanted to give them a hero's welcome, but instead they were being put into police vans. "Keep an eye out for Simon," said Harry. "He's never been in a police van before."

"What will they be charged with?" someone asked me.

"I don't think the police have worked that out yet." I wondered myself.

Watty walked up with a bundle. "Present from the boys," he said. It was footage that they had taken from the top of the column.

"Fantastic."

The filming team ran to edit the EPK. The helpers from Greenpeace were putting away the climbing equipment. Steve had suggested to the police that we "grab the banner immediately to prevent it blowing into the road." Not to mention the fact that we wanted to make sure it wasn't confiscated.

"Haven't the police been brilliant?" I was so proud of our police force, proud that I could talk about fantastic policing.

"You know what I heard one say?" Steve grinned. "He said that this was the best event that he'd ever been at and that if all activists were like you lot, then they would never have a problem."

We hadn't heard a raised voice or a cross word. "I hung around and eavesdropped a bit. That Indian sergeant, I think he was actually quite moved."

"Katrina's dashed off to her mum's seventieth birthday party. She says she'll call later," said Rachael. "I'm going down to the police station with the boys. I've rung the solicitor, and she's on her way."

"OK, see you later."

I shook hands with the folks from Greenpeace who had come along for support, and they all vanished, taking their van with them.

On the ground a man with a laptop was looking at photos of the event on his screen. It turned out that he was Russell Boyce, the deputy chief photographer from Reuters.

"I'm actually quite angry," he said. "No one rang us about this. It was luck that I got here in time. Why didn't anyone let us know?"

We looked at each other helplessly. I didn't like to say that I'd been told there wouldn't be much interest.

"Never mind." He said, "I made it anyway, and these pictures are all over the world now. They've just picked this up in the USA and in Australia. It's international."

"Thank you, Mr. Boyce," I said. He gave me his card. "Just ring me next time." And off he marched.

So there we stood: PS, Kate Saunders and her encouraging smile, Steve.

"Time for breakfast, I think. There's a coffee shop in Waterstone's."

The phone was still ringing, and two journalists who were a bit late in the day arrived. "Come and have coffee with us," I said. "We are waiting for the boys to be released so we can buy them drinks." We sat while they asked bemused questions until the phone rang again and it was Maggie, the solicitor, asking us to come down to the police station.

I'd not met Maggie before then, but now I felt sorry for the police. She looked like a fairy godmother from a storybook. Or to be specific, she looked like the cartoon fairy godmother in the Disney version of *Cinderella*. I knew the "boys" would be out soon.

"No trouble," she said. "They aren't going to fine them or hold them or anything. They aren't even going to interview them. They have given them a caution for 'Displaying a picture and taking part in a "performance" without a license.'"

We shook hands, and I took another deep breath. No penalty, and the pictures all over the world. The phone rang; it was Katrina. "You are on the front page of the *Evening Standard,* half-page picture, full color."

Steve ran off to find it, and by the time he got back, Gary and the guys were out. Rachael and I threw our arms round them one at a time. How we loved them all. "Great morning at the office," said Damian. "Where's the pub?"

Two policemen strolled by, and when they saw us all, their faces broke into smiles. "I probably shouldn't say this," said one, "but well done. Where's the crazy bloke that jumped?"

"That'll be me." Gary held out his hand, and the policeman shook it warmly. That would have been a moment to have photographed.

"Pub's over there," said Rachael, who had anticipated the guys' needs. So we piled in.

"You can't imagine what the atmosphere was like up there." Harry's face was one huge smile.

"Damian, did you film the moment that Gary jumped?" I asked him.

"I missed it. I filmed him walking to the edge, and then I had a moment of awe when I looked at the sky, and when I looked in the camera again, he'd gone."

We laughed. I began to feel my breath in my lungs again, and the knot in my stomach started to undo itself.

We passed around the *Evening Standard;* it was a story about Gary, and at the bottom, under a portrait that said "Reward the Dalai Lama," they had written, "They unfurled a protest banner calling for a Free Tibet."

I had to smile. "As long as one of the papers gets it right. That would be good."

The Saturday papers were good to us. The *Telegraph* and *The Times* both ran a picture and an article even though they hadn't been invited. The *Mirror,* despite their exclusive, ran only two paragraphs, including the quote "I was scared s***less" from Gary and no quote about nonviolence. The *Independent,* inexplicably, ran nothing at all. Steve rang me excitedly to say his plumber and bricklayer had seen it in the *Star* and the *Saturday Sport,* respectively. Alison Reynolds called and was lovely. "I have to hand it to you, Isabel. As far as I know the Dalai Lama has never before appeared in the tabloids."

The *Guardian* was the paper that reported it as I had wanted them to, and they quoted the reasons for the action in full, saying: "Governments don't put real political commitment behind the Dalai Lama. If there is a war on terror, then surely we need to reward and support nonviolence." The front page had been taken over by a tragic plane crash, but they ran an amazing photo of Gary in midair with the whole length of the banner in a full half page on page two.

The TV footage made the BBC and ITV main news, it was shown on the half-hour loop all day on Sky, and someone emailed Alison to say that it had been shown on NBC all across America.

Emails flooded in from everywhere. As I'd suggested on the website that people visit their member of Parliament, asking for support for nonviolence, I had emails offering to do just that. We had messages of congratulations from India, Tibet House in London, Washington; Radio Free Asia interviewed Isabel Kelly; two radio stations in the United States ran serious half-hour interviews with me, giving me a chance to talk about nonviolence and about Tibet; requests for copies of the film came in from Norway, from France, from Germany. We had a response.

And of course I sat and reflected on all this two weeks later as the emails started to slow down. Maybe if more and more people did visit their MPs in a friendly and persistent way, then it could directly influence Parliament. It was good that Tibetans everywhere had felt encouraged and that they knew once again that they were not forgotten. We had made a ripple. We had made lots of ripples.

But we hadn't rocked the boat.

PART: THE THIRD

And the Wisdom to Know the Difference

A TRIP TO DHARAMSALA

THE MOST EXCITING LETTER EVER

I had thought, when I began this self-imposed exploration of the serenity prayer, that I could research it neatly. I could consider serenity and then explore courage and maybe, even, eventually, perhaps, albeit very unlikely, acquire a microgram of wisdom.

But life isn't like that, is it? The world doesn't throw us challenges in neat packages. Relatives and friends don't have crises in their lives when we have a free weekend. And the muddle is part of it all.

One day a letter came. The Office of Tibet in London, having been moved by my attempts to support them, seemed to have worked a gentle piece of magic. The letter was an invitation to meet the Dalai Lama.

I had written several months before, half daring to hope that such a meeting might be possible in a dream world. I knew that the waiting list was three years, and I'd imagined that by then I might have had some time to read a little about Tibetan Buddhism, have some intelligent questions, or maybe even have made some small but genuine contribution. But now?

I knew that he had recently been in poor health, that he was nearly seventy, and that he met each and every Tibetan refugee that escaped from China. That thousands risked their lives every year in the hope just of laying their eyes on him. That world leaders took second place. That major sponsors and celebrities who could donate large sums to help build schools and hospitals would have to come third. Then there were those appealing for help from all over the world, those who believed he had magical powers and could cure them. Then devout Buddhists, for whom he was not just a spiritual leader to be admired but a figure to be venerated. I didn't come into any of these categories. Yet here was an invitation.

I drew breath and sat down. I was stunned, humbled, and excited all at once. I thought of all the people in Tibet who were imprisoned for their devotion to him and would never meet him. I didn't have courage like theirs. Why should I be so honored?

Then in another moment I would notice a rush of simple affection and excitement as if I were simply going to meet an old friend. Was this a kind of projection? Was it because I'd read so many of his books, because I'd seen him on film, touring Northern Ireland, or even because of the now familiar photo sitting among those of my friends? Whatever the reason, I felt as if I knew him already.

Many people seem to feel this. Not only Tibetans for whom he means everything but Westerners who have only seen his picture. Everybody likes him. The strange feeling that I had of knowing him already was not mine alone but seemed to be shared by everyone I spoke to. I felt as if, on meeting me, he would shake my hand and say, "Isabel, what took you so long?" And that instant familiarity would be natural and even appropriate.

I couldn't think of any other world leader of whom this was true. Even Mandela, who is similarly loved—I didn't feel as if I knew him.

But I'd had a dream. The Dalai Lama walked smiling and joking, so at ease with himself and with the other characters appearing in my head. When I woke I couldn't remember what had happened, but I felt that I'd met him. The followers of the controversial Indian spiritual teacher Sai Baba say that you never dream of him unless Sai himself wishes it.

I don't think that His Holiness, or HH as people call him, would make any such statement. I would imagine him throwing back his head and laughing and saying that people were free to dream of him if they wished and he hoped the dreams would be useful. But I did feel, superstitiously perhaps, that the dream meant I would meet him. So when the letter came I was half amazed and half not surprised at all.

I realized that Tibet House in London must have told his office about my efforts to support them. Or at least of my persistence. They must have given me a recommendation. This simple kindness must have created this letter. Without it this would have been impossible.

I read:

I am happy to inform you that because of a change in His Holiness' visit schedule we may be able to schedule a brief audience for you, here in Dharamsala. Before being able to confirm the audience, we will need to know exactly what you would like to inform His Holiness and if you have any specific questions.

It was a month away. Far too soon. I wasn't ready. I needed at least six months to study Buddhism. I probably needed that long just to learn to clear my mind of busy thoughts for a second or two. I hadn't read enough of his books. I didn't know enough about Tibetan history and culture. I hadn't done anything or learned anything or changed anything. I wasn't ready. I would have to change the date.

I rang Tibet House in London and told them I'd received a letter. The reaction was spectacular. They were as excited as I was.

"You must confirm it immediately."

I tried, indirectly, to indicate that I wasn't ready, that it was too soon.

"This opportunity has come before . . . I haven't studied . . . er . . . I thought that perhaps next year . . ."

A silence.

I spoke again. "Yes, of course, I'll confirm today."

"Be sure to tell them that you have already made your travel plans."

The message was clear. One does not rearrange.

I put the phone down and tried to gather my two brain cells together. I opened my diary to look at what I thought I had been going to do. This meeting, that meeting, a talk I was giving. Oh heavens, an event already publicized with my name on it. A day of phoning to let down individuals and organizations. But I needn't have worried.

"You're doing what?"

"I've had an invitation . . . you know this Tibet project I've been working on?"

"Who's the invitation from? The Dalai Lama?" (Raucous laughter.)

Pause.

"Yes."

Pause.

"You're kidding? You *are* kidding?"

I'd laugh. "No. Really."

There would follow a sentence that would begin "You lucky . . ." and continue with a row of interesting expletives. It was a most enjoyable hour on the telephone. Sometimes it's fun being hated by everyone.

Preparation for the journey would be easy. India is hot. And it presented some interesting challenges. What would I take as a present? What would you take the Dalai Lama?

I had something that, if I was very lucky, would be a special gift. In his autobiography HH describes how, as a boy, he looked forward to the day when he could leave the Potala, the winter residence of the Dalai Lamas, and travel to the Norbulingka, the summer residence. In the Norbulingka is one building that the present Dalai Lama built. Unlike so many of the dimly lit ancient Buddhist temples it is light and full of glass. One especially magical room is where HH took his lessons as a boy. It is painted in bright yellows and reds with wonderful murals and Buddhas on the wall. It contains two benches, one for the young Dalai Lama slightly higher than that for his teacher.

Now the room he had loved is filled with Chinese guards and rules and regulations, with one particularly stringent rule: "No photography." But I had waited for my moment and broken all the rules, stepped over a rope, and taken a photograph.

It was possible that no one else, having read about his love of that place and then traveled there, would have risked the wrath of the Chinese guards and then had an opportunity to enlarge the photograph and make a gift. Or he might have a huge file of hundreds of photographs brought to him by crazy souls like myself full of the hope that their gift might be unique.

I smiled, thinking that if it were the latter he would no doubt be so gracious in his acceptance that I would think it was the former. Or maybe, as a monk, he wouldn't accept gifts. I set out like an excited six-year-old to enlarge my prized photo to an 8-by-10 and have a simple clip frame made.

"You may like to know that you are making this as a gift for the Dalai Lama," I announced excitedly to the man in my local frame shop on Battersea Park Road.

"Who?"

"The Dalai Lama."

"Who's that?"

I couldn't think of where to start. History, geography wouldn't do it.

"Have you heard of Nelson Mandela?"

"I have, yes."

"Well, the Dalai Lama is a friend of his. I have a picture at home of the two of them holding hands."

"Oh? A friend of Mandela's? I'll make a good frame, then."

HH would like that, I thought. "A friend of Mandela."

Then more fun. I can't imagine life could have many more enjoyable experiences than choosing wrapping paper for HH.

"Take something with suns on," a friend suggested. The Dalai Lama is often described as the sun and the Panchen Lama as the moon. So that would have been appropriate but not what I wanted. I wanted something silly. To make the smiling face smile. I found something ridiculous: dogs with cakes on their heads. Perfect.

Then I wanted toys for the refugee schools. I went to the Early Learning Centre. What a fantastic experience—shopping for children who have nothing. So many children in the West have too much. Too much Fisher-Price. Too much everything. I'd read in one of my Buddhist books that "too much 'mine' leads to too much 'me.'" So I needed to buy toys that could be shared. I found a huge set of indestructible plastic farm animals. I winced as I noticed that they each had "Made in China" across the bottom and, offering a silent prayer that they had not been made by prisoners in a labor camp, I threw them into my shopping basket. I found books with toughened pages and bright pictures without words. Boxes of thick chubby wax crayons. Even a man could have enjoyed this kind of shopping.

Then film. I knew that I'd have the opportunity for a photograph. At the thought of this, vanity kicked in immediately. The Dalai Lama, perfect in every way, and myself, eyes half closed, mouth open on the bad-hair day of the year. Was there no end to my vanity? I wanted to have a photo with the Dalai Lama and look good? I bought film, put sundry items into a backpack, and I was as ready as I would ever be.

I had one more question nagging in some persistent corner of my head. Could I possibly cross the world and not see Khenpo? We had been emailing about the possibility of his sister coming to Britain to do an MA. He'd been driving me crazy by not giving me the simple information that I needed to help her. How old is she? What was her degree in, and where had she taken it? What was her email address? And he'd reply and answer a group of other questions that I hadn't asked.

In spite of all this I had an opportunity that I felt should more rightly be his and I should, at the least, offer to share it with him.

I emailed: "I am coming to Delhi next month and then traveling to Dharamsala to meet His Holiness. Do you want to come?"

Amazingly a logical reply by return, addressing all my points with precision: "I will not come to D'sala but will come to Delhi to see you. Send your flight details."

WALK THIS WAY!

The plane touched down and I emerged, rubbing my eyes, into the pandemonium of the Delhi airport lounge. There among a thousand faces was a smiling face looking at me and then away from me, welcoming me and not daring to make eye contact with the person he'd come to meet. He presented me with a *kathak,* the traditional scarf that is a welcome greeting in Tibet and a sign of honor and respect. Already I felt overwhelmed.

"Welcome to Delhi."

"Thank you, Khenpo La."

"Come! I have a taxi."

I wasn't used to being given orders, but it was good to relax and just do as I was told. "You are OK?" "Put your passport away carefully." "Walk this way!" I walked through the lounge, smiling to myself and thinking of John Cleese.

It seemed a second ago I'd been at Heathrow. And now I stepped out into the air of Delhi, the heat at midnight engulfing me as if I had wandered into a sauna. We climbed into the back of a taxi with Khenpo giving out coins to the beggars that surrounded us in seconds. I had no coins or small notes but they all went away happy with what he'd offered them.

"Get in taxi!"

"Yes, Khenpo."

We drove away with the horn honking at two cows who knew that the night was long and they had no pressing engagements. I gazed at them, trying to adjust to the wonders of Delhi, when suddenly the monk spoke: "I have a gift for you."

Out of his bag came a Tibetan necklace with traditional turquoise and coral.

"Khenpo, it is beautiful. You are so kind."

"Oh yes."

And then he talked to the taxi driver constantly for the half-hour journey to the hotel in the Tibetan quarter of Delhi that he'd booked for us. Separate beds? you are wondering. Yup, so was I.

Then the taxi stopped suddenly in the middle of nowhere. A big wide road in the dark and a little roadside hut. "You drink masala chai?"

"Yes. I do."

"OK. We drink tea." And out we got.

I was blissfully happy. I examined my feelings and found that I was genuinely completely neutral about what his intentions might be. If his intention was to begin a practical study of tantric practice, then, whether it was appropriate or not, I would generously offer myself for his learning. If it was not, then I looked forward to a good night's sleep. I would leave this, along with all other decisions while I was with him, up to him.

The night air smelled of an exotic mixture of Indian spices, unwashed flesh, and rotting food. A group of faces gathered around us in minutes. Khenpo talked to them all. I drank my tea, the best I'd ever tasted, while great fat drops of rain started to splash down. Even the rain was different, as if the spaces between each drop were too wide. Then it stopped raining immediately. "Only joking," said the clouds. It was too hot for them to trouble themselves.

Burnt faces around me, all with identical haunted eyes, looked at me as if I knew something they didn't. They talked and laughed. Whatever cares they had they evidently didn't bring them out at night to serve with the chai. They all wanted to talk to me—except Khenpo, of course, who appeared totally uninterested in his Western visitor.

"We go now." He stood up abruptly.

"Yes, Khenpo La." I was reduced to total smiling obedience.

As we drove through the night, I noticed one place that stood out. It was the Gandhi Museum and Institute. I pointed it out excitedly.

"Look, Khenpo. A museum for Gandhi. Would you like to see that tomorrow?"

"If you want."

"No, I said, 'Would it interest you?'"

"Oh, yes. We will go tomorrow."

He spoke with complete indifference. I felt sure that if I'd suggested the Lotus Temple, which I'd not seen, or the local shopping mall, his response would have been identical.

"I'll come to your room at nine, and we go for breakfast, OK?"

That was one question answered. "Yes, Khenpo."

Silly of me to have thought that, having crossed a country to see me, he might want, at least, to have a conversation. He carried my bag up to my room.

"It is very good to see you," he said as he left the room.

"You, too." I smiled as the red of his robes fluttered away. I collapsed gratefully onto the bed. A huge old fan whirled around above me, and I lay and watched it with a huge grin on my face. I needn't have wondered whether his intentions might not have been strictly honorable. He was obviously going to remain in the category of total mystery. Wonderfully, some people are like that.

WORDS FROM BAPU

I had wanted to see the Gandhi Museum as I knew that he had been a great inspiration to the Dalai Lama. HH writes that young Tibetans have often challenged his policy of nonviolence, claiming that only violence gets noticed. It has even been argued that the terrorists were more effective in telling the world about poverty in Afghanistan than fifty years of nonviolent opposition to China. Many young Tibetans are very angry with him and feel that his policy is one of weakness that has destroyed their country—another monastery razed to the ground, another massacre of innocents. At times he has had to listen to their demands that he allow them to take up arms against their oppressors.

At times like these, as a young man leading his country, the Dalai Lama imagined himself going to talk to Gandhi. He knew that the old man, had he been alive, would have understood but told him that never, under any circumstances, must violence be repaid with violence. For that way, madness lies. As we know.

The institute interested me more than the museum. I knew from friends in London that the Gandhi movement is alive and well in India. People were still attempting to follow him, living a simple life in ashrams and practicing his teachings. I hoped that I had found such a place.

Khenpo arrived punctually and took me for a light breakfast while he chatted in Tibetan to the restaurant owners, and then we clambered into a rusty rickshaw and he chatted in Urdu to the driver. We arrived at the Gandhi statue.

"Institute for Gandhi Studie" it read in huge letters. Not sure the spelling bodes too well for the academic standards.

"So where is the institute?" I had assumed it would be behind the statue. Khenpo asked the locals. A lot of waving and head shaking went on for what seemed like an unnecessary amount of time for directions. Finally Khenpo laughed.

"There is no institute," he said.

"But it says there . . ."

"I know. It doesn't exist. It's just a statue."

"I see. No studie?"

"No."

"And the museum?"

"That exists. On the other side of this road."

We clambered on to a pedal rickshaw to be driven across eight lanes of traffic. "May all the Indian gods I've never heard of be with us," I murmured devoutly to Khenpo, momentarily forgetting that he didn't believe in traffic gods. I gave the driver fifty rupees for the two-minute ride, about sixty pence, and he cycled off as if he'd won the lottery.

The old museum looked so neglected that it almost hurt. Everything he had stood for—his teachings were displayed along with his life in photographs and pieces of his clothing and possessions—it all looked forgotten.

I walked around and looked at the captured seconds of Gandhi's life. A young boy with intense eyes, a law student in London, a political activist in South Africa, and then a world leader in a simple piece of cotton. He was so tiny, half the size of the rest of the gray-suited men who stood beside him. A solitary figure standing for the independence of his people against the might of the British Empire. Bapu, they called him.

"I want world sympathy in this battle of right against might," he had said in 1930. It all seemed uncannily familiar.

"It's not the same," said Khenpo, apparently reading my thoughts. "The Chinese are not the British."

"What's the difference? It's still right against might."

"Yes, but he represented four hundred million Indians against one and a half million British. The Dalai Lama represents six million Tibetans against one billion, three hundred, and sixty-five million Chinese. There is no comparison."* His mind was like a reference book, but that still wasn't the point.

"But it's not the level of impossibility that interests me, Khenpo. It's the inspiration. Look at him. Look at the size of him."

"The British were not as the Chinese are."

"Do you know what the British did in India?" The story was familiar to me, not from reading but simply from Richard Attenborough's epic film *Gandhi,* which I had watched with my daughter every two years since she was fourteen.

---

* These figures, like all figures, are disputed by various experts. For example, one source says there are not 1,286,975,500 Chinese. I have also read that the population of China grows each year by the size of the population of Australia.

He strolled off dismissively, and I wondered whether he was right. Maybe it was hopeless. Maybe I was just a stupid Westerner who knew nothing. But I felt angry with him for being so dismissive. At least I was trying to change something—no matter if I was failing. And why wasn't he doing anything anyway? So I decided I'd challenge him directly. But later.

I looked at more photos: "Gandhi's 241-mile walk," "Gandhi and Nehru," "Gandhi's first fast," "Gandhi with a spinning-wheel, making cloth," "Gandhi's second fast," and then a frail old man on a bed: "Gandhi's third fast."

The warmth in his face was palpable, the tiny stature shrinking more and more as he became an old man. And there it was again in me: a huge affection for a man I'd never met. I wanted to thank him.

And then the next picture. Just like today. All it takes is one extreme fundamentalist. A brave and vulnerable old man with nothing but a piece of cotton between his wrinkled skin and a bullet. Tears pricked the back of my eyes.

Who the hell did I think I was, trying to change anything, anyway? It was all very well as an experiment—the idea of taking on a huge and complex issue—but maybe I'd messed up on the wisdom to know the difference from day one.

I wasn't angry with Khenpo any longer. I had nothing to challenge him about. He knew what he could do, and he knew that he could do his job well. He taught his monks. Maybe it was time that I found myself something that was achievable and concentrated on doing that well. What was the opposite of wisdom? Stupidity. I had that by the bucket-load.

And then, as if to correspond with this train of thought, the electricity generator failed, and we were plunged into darkness. I was glad. I didn't want to see any more. I wanted to sit in the dark. Khenpo walked up to me, "What are you doing?"

"I don't know. Sitting in the dark."

"You want to stay here?"

"I suppose not."

He took my hand and led me out into the sunshine. It was hot and bright and kind of demanding. I blinked, looked behind me, and read what was written on the wall:

Whenever you are in doubt or when the self becomes too much with you, apply the following test. Recall the face of the poorest and the weakest man who you may have seen and ask yourself, is the next step you contemplate going to be of any use to him? Will he gain anything by it? Will it restore him to control over his own life and destiny? In other words will it lead to Swaraj {literal translation: "rule over the self"} for the hungry and spiritually starving millions? Do this and you will find your doubts and your self melting away.

M. K. Gandhi

"When the self becomes too much with you"—we don't tend to think like this in the West, but perhaps the answer was that simple. This was exactly where my thinking had gone off course. Where would focusing on my own inadequacies get me? I could write a book about those. Except I'd already done that. This challenge wasn't about me. My inadequacies didn't matter. The point was to go on anyway.

"Thanks for that," I said to whomever had decided to put these particular words of Gandhi's on the exit wall.

"Hey, Gandhi—what should I do about this?" You can ask the air whenever you want. But you almost always get an answer.

WHATEVER YOU SAY, KHENPO

Then a real voice spoke. "Lunch now!"

"Oh. Yes, Khenpo." I was determined to talk with him at lunch, and I had a plan. Keep away from the Tibetan area. Go to lunch where I would be certain that no one would know him. It was a drastic plan.

"Can we go to McDonald's?"

Yup, it was that extreme. I hadn't been into a McDonald's for years, but it worked. We sat in a building that could have been in Oxford Street. I had his undivided attention.

"So, how are you?" The french fries were as bad as ever.

"Very fine."

"No. How are you? How is your life?"

"Very fine."

I smiled.

"I teach two hours morning and two hours evening. It is very demanding. I have twenty-eight monks in their twenties and thirties in the first class and thirty-five monks between the ages of eight and fifteen in the second class."

"What about the ages in the middle?"

"At eighteen some of them leave. So the ones who stay are the serious ones. I've been asked to teach in a second monastery, and they have over two hundred monks. I think I may teach there between ten and twelve. I don't know. I would also like to travel."

"Do you want to come and visit me in London?"

"I can come, but I have to bring a young monk with me. He wants to live in Ireland."

"But you can't just bring a monk. He needs papers."

"He has them. He has everything. He is monk with refugee papers. It is all OK. They will let him in. I am not a refugee. I will come back."

"I don't understand when you are serious and when you are not. Or what you want. Are you asking me if you can visit?"

"There are many possibilities. I have taught for eight years since I completed my studies. If I take a break, then I have to take two or three months, and they have to try to replace me. But they won't find a replacement. I have an assistant, but he has only studied for eight years, so he can't replace me. To be a khenpo isn't easy. I'm not a full abbot."

"I don't understand."

"I have the title Khenpo because I teach Buddhist philosophy to the senior monks, but I don't participate in the monastic lineage. I don't ordain or do the rituals. I have a qualification from an eleven-year course of higher studies. I am a master of Buddhist teaching. I give classes, that's all."

"What would you like to do? What would your choice be?"

"I don't know. I haven't decided yet. When I'm thirty-eight, in two years' time, I'll decide."

"Why not now?"

"It's not the right time. I'm not going to decide anything in Delhi." He laughed.

"So do you want to bring this monk?"

"It's possible. Maybe I'll bring him and give him to you."

I stared at him, totally perplexed.

"He's Tibetan. From Mustang with its Tibetan language, culture—everything is Tibetan. It's this side of the mountain."

"So are you saying that you think you may bring him? Take him? One day?"

"That's almost right." He laughed, and I was as lost as ever. I drank my coffee.

"Tonight we will walk by the river, and tomorrow you will get the bus?"

"Whatever you say, Khenpo."

And that night we walked by the wide black river in the dark, and he did touch me. He put his arm around me as we walked along, as he must have seen American college boys do in films. And I learned that friendship can sometimes be an uncomplicated thing, and some things we don't have to change. Because we wouldn't want to.

DON'T TAKE THE BUS

If you ever decide to go to Dharamsala, I wouldn't recommend the bus from Delhi. It had been PS's suggestion.

"I love the bus," she'd said. "It's so simple because you get on in Delhi and you get off in Dharamsala." On top of that, I'd imagined that it was the right way to travel. To spend £3.50 to cross India with monks and pilgrims—it sounded like an essential Indian experience.

Khenpo had been insistent that I take two seats.

"You must pay double so that the seat beside you is free. Then you will not have a strange-smelling man falling asleep on you, and you will be able to stretch your legs."

It was obviously a sensible suggestion. And for less than a £10 London taxi fare I bought two tickets.

But even with two seats I wouldn't recommend this journey.

Leaving is fun. The whole area gathers around to try to sell you things. More *chai* tea is served. Hot chapatis are wrapped in paper and sold to everyone, and for the first hour the journey looks as if it will be fantastic. India rushes by outside, and soon Delhi is left behind for an open motorway. In the seat in front of mine two elderly Tibetan monks were chanting their prayers. It was exactly the experience that I had wanted.

Then I noticed that there was, of course, no toilet on the bus. The journey was fourteen hours, and only two stops were scheduled. Also, as we came off the good roads, I noticed that there was no suspension in the bus, either.

Discomfort gave way to pain until I was seriously considering creating an adventure for myself by just asking the driver if I could get out.

"Toilet stop?" I asked hopefully.

"Half an hour, madam."

That was OK.

One and a half hours later we pulled into a restaurant, and I found a sign pointing out to the back of a yard. The loo had four walls and an electric light, but it also had an open roof and an open drain. It had become a small sanctuary for every mosquito in Himachal Pradesh. And there was a large neon sign: "Catch your malaria here."

My antimalaria pills were in an unopened box in London. Panic seized me, and I ran away down a dark alley. No doubt a band of lunatics bent on the murder of an innocent tourist would be passing at that exact moment, but being hacked to death by sabers seemed preferable to facing the killer bugs.

It was only later back in the restaurant that I noticed I was the only female on the bus. Now I knew why. I'd always thought PS a little crazy. Then I ate a veggie Indian meal that tasted like my Hindu friend Nim's home cooking and felt happy again. I resisted the tea.

I think I can truthfully say that the next ten hours were among some of the most uncomfortable I've ever spent. There was no surface on which I could lay my head without being in danger of concussion. Nowhere could I put my feet without having to fold myself up, or risk disturbing the monks in front of me by waving my socks next to their heads, or let my legs protrude to the side—onto the laps of two other monks. They were all sleeping the pure sleep of the sinless. I hated them.

Exhaustion made me long for sleep, but the struggle proved so ridiculous it was easier to give up and stay awake. I looked out of the window into the darkness and told myself that just as all things come to an end so would this journey.

But no, I had found an exception. A way to make time stand still. Hours passed into days, weeks into months and years, and still I was on this bus traveling through a hot and dusty night. My skin began to dry out, my hair turned white, teeth fell from my mouth onto the floor of the bus. The monks, in luminous shades of red, their faces aged by deep lines, began to recite prayers for the dying. I was on the bus ride to eternity.

And then I woke up. It was daylight, and the bus was swerving violently as it climbed up what seemed to be a vertical mountainside. Everything around us was green and lush. I looked at my watch: 7 a.m. Only one more hour to go. I felt sick and aching, but outside was some of the most beautiful countryside that I'd ever seen, and I was glad to be alive and to be in India.

And then it stopped looking like India. Hotels started to assume Tibetan names, prayer flags were draped from houses, and wall banners read "Long Live the Dalai Lama." I noticed a sign that said "India/Tibet Friendship for Ever." The shops stopped selling statues of Ganesh, and Buddha statues appeared, then prayer wheels, then Tibetan costumes, and then the bus stopped. It was a lifetime later. But I was in Dharamsala.

"Go to the Om Hotel," Kate Saunders had told me. "It's cheaper than the Tibet Hotel, where all the important people go, but it's got the best view in town, and the family that runs it is lovely." And as I got off the bus I saw a sign—"Om Hotel this way." I said a prayer for the long life and happiness of Kate Saunders, picked up my suitcase, and swayed in that direction. The Tibetan at reception looked at me. "Journey from Delhi not good?"

"No."

They showed me a bed. "Sleep."

WOULD YOU LIKE SOME MASALA TEA?

If you ever go to the Om Hotel and take the balcony room, bring a clothespin because the smell of the drains at night is something you'll not otherwise forget. Apart from that it has the most fantastic panoramic view over the mountainside. The drop is so steep that you can watch hawks hovering above their prey at eye level. It's an excuse to sit for an hour just watching the way that they casually lift one or two tail feathers to ride a new breeze or spread out their wingtips like fingers to turn. I didn't see them dive to hunt at all. Perhaps, like me, they were just enjoying the sunshine.

Monkeys, too. I don't think anyone raised in Europe will ever cease to be ridiculously excited at the sight of a real monkey running around free. I had to force myself not to gasp, "Oh, look! A monkey!" to the other guests or to the locals, for whom the antics of the monkeys were a daily nuisance.

They were just so watchable. The mothers would strut along with one baby on their back and another clinging upside down to their tummy. The young ones would run around chasing each other and taunting the females. The males would jump up and down and screech at each other. Screeching seemed to be the main game. Wouldn't it be great if we could just jump up and down and shout "Eeeek! Eeeek!" at people?

Anyway, where was I? Oh, yes.

I'd been given a number to ring, and someone had evidently been told of my various schemes because I was summoned to meet a local government official who provided me with a driver and a guide to see whatever I chose. I was asked if there was anyone that I'd like to meet, so I requested a representative of the Tibetan government-in-exile and then added ambitiously that I'd also like to speak with the new "prime minister," Professor Samdhong Rinpoche. To the audible sound of eyebrows being raised I was told that they'd see what could be arranged. Meanwhile I'd be collected for a day's visits the following morning. I was shocked and even a little embarrassed to be treated with such generosity. Once again it seemed as if I were being looked after.

The remainder of the day was free to do a little shopping.

I hate haggling. Do you? It seems that some people love it and consider it a game. The Israelis are great at it, which is unfortunate because 80 percent of the visitors to D'sala seem to be Israelis. The shop-owners must hate it when they hear an English accent. I was imagining them thinking, "Oh no, not one of those mean scrooges."

I was innocently walking along browsing, as one does, when I was caught by an excellent English accent. "Hello! How are you? I do know you, don't I? You've been to Dharamsala before, surely?"

"No."

"But you seem so familiar to me. I feel as if I know you. Would you like some masala tea? It's my shop up here."

It was obviously the young salesman of the year. "What are you looking for? But I'm not selling today. I'm tired. You can just come and look."

The clothes, cushions, and carpets looked amazing. I stepped in to look for light trousers. He made me masala tea. He invited me to sit down. He told me the story of his life. I laughed; I drank tea. The sales patter was even better than the Irish antique dealer's on Battersea Park Road.

I looked at the cushions. They were "only about £2 sterling." They were beautiful. I thought about what I spend on coffee in London. No point in buying one of these amazing cushions; as a present you would have to buy a pair. Then my daughter would want a red one and this friend would like blue, this friend orange. They all seemed so cheap.

"You have such a good vibe." He went on, "You seem to me to be a very special person." He poured out more tea with his flattery.

"Do you teach classes in how to sell?" I asked him. "I actually came in to look for some cheap cotton trousers. I brought jeans, and they are far too hot."

"Something not too ornate would be your taste, I guess?"

"You sell trousers, too? Oh dear."

"Don't worry if you don't want to buy. You can go and compare prices elsewhere to be sure and then come back if you like." He made yet more *masala* tea with the best spices and honey. It tasted wonderful and sweet.

I left his shop, having spent £25. It did seem to me to be a huge sum, but I loved the trousers and the nine cushion covers that I'd bought for friends. I justified to myself that I had to shop a bit to support the local economy. I'd been asked for a wooden chess set, and I turned into a tiny shop with an extraordinary selection. They were lovely, but I explained to the owner that I'd just spent 1,800 rupees and I was feeling broke.

"How much?!" He looked at me in amazement. "What did you buy?"

"Some cushions. Lots of cushions."

"Show me," he said, shaking his head sadly. I showed him my cushions.

"You've been robbed." He sighed. "It must have been a Kashmiri."

I smiled. "Well, yes. He did mention that he was from Kashmir."

"And he probably made you tea?"

I laughed. "Yes. Obviously I have 'Fair Game' written across my forehead."

So I walked away from the second shop feeling sad. As if I'd been robbed and I was foolish and gullible. Until I noticed what had happened. After leaving the Kashmiri I felt happy and amused. I'd been well entertained, and I was pleased with my purchases. After leaving the second shop I felt dejected and stupid. So which one had robbed me?

TWO DOGS DOING IT

The following morning as I strolled out to meet my VIP guide I was greeted by the sight of two dogs shagging. Now, there's a bizarre thing. It had never struck me before that if you live in a city the only things you ever see doing it are pigeons (she doesn't like it much) or people on TV (the earth moves for her). No wonder we are all a little confused.

Our bizarrely artificial life has become so sanitized that reproduction, like death, is something that we just don't come face-to-face with. Maybe if we had dogs and cats and monkeys and cows and horses all copulating merrily in the streets, then we wouldn't have parents who don't know how to explain the much-dreaded sex issue to their kids. This ends my short homily on the subject of the reproductive act.

While I'm on this digression and keeping you hanging around for the continuation of the narrative, do you know the story of the native American who goes to the great chief White Eagle to ask about the origin of names?

"We name our infants according to the first event that is noticed after the birth," explains the chief. "So Rising Sun over there was born just at the moment of the dawn. Sitting Bull was named after the great bull that sat down after his birth." There was a pause. The young boy did not seem content with the explanation. "So tell me," asked the chief, "why do you ask, Two Dogs Fucking?"

DAVID BECKHAM, VERY GOOD FOOTBALLER

My guide was a young Tibetan women called Yangchen, who had taken an MA in Norway and whose English was almost perfect. She wore the traditional Tibetan clothes and was unnecessarily polite. I explained to her that I wasn't anyone important and would she please just call me by my first name. If she and I were to spend a week together, then the guide and guest roles would have to go. I told her about my life in London, and I noticed that she relaxed very quickly.

Our first stop was to be the Tibetan Children's Village. Two thousand children of refugees, up to eighteen years old, are educated in this huge complex, along with some Indian children whose parents have noticed, as I did, that the children all look ridiculously happy.

They are almost all boarders. I was taken into one of the "houses." Thirty-six children in one house. The two bedrooms, one for boys and one for girls, house an equal number of each gender, with beds in rows like something out of a *Matilda* storybook.

"How old are the children who live here?" I asked admiringly of the woman with all thirty-six of them in the house under her single individual care.

"They are aged five to sixteen."

"That's a very wide age range, isn't it? Do the older ones enjoy having the younger ones around?"

"They love them. Each older child has a younger child that they look after. They act as mothers and fathers and take care of them and help with schoolwork.

"They sleep two in one bed. The older ones with the younger ones. It's nice for them all, and in winter it helps them to keep warm."

My mind boggled slightly. Everything seems so simple here. We are so used to the idea of sexual dysfunction in the West and there are so many kids that have been messed up that this simply wouldn't be possible. Of course most of the damage to our children in children's homes is committed by adults and very little by other children. But even then I couldn't imagine the outcry in Britain if older boys in children's homes were asked to sleep with younger boys. Here it simply wasn't an issue. I wasn't going to ask, "Do you have any problems with sex?" I could see the answer. These were normal healthy kids who had never known cruelty and for whom cruelty would not therefore be possible.

It sounds as if I'm being all pie in the sky, doesn't it? But the only time I'd heard a raised voice all the time I was in the Tibetan community, it was raised in song. Honestly. It was only when I got back to London and heard a mother screaming, "Don't you bleeding speak to me like that!" to her six-year-old that I fully realized what I'd just left.

We walked past the classrooms, and the children sat in huge classes, chanting spellings.

"This teaching by rote," I said to Yangchen. "We don't do it any more."

"Why not?" she asked. "We find that children singing the word spellings works very well."

I was tempted to say, "We found that rote learning didn't work." But then I could have added, "And we have children who can't read or write when they start secondary school."

In another classroom children strained forward at their desks to answer questions. It all looked too good to be true. The classrooms of the older children were decorated with notices that made me reach for my notebook.

*Look for the good in a person if you feel like
saying something mean.*

*Apologising doesn't always mean you were in the wrong—
it means you are sorry.*

When someone has been successful, compliment them.

Try to make others feel better when they make mistakes.

Let your friends have other friends.

Goodness, there seemed to be something in the syllabus other than the grade levels. What a concept. Maybe it was all an illusion. I wondered if they had children manacled to walls in the cellars, locked up for the slightest misdemeanor?

"Do you have corporal punishment?" I asked her.

"What's that? I don't understand."

"Smacking? Hitting? Do you hit the children if they are naughty?"

Yangchen looked horrified. "Oh no. Many years ago they did this but not for many years. No."

Maybe here it was possible for education to be an enjoyable and effective process.

"I have some gifts," I said. "This class looks about the right age. May I give them to the teacher?"

"She will be very happy."

I proudly presented her with my "Made in China" farm animals. "Oh! Look!" She passed them round the class to delighted laughter. "I can use them as a teaching aid." She looked at me as if I were Father Christmas. I then gave her the eighty chubby wax crayons. I've never seen anyone's eyes go wider. Then I produced the books with the stiffened pages and the lovely pictures.

What it says in the New Testament about giving is true, you have a witness, because receiving presents never felt as good as this.

It all looked so lovely, and I wanted to stay. I thought of my own childhood. No brothers, no sisters, no friends around me to play with. I wondered what kind of person I would be now if I'd had thirty-five brothers and sisters but no mother that loved me and let me know that, for better or worse, for her I was "special."

This "being special" thing we do in the West. Does it really help anyone? It is evidently not true—a quick trip through India for anyone who needs to be reminded how unimportant the individual is. And the truth is there are millions of us.

The next stop was the Tibet Museum. A short history of Tibet. I smiled and nodded. It would have been interesting if I'd been a tourist and hadn't spent the last six months reading every book of Tibetan history I could lay my hands on. I walked around thinking of a hundred ways the museum could be improved but decided in one of my rare moments of wisdom to keep my bucket-loads of unsolicited advice to myself.

Walking out past some copulating monkeys, we grabbed a quick lunch before being escorted back to the car for a trip to the Norbulingka Institute.

Now, the Norbulingka, as you now know as I'm sure you've been paying attention, was the Dalai Lama's summer palace in Lhasa. Here he has recreated the beauty of the gardens and the Tibetan buildings to house an arts college for all the traditional Tibetan arts.

Like tourists we were able to stroll into a room where, in total silence, twenty artists sat on the floor painting holy *thangkas*. These paintings of the Buddhas are used for devotion in the way that Christians use icons. Each one would take twelve months or more to complete, the detail on them requiring hours of painstaking perfectionism.

I was lucky to see a Buddha drawn with all the perspective lines still in place, each angle measured out with perfection to create an exacting symmetry. Instead of Leonardo da Vinci's man standing in his measured circle, the Buddha sat serenely meditating in his. Before seeing the real thing I'd found *thangkas* too obscure to be interesting, and I now realized that I'd only ever seen cheap prints. This was a conversion experience such as someone might have if they had only ever heard music on a poor-quality radio and then, one day, heard an orchestra.

The paintings had a beauty that took my breath away. Twenty artists in a room that is completely silent all day. As they paint they sit cross-legged on the floor, and while they paint they pray. They were all in their twenties.

Then we moved to another building, which housed the furniture painters. How different this was. They chatted loudly to each other, and when we arrived they chatted to us. I looked around. Traditional Tibetan designs are often red, like so much else, and the ornamentation uses bold primary colors and intricate designs. Then a portrait photo on the side of a work desk caught my eye. It was not of the Dalai Lama, whose gentle eyes smiled down from numerous portraits that had been pinned up over the years, but I thought I recognized the face. Have you guessed? Yup, it was David Beckham.

"What's this?" I demanded in a mixture of amusement and horror.

"David Beckham, very good footballer," said the young man.

"Yes, that may be. But why do you have his picture here?"

"He my favorite footballer."

Well, obviously.

The next room, where they made metal Buddhas, I didn't like. It was noisy. No matter what you are making, metalwork involves hammering. A half-made Buddha lay on the floor, his head not yet on his shoulders and mainly in pieces.

I smiled at him. If all Buddhas were like that, we wouldn't have such trouble recognizing our Buddha nature. I put my camera together and took a photo of him—the only photo I'd taken since leaving London. Yangchen looked at me quizzically.

"Look, he's just like us," I said. "Only half made, all in pieces, and with our heads not yet on our shoulders."

"You don't move the hammer to take the picture?"

"I don't think so. What else are they going to beat him into shape with?"

"And the old bits of metal beside him? Shall I take those away for you?"

"The thing is, Yangchen, that I think he's perfect just as he is." I took another photo.

I think she was coming to the conclusion that I am a little odd.

The day ended perfectly by my being able to slip off my shoes and walk into the Norbulingka temple. A huge shining Buddha sat looking happy, and in front of him, in his rightful place, was a photo of the man who had inspired all this: the fourteenth Dalai Lama of Tibet.

I couldn't even begin to meditate on the fact that I was going to meet him. I sat for five minutes in front of his picture and the Buddha statue. I just looked at them both while they looked at me.

And then I got up and walked out into the greenery of the blissfully beautiful journey up the mountain to the little hotel room that already felt like home.

CHICKEN TONIGHT

"I am never going to eat chicken again. That's it. From today I'm going to be fully vegetarian," I exclaimed to a guest innocently sitting having a coffee on the veranda of the Om Hotel.

"Why's that?" he asked politely.

"I've just seen the most terrible thing. Three chickens alive in bags with their feet tied together and terror in their eyes. I asked the man who owned them, who evidently wasn't Buddhist, whether he felt any compassion for them. 'I have an English guest for dinner,' he said, smiling. 'He said that he wanted to eat chicken.' So I said, 'But couldn't you let them out of the bags until you kill them? Look at them.' And he looked at me, the strange English woman, and took them out of the bags. I thought about buying them from him and letting them go."

My fellow guest stirred his coffee. "He'd only have bought three more."

"That's what he said. And then a friend of his arrived with a large knife. They saw me wince. The man with the knife smiled at me and asked, 'Are you a vegetarian?' The answer until that moment would have been that I don't eat red meat, but I eat chicken. But today I answered with certainty, 'Yes, I'm a vegetarian.' I knew that I would never eat chicken again."

"Then what?"

"He picked up the terrified creatures by the legs and, looking at me with a mixture of amusement and disdain, he threw the poor creatures in the back of his van."

"Thank God the story ended like that. I was afraid you were going to put me off my breakfast," said the young man, a Buddhist pendant around his neck.

"It's not really the end of the story though; it feels like a beginning," I said.

"So I have a question for you." He smiled at me as if holding the winning card.

"Yes?"

"What about fish?"

IT IS HELPFUL, YES

Then suddenly one day I felt quite cross. I had been welcomed royally by the Tibetan government and shown around with magnanimous generosity. The point of the trip, however, was not for me to enjoy myself but to learn something about how individuals can support the Tibetan cause and hopefully to acquire a little wisdom. So with that end in mind I'd asked if I could interview a senior government politician, someone with energy who was going to be positive and would have ideas for the way forward. Tibet House in London had given me the name of a man who was "young and dynamic." I anticipated the meeting eagerly.

The thing about politicians (our own, that is) is that we may not trust them, but we must at least hope that they are clever as their decisions affect us all. Many years ago I met my first member of Parliament because he was also the director of a TV company that I worked at. His name was Phillip Whitehead, and he had a brain the size of a planet. In the year I worked for him I never discovered a single subject about which he was not fully informed. And I'm not just speaking about British history and politics; his knowledge was international and encyclopedic. As well as this he had a passion for his work and the energy of ten men. More impressive still, he was a good listener, polite and generous and with a razor-sharp wit to match his intellect. I assumed that all MPs were like him.

Subsequently I've met some more and discovered why our country is in the mess that it's in. It's scary when people in positions of influence are not cleverer than I am. I find it very confusing. How did they get the job? And why?

These are questions I asked myself this morning. There are many brilliant Tibetans in the world. There are Harvard graduates, acclaimed scholars, and fantastically successful businessmen. So why on earth, I wondered, was this man in this job?

There is, of course, nothing wrong with not speaking English. But if you are giving an interview and don't speak well enough to answer the questions, wouldn't you bring a translator?

I smiled in a friendly and approachable way and launched into my first question: "What do you see as the relationship between Western campaigning organizations and the attitude of the Chinese government on the Tibetan issue, or do you consider that these issues are unrelated?"

I turned on my tape recorder expectantly. Then I sat with a be-mused expression on my face while I listened to the answer. He was speaking in English, as far as I could discern, but the sense of the words was eluding me.

"Could you please repeat that more simply?" I asked. "I'm not sure that I fully understood you."

He obliged, talking for some length of time. I stared at him blankly. Honesty was the only way forward. "I'm sorry. I don't seem to understand you."

"My English is not so good," he said.

I didn't like to be impertinent, but decided I would be.

"Would it perhaps be easier for you if we invited a translator to join us?"

"Oh yes. Very good idea."

So then I had two of them. But I'm still unable to provide you with a coherent answer to the question. I thought I'd try an easier question.

"What do Western groups do that is helpful, and what is not helpful?"

"It is helpful, yes."

"What is?"

They talked Tibetan between themselves. The translator said. "Groups help us, yes."

"But what exactly is helpful?" I thought I'd help them out a little. "Don't they put letters in the rubbish bin? Does the Chinese government really listen?"

"Lesson?"

"Listen." I spoke calmly, taking on the air of a very patient lan-guage teacher.

"Actually they don't listen anything."

"So is it better if people write to their own governments?" I think we were now on to what is called "a leading question."

"First they should do. Then there are so many pressures to Chi-nese government."

This was not the interview I had hoped for. "Would it perhaps be wiser for Tibet support groups to work specifically for genuine Tibetan autonomy within China? Or not?"

"Yes. They should know the Tibetan problem. Tibetan government is for the Tibetans. What the Tibetan government policy is. So let them forget Tibetan government we are doing and other things. That's not good. They are for the Tibetan curse."

I think he meant "cause."

"So if they are seeking to support Tibet, shouldn't they be giving the same message to China as His Holiness?"

"Yes. It is Tibetan problem."

I began to feel exasperated. "Have you approached them, then?"

"We cannot instruct them. They are independent."

OK, I'd been here before. I was going to make no progress down this line.

I struggled on for a while. Maybe I was just talking to the wrong person. Either this man wasn't very bright despite his position, or he thought that I wasn't. I hoped dearly that it was the latter.

At the very least I needed a statement of what the Tibetan government wants, to put on our new website.

"Would it be possible for you to give me a brief statement, with your name and today's date, of what the Tibetan government wants?"

"We want negotiation without any precondition so that Tibet and China problem can be solved. Yeah. This problem is not only Tibet, it is Chinese government problems also. First they should know that problems for both of us. We have problem, our problem. Both problem, so if there problem we should solve."

I had a problem. "Yes. I understand, but would it be possible for me to have a formal statement in writing? Five or six lines?"

"Tibet means not only autonomous Tibet. What we call Tibet is three provinces: central Tibet, Kham, and Amdo."

"I know. But, er, for a website, I'd like something in writing about what your government wants."

"Genuine autonomy."

"Yes. I know what you want, but I don't want to use my words."

"Negotiation should be as soon as possible."

The translator tried to help. "He wants to say that there must be self-rule comprising for all three provinces. Negotiations didn't come on table, problem didn't solve each other's."

I started to tear out my hair and scatter it over the floor in front of them. "Yes! I understand! And would it be possible for me to have a formal written statement?"

I gave up. A different question. "Tibet House in London has only two staff members for the whole of northern Europe. It's impossible for them."

"We are refugees. We have no funds. Without funds how we send more staffs?"

I felt sure that it should be possible to create interesting voluntary short-term opportunities for their brightest graduates, but this obviously wasn't the place to discuss the concept of work experience. "Do you have any advice for people who are trying to help gain freedom for the eleventh Panchen Lama and his family?"

"The United Nations declaration because we have to see it. Because China is also in the UN. They should follow all these child-rights declaration."

I wasn't sure where this was leading either. "You mention the UN? Do you think the UN is helpful at all? As far as I recall it has never helped Tibet."

"UN is helpless. Actually United Nations not all world. Not for all countries. They have five countries that we do power."

So what was he saying? I was asking about what could be done, and like so many people involved, he was telling me what couldn't be done.

"So if the UN can't help, then what can help?"

"Same thing what I told people. Tibet support groups should pressurize their own governments. He is not just a political prison.

This is time for education for that Panchen Lama. What we told before."

"Yes." I sighed deeply. I stood up and held out my hand to shake his. "Thank you for your time."

So! Do not let it be said that in this book I have painted a glowing picture of Tibetans or given them unadulterated praise. I had heard stories about their ancient and bureaucratic systems and the inefficiency of the people running them. Now I had experienced it firsthand.

I had been impressed by almost everything else I'd seen. People with compassion at the center of their belief system, a profound spirituality, gentle schooling, dedicated artists, and hardworking businessmen. But it seems that in one way they are the same as many other countries. They are let down by their politicians.

TORTURED AT NINETEEN

I'd never met anyone who had been tortured before. Are you tempted to skip this bit? Perhaps you're not as bad as I am, but I think that has always been my attitude. I know that people are being tortured as I write this, but I like to forget it. Or imagine that somehow it happens in another world far away from mine, or at least that there is nothing that I can do about it.

They had asked whether I'd rather meet a man or a woman. I'd said a woman. We are physically so much weaker. I'd found it even harder to believe that it would be possible.

I was shown into the office of a tall smiling monk who turned out to be the president of Gu-Chu-Sum. A notice on the wall read:

We, the members of the Gu-Chu-Sum Movement of Tibet, are all ex-political-prisoners or their families. Most of us have spent many years in prisons and endured brutal torture, just for exercising our right to call for basic human rights in our beloved Tibet. After years of oppression we have all had to flee Tibet. But we can never be happy until all Tibetans are free.

I hadn't noticed that, as I was reading, a tiny, mousy woman had come in and sat down. She barely looked at me. She barely looked up from the floor. Could this woman have been a victim of torture?

The monk offered us all tea and left his office. Yangchen and the girl talked for a while in Tibetan. The girl looked up at me. "Her name is Tenzin." It was a strange introduction. I smiled, not daring even to hold out my hand to shake hers. I felt strangely ashamed to be asking her about what had happened to her. To ask her about being tortured was, in my eyes, to torture again, to put her focus back to a past that was ever present for her. But I knew that she wanted to tell her story. I had asked them specifically to choose only someone who wanted to talk to me.

"Please ask if she has interviews like this often?" I asked Yangchen.

"Five or six times in the last couple of years. Not as often as she would like."

They talked softly to each other in Tibetan while I watched them.

"Could you ask her, please, how she feels about talking about these things?"

"She wants to talk, but sometimes journalists who don't know about Tibet and the Chinese don't believe her. Then when she tells them what happened and they don't believe, she is very sad."

"Why would she lie?"

The question was repeated.

"She says that she doesn't know. She has never lied in her life."

I almost didn't need to ask her about her life; I could see with my eyes. She looked as if someone had broken her. Picked her up and snapped her and all the energy and life force had been drained out. But I was here to listen, so I switched on my tape recorder and began. "May I ask how she came to be arrested?"

They went on talking softly, and I noticed how she kept constantly moving her hands, touching one with the other, stretching out her fingers.

"She was nineteen years old. It was the year His Holiness won the Nobel Peace Prize. 1989. They went out, she and five friends, some younger, some older. They sat on the pavement and started to say "Long live the Dalai Lama" in the Drepung square. They were there less than five minutes. Chinese guards came from everywhere. They threw them all in a van." Yangchen looked shaken translating the story. "The people around in the street began to cry and shout, "They are taking our people away!" And then she doesn't remember any more of the arrest because they hit her hard on the head."

I tried to imagine the courageous young girl that she must have been then. If the Chinese had wanted to crush her spirit, they had succeeded.

"Then they interrogated them for fifteen days constantly. They beat them and tortured them."

She demonstrated how they had used a form of Nelson's lock—one hand twisted up behind and the other reaching up and then pulled down between the shoulder blades. Then they joined the two with a chain that they tightened until the screaming was loud enough.

"Is it a stupid question to ask why they tortured a group of teenage girls?"

"It was because they didn't believe they had chosen to support the Dalai Lama themselves, as they had been brought up in China. They were convinced that they had been organized by someone else from outside China. They wanted them to tell them who it was. They tortured them to try and make them confess to who had organized them, but it was no one. It was they who had wanted it. They had known the truth of Tibetan history for many years, so when they heard that His Holiness had won the Nobel Peace Prize they were proud. They considered him to be their true leader."

She turned to Tenzin, asking her to go on with her story. They were not allowed to sit or sometimes not allowed to stand. They were given only one half cup of black tea a day to drink. She says she was so thirsty she would cry and beg them to allow her to have water, but they refused."

"Was she in a cell at night with her friends?"

"No. She was alone."

I couldn't imagine it. Even with her here in front of me. Perversely I could understand why journalists were not able to believe her. But I believed her. I could see it in her eyes. A look that I'd only seen before in terrified dogs at Battersea Dogs Home, dogs that had been beaten. I'd never seen this fear in the eyes of a human being.

"So what happened then?"

"This went on for fifteen days. Then they sentenced her to five years in prison. Some of her friends that were slightly older were given eight years."

And this country has been given the Olympics. Human-rights organizations are not being allowed the right to peaceful demonstration because the National Olympic Committee insists that they must not mix sport with politics. Can someone explain this to me?

She told her story without tears. Just a heavy, heavy sadness.

"Her family wasn't allowed to bring her anything. No clothing or food. Not even a sweet."

I imagined what I would do if my daughter were in prison in these conditions and I could do nothing for her. I think that might genuinely drive me mad.

"They were six women in a tiny room with just one open bucket in the corner. One of them was allowed out each day for fifteen minutes to empty the bucket. The food was pushed in through a small hatch. There was one electric bulb that was on both night and day."

No. I couldn't imagine it. She got up and indicated the size of the room. About six foot square. I didn't really know what to ask next. I struggled to find something half positive to say.

"It's a miracle she's alive."

"She has a blood problem, and her kidneys are not so good. She has to go often to hospital, and she has had an operation on her kidneys. She had stones in them."

"How old is she?"

"She is thirty now."

"Does she work here?"

"Yes. She learns computers, but she is very weak."

I looked out of the window at sunshine and smiling faces. "It can't be easy, living here in the exile community after that. I mean, most Tibetans are passionate about your cause. But many that live here are second-generation and don't really understand."

"Yes, she says it is difficult. In Tibet all they wanted was their freedom, and here people have it."

I knew she meant "and don't know what they have."

I looked at her. She had been free for years now, but she didn't seem to have even begun to recover.

"Is her health better now?" I smiled, clutching at a straw.

"They tell her that she will never be well again."

I suddenly started to sound as if I were in a "new age" seminar. Later I sat and listened to myself on a tape, saying these things: "Please tell her not to believe them. Tell her the mind is strong, she should imagine herself strong and well and discover what will help her to get there. Tell her anything is possible."

And even as I heard her translating, I knew how ridiculous I sounded. "Anything is possible?" In what Californian seminar did I hear that? Maybe it was possible that she could recover fully, but maybe it wasn't. Not everything is possible. To change the past isn't possible. To go back in time and say to her torturers: "Why are you doing this to a girl of nineteen?" Or to break open the doors of the van and let her out and say, "Well done for demonstrating. It was a brave and courageous thing you did. But don't do it again because your Chinese government is crazy, and you don't even want to imagine what will happen if they drive you away."

As I left I saw a some faces of prisoners on the wall and stopped to read just one story.

Phuntsog Wangdu joined Ganden Monastery when he was fourteen years old. In 1990 during the re-education campaign he, along with seventeen other monks, was expelled from Ganden Monastery. In October 1990 Phuntsog fled to India and joined the Buddhist School of Dialectics in Dharamsala. In 1993 he returned to Tibet to visit his ninety-year-old grandmother and while still in Tibet was arrested and detained without charge for six months. After being released his movements were restricted so he stayed in Lhasa for the next three years. On the eve of the Tibetan New Year he was arrested and taken to Gutsa Detention Center, where he was beaten mercilessly. While at Gutsa he was also handcuffed and put in leg irons. After continued beatings he became so weak that he could no longer pick up his own bedding. He tried to commit suicide, but failed. In June 1998 he was charged with "espionage" and sentenced to fourteen years' imprisonment. His appeal was rejected and he was transferred to Drapchi prison. He is due to be released in 2011.

At the time of writing this, of the 135 political prisoners in Tibet's notorious Drapchi prison, 99 are monks, 21 are nuns, and only 15 are laypeople.

It had seemed bizarre to me when I had first read that one of the biggest threats to Communism was Buddhism.

A DAY OFF

So Sunday came, and me being brought up a good Christian girl, like wot my grandmother tried to do, I had a day off.

I had spotted a couple of interesting white faces around and decided to have lunch with them. I climbed into one of my beloved motor rickshaws for a journey out of town to a village called Bodi.

If this had been England, there would have been a sign, "Designated as area of outstanding natural beauty," and a hotel would have been built. And then I spotted a little hotel. Someone had created a typical English-style guest-house. There was a little veranda surrounded by a lawn for serving drinks. And at the edge of the veranda, the mountainside fell away to a distant valley. The little terrace looked very out of place but utterly delightful. On it sat three figures sipping drinks in tall glasses under a large white umbrella. They turned and waved, and amid general exclamations of "Aaahh, you found us!" I pulled up a chair and joined them.

The white faces I'd stumbled on, in one of the posher shops into which my feet had led me, were no ordinary tourists. When I'd asked Helen, from Switzerland, when she had first come to D'sala, she'd said, "About thirty years ago, and I've been every year since." The second, Sue, from Oregon, was on her first visit but was also not just here to enjoy the views. "I'm teaching Montessori to the teachers of the three- to six-year-olds." She talked about her work with a passion that was good to drink in.

"If you get education right at this age, you have no idea what a difference it makes. I find that the younger the children I work with, the greater an impact I can have."

The third white face had already gone red sitting in the high-altitude sunshine. "I don't need suntan lotion," said Ed, the other American, before removing his sunglasses, revealing two white circles and making me hoot with laughter rather unkindly.

"Thanks for that," he said. Refusing Sue's offer of lotion, he went on sitting in the sun.

Ed was a business executive who had run his own company and done very well. He had tired of the rat race and, joining an organization called Tibet Volunteers, had traveled to India for the first time to stay for a year.

"What do you do?" Sue asked him.

"Whatever they want me to. I'm available to the Tibetan government-in-exile for whatever they need. I've just finished teaching a series of three-day courses on starting small businesses in the various Tibetan settlements. I know about business, but I've never taught before so it was, ah, kinda interesting."

He had in front of him a copy of the *Tibetan Book of Living and Dying*. "I've been meaning to read that," I said. "Do you recommend it?"

"If you have an interest in the various states that you'll experience between one life and another."

"There is so much to learn in Tibetan Buddhism."

"Yes, but don't worry because you have an infinite number of lifetimes to learn it."

What a fantastic thought. In the West, where we think that we only go around once, people are sad because they think their childhood is gone forever; and they are in a rush because there is so much to fit in before we get old. Or at least—when I say "people," perhaps I should speak for myself? I'm in a rush most of the time anyway. The Tibetans and Buddhists I've met who genuinely believe that we have an infinite number of lifetimes are full of patience and serenity. They have more than all the time in the world.

"And Helen, what brings you back again?" I looked at her with admiration. She, too, was one of these calm types—so elegant, so relaxed.

"Pleasure, this time. I sponsored two girls in the Tibetan Children's Village years ago. They had escaped with their mother and baby sister, but both the mother and baby sister died, and they were left here as orphans aged three and four. I sponsored them both. Anyway the older one is at Madras University now, doing a master's in economics, and the other one is just finishing her degree. I used to come to see them, but this year I've just come for the teachings in the temple."

"How amazing to have extra daughters like that."

"Yes. That's how it was. They were just like my own only they cost less to bring up." She smiled. "Considerably less."

So these three had all found a positive way to contribute, each using their own skills. I thought I'd run my question by them. "I'm exploring the serenity prayer . . ." They all nodded. "Do any of you have any thoughts on how the individual can apply it to the wider cause of Tibet?"

Helen spoke first. "I don't think there is much that one person can do. I think we need to look at everything that happens in the world from a much larger perspective. People often get very upset and very unhappy because we look at the situation closely, especially when it affects ourselves. So many things have happened, so many disasters, and we have thought, 'If this happens, it will be the most dreadful thing, and we, as a race, will never survive it.' In the final analysis it doesn't always work out like that. We have to have a really large perspective, historical and international."

I listened carefully.

"You are so young," she continued, "but if you'd been in the last war . . . it was so dreadful. We thought it was the worse thing that had ever happened with the concentration camps in Germany . . . but now we've gone beyond it, and there is another conflict looming."

"But people died."

"Yes, but life is this."

This sounded like the historical and internationalist perspective on reasons not to do anything.

"Are you saying that people shouldn't try to make a difference?"

"I think one needs to make a difference in one's own surroundings. Not hurting anyone else and helping them if you possibly can. Doing absolutely the best you can. If you can be a good example in your own family, I think it makes a difference. There may come a time when we can do something physically for the wider world. There may never come a time. I think we have to accept that."

I did not accept it. I would not accept that such a time would ever come if I did not keep creating it.

"'Courage to change the things we can'? Everyone knows that the only thing that we can change is ourselves." Ed looked at me as if he were having to explain the bleeding obvious.

Sue smiled agreement.

"You need to meditate."

For the first time in months I felt a wave of anger.

"Well. That's fine, then! I'll listen to you three and go off to a nice comfortable Buddhist temple and learn to meditate, which I'm sure I'd enjoy very much. And meanwhile political prisoners in China will continue to be tortured." I was off on a little tirade. "I think you'll read that the Dalai Lama teaches 'My religion is kindness' not 'My religion is meditation.' He teaches about compassion. Surely kindness and compassion are actions." Suddenly I liked the name Act for Tibet. At least it wasn't Meditate for Tibet.

"We have to change ourselves." Sue looked at me in a Buddha-like way.

I took a deep breath. "I need to explain that I do agree with you. I know that we have to be responsible for ourselves, to change ourselves." I'd written a book on the subject, as it happened. "But it can be such a cop-out . . ."

"I have a question now," said Sue grinning at me.

"Yes?"

"Do you meditate?"

"I, er . . . not often."

They all laughed.

"How can you hope to be effective if you don't meditate?"

I could still reply. "And how can you be effective if all you do is meditate?"

"I know that what I do is effective. I've seen the changes in the children." Sue had a reply every time, and so did Helen.

"My sponsees are at university. I'm very proud of them."

"And without meditation, what have you changed?" asked Ed.

I was in a corner. "Not much."

Then Sue piped in again, "Why do you think His Holiness meditates for three hours a day despite being one of the busiest people in the world? Look at what he has achieved." She obviously had the eternal truth on her side.

"Like the Nobel Peace Prize, for example," Ed added. Rather smugly, I thought.

Sue was enjoying herself now. "Without meditation you are simply running around like a headless chicken, giving no deep thought to what you are doing."

That was rather how it had felt. "But if everybody did what you suggest, where would that leave Tibet?"

"We never said, 'Just meditate.'"

I agreed with them on one point. "I know that we need to change ourselves first and be at peace with our families and those around us."

So in theory we were agreed. I could see that choosing some small way that I could make a tangible difference might be better for my peace of mind. If I could convince myself that it was enough. But I still felt thankful for all those people who tried to take on the wider issue. Geldof didn't sponsor a child, he tried to feed the world. And yes, Helen was right, there are still people starving. But he still fed a lot of people. And there is still a caste system in India despite Gandhi's attempting to send this wretched belief into the history books. But I'd take Bob and Bapu for inspiration, and if that meant that I still didn't have the wisdom to know the difference, then I was happy to remain crazy and misguided.

I do realize that sponsoring two children from childhood through to university may certainly be a better contribution to the world than putting a picture of HH into two days' worth of newspapers that are soon forgotten. The sponsorship in the Tibetan Children's Village works well, and it doesn't set sponsored children apart from their peers. Of course it's important for each of us to ask, "What can I do?" If Sue decided to teach Montessori here or any of us contribute where we can by helping a child in our own community, that's one way to change the world.

But what I had wanted to do was not just to look at the local level but to take on the larger issue. It may be that these three, older than I am, were also wiser, or maybe sometimes it's good not to have the wisdom to know the difference. What's the old line? "Fools rush in where angels fear to tread." I had no regrets about grappling with the attempt to make real change. Through the Act for Tibet website, individuals were now talking to their MPs about Tibet, applying persistent, friendly nagging, one MP at a time.

So the stunt wasn't a one-off event but maybe the beginning of a commitment to Tibet that would last a lifetime or several. Maybe that's how long it would take me to find the wisdom to know the difference.

I sat with Helen, Sue, and Ed, and we looked at the view. We ordered some Tibetan tea and sat and sipped it before we turned with amusement to watch, just a few feet from where we sat, the merry sight of two goats, er, doing it.

OVER THE HILLS TO FAR AWAY

The following morning I was taken to the reception center for recent arrivals from Tibet. To the question of whether I'd rather meet a man or a woman, I again said a woman. I couldn't imagine ever being that brave.

We arrived in what looked like a large barracks with about thirty beds in one room for the men and another big room with mats on the floor that was empty apart from the woman we had come to meet. She was lying in the corner on a mat. As we crossed the room she sat up and rubbed her eyes sleepily. She must have been at least six months pregnant.

Yangchen started to ask her questions while I looked at her. A round face with burnt skin, beautiful thick black hair. I recognized the look in her eyes now: a mixture of sadness, fear, and a weariness far beyond her years.

"She's twenty-three years old. A nomad from Amdo. This is her first baby, and it's due soon. She came out of Tibet with her nephew, who was eighteen months old, and two children aged eight and nine."

"Hold on, Yangchen. Could you please ask her what her name is?"

"Her name is Rinchen; she escaped five months ago. This is very unusual. Normally only recent arrivals stay here for up to three weeks. It seems that normally she would have been sent to the school or to work, but as she was pregnant she couldn't do this, so they found a room for her, but she didn't know anyone there so she came back here. This doesn't normally happen."

"How did she get out of Tibet?"

They chatted animatedly. A group of refugee children gathered around us to listen and stare at me. "She traveled for four days from her area to Lhasa, the only adult with all these children. Then in Lhasa she was able to meet up with some others who were getting out. They traveled together in a jeep from Lhasa to a point at the border that she can't disclose. Then they paid a guide, and it took them three days on foot and under cover of night to get out."

"And she did all this pregnant and with three children?"

"Yes, she did. She says that she took a great risk and came out in summertime. She says that those she traveled with were very kind to her."

"What would have happened to her if she'd been caught?"

"She'd have gone to prison like the other girl we met." I tried not to imagine her being beaten and wondered if they show mercy to pregnant women.

"Why do they take such risks? Please ask her."

Hollywood makes films about escapes like this. She was so young, and I doubted that she could read or write. But does education teach courage?

"She wanted to be close to His Holiness and to have a chance for an education for herself and her child. In China she can't afford to go to school, but here her child will be educated. Also it will have Tibetan education."

There are many more like her. Another group of recent arrivals was expected the following day.

"She will have to give up her baby to be looked after at the orphanage otherwise she won't be able to work."

"What? She can't keep her child with her?"

"Who would look after it when she went out?"

"When I was a young mother someone would have had to kill me before I would have given my child away."

"But if you had known that it would be well loved and well cared for and that you could visit whenever you wanted and that if you kept it you wouldn't have been able to feed it?"

I didn't like to think about it.

"What can we do for her? Will you follow her progress to see if they have a room for her? Will she manage to get work?"

"I don't know. There is very high unemployment here."

"What does she hope to do? Can you ask her?"

"She says that she hopes to go to school. She has never been to school."

"So she can't read or write?"

"No. This will make it almost impossible for her to find work."

"You couldn't help her get work as a cleaner in your office?"

"Even to work as a cleaner in the government buildings you have to do basic administration tasks, and she wouldn't be able to do these."

"How much money will it cost your government to house her and educate her child for her? Will the child need a sponsor before it can go to school?"

"No. The Tibetan government manages to provide education for all who want it."

"And nobody goes hungry."

"No."

And no one would be unkind to her. I imagined myself or my

daughter in her position, but it seemed impossible. Twenty-three years old and she felt like a heroine to me. I tried to remember why we treat people so badly who risk their lives to get into Britain.

"Do you ever have incidents here of racial violence? From the local Indian community?"

"There is some resentment of the Tibetans because they work hard and, compared to many local people, they become well-off. But there are also many people employed here because of us, and we bring many tourists. We do not have race violence. No."

"So can I give her a gift?"

Yangchen asked her if she would receive a gift as payment for our talk. We had agreed that I shouldn't give her money, so I took a Tibetan necklace I had bought, in the style preferred in the area she came from, and presented it to her. Suddenly she looked her age, and her tired face broke into a broad smile. I wanted to give her something a little more practical, and I remembered the Kashmiri carpet seller had offered me a free woolen shawl that I had declined. I would go back and claim it and pass it on to her.

"We have to go now." Yangchen looked at her watch. And we helped each other up to our feet. The pregnant refugee, the government official, and the English visitor. Much nodding and shaking of hands, and my guide and I left. She lay back down on her mat to go to sleep.

WEARING A CHUPA

I had a few hours to spare before a meeting of a very different kind. I was thrilled to have a private meeting with Professor Samdhong Rinpoche, to whom the Dalai Lama had passed all his political authority. He was the newly elected Kalon Tripa of the Tibetan government, rather like a prime minister. The big boss. But before the meeting I could play for a while.

I wandered the muddy streets filled with the best mixture of Tibetans in their traditional costumes, Indians in their fantastically colored saris, Israeli tourists in their newly purchased pashminas, more beggars constantly challenging my conscience with their hands outstretched, and an amazing assortment of cows and dogs wandering around the street stalls. It was all so busy, so friendly, and so cheap.

I'm sure you've discovered this when traveling. It's easy to spend money because the prices, relative to Europe, are so low that it becomes a crime not to spend huge amounts. You walk up to a beautiful exotic item that catches your eye on a street stall, and it is so ludicrously cheap that it feels like an affront to the stall holder not to purchase it. Along with sundry items on the next stall.

So far I had purchased nine cushion covers, one wooden chess set, one pair of trousers, one Indian silk scarf, three T-shirts, one roll of Tibetan prayer flags, one small sandalwood pot, two pairs of earrings, one ring, one bracelet, and one small Buddha statue. Total cost? Well . . . not much. Relatively. I suppose.

Today was the day I was going to buy a *chupa,* the traditional Tibetan dress. I could have it made to measure for £2.50, and the justification that I could wear it to meet the Dalai Lama and then for Tibetan events in London was all the excuse I needed.

First you choose a blouse, and the *chupa* is worn over it. It's a specially shaped dress that folds over at the back to ensure that, whatever the size, one's bum does not look big in it. Most excellent. Then, if married, you wear a colorful stripy apron. By not wearing the apron you are advertising "Woman available here." The men, of course, have no such dress code. But then I amused myself by remembering that, in traditional Tibetan homes of old, one woman had several husbands. I would have lived very happily with this system. One husband who was intellectual, one who could put up shelves, one who had money, one who played the piano by ear and could transpose, one who spoke Spanish and Italian, and one who was good, er, who enjoyed doing physical things. And they could all see me by appointment only. What do you think, girls?

But back to my new *chupa.* "In some areas of Tibet all women wear the aprons, and even here, on festival days, unmarried women wear them, too, so the men can never be totally sure," Yangchen had assured me. But I was young(-ish), free(-ish), and single(-ish), so no apron for me.

I'd asked the Tibetans in India if they thought that Westerners wearing *chupas* were silly, and they'd said that only those who were really interested in Tibet wore them, and so Tibetans liked it. Daring to hope that Tibetans in Britain thought the same, I bought my dress.

I walked out of the shop like a six-year-old. How can any woman not be thrilled with a new dress, all in red and made specially for me. Now I was ready to meet the prime minister.

AN HONEST PRIME MINISTER

There were some who were not happy with the election of Samdhong Rinpoche to the top job in Tibet, because he was a monk. Many Tibetans have had enough of the world thinking that they are all monks. But he was obviously the best man for the job.

He didn't want the job either and, rather fabulously, wrote a ten-page rejection outlining why he didn't feel that he could do justice to the job or the Tibetan people. He was then instantly elected, and the Dalai Lama confirmed him as his own choice for the post. So he has the job.

Of course the world still thinks of the Dalai Lama as the political as well as the religious leader, but this has ceased to be the case. HH has insisted, since 1962, that the parliament be elected by the people in order to exercise true democracy. He had to change a constitution that was nine hundred years old, to do himself out of a job. But he has succeeded. He has enough to do being the spiritual head.

I was secretly amazed to have been granted an appointment. I had remained in doubt until the last possible day that it would happen. I'd made my request, but days had passed until I'd had the meeting confirmed. Parliament was in session, and a huge delegation from the Italian parliament had arrived to discuss Chinese intransigence. There were queues and much frenetic coming and going. I could see why, as a monk dedicated to the inner life, Samdhong Rinpoche had been keen to avoid all this.

He walked in briskly and shook my hand. This was an altogether different kind of monk from the stereotype of the smiling Tibetan that we in the West have come to expect. He was thin, almost wiry, with a long drawn face and a very serious expression. He looked like a man who took the fact that the plight of six million people rested on him very seriously indeed, and he wasn't about to waste two seconds. No ceremonial scarves here. I'd asked Yangchen to join us in case of any language difficulties, but his English was fluent.

I sat up straight, opened my notebooks, and began my questions: "What do you feel is the role of Western campaigning groups in your relations with China?"

"The role Western groups play is always a positive one. In the seventies and early eighties some Western pressure was negative, and China's response was negative. Today of course China claims that they do not take any notice of Western pressure, but we know that, these days, only Western pressure works. The recent good gestures of the release of some long-term political prisoners and allowing Tibetan people, such as our delegation, to visit China—in my opinion these are basically to appease Western people."

"Do you have any thoughts or advice for Westerners who are interested in helping Tibet?"

"Any show of solidarity and support from Western people is good because it is spontaneous and voluntary support. This support is not political, it is just loving people supporting us, and this is a very strong message. In spite of China spending a lot of money and using all kinds of political and economic tactics they are not able to . . ." He hesitated.

"Prevent people loving you?" I smiled.

He laughed. "Yes. And on the other side the Tibetans have nothing to offer—we have no political power and there is no economic incentive, and yet groups to support Tibet are growing like mushrooms everywhere."

"Isn't that fantastic?"

"It makes China . . ." Again he paused, choosing his words carefully. "Nervous. But if I may add that, at the moment, in order to encourage the possibility of negotiations between China and His Holiness, we would like everything to be as positive as possible."

"So if I can take a specific example, this question of writing letters, do you really think that it makes a difference, and if so should we be writing letters to our own governments or writing to China? And surely if we are writing to China, then the letters should be in Chinese?"

"Letters to China in Chinese are certainly most effective." Did I detect a slight smile in his eyes? A hint of irony in his inflection?

"Do you think writing to the Chinese leadership directly, works?"

"Yes, I think when you write to China they feel it very much. Especially when many people write."

"And do you think that this is more important than contacting our own MPs?"

"It is necessary to do both."

A simple answer.

"May I ask you about the Panchen Lama? One of the things that we would like to achieve is for the United Nations to be allowed to send a delegation to confirm that he is alive and well."

"You know China's position on this, I'm sure. They say that he is alive and well and receiving a good education, and this I'm sure is true. But he has not of course been allowed to learn the Tibetan language or to learn about Buddhism or that he is the Panchen Lama."

I sighed rather wearily. "And what do you think will happen to him?"

"My personal belief is that China is preparing him so that he will come to the public and state that he is alive and well but that he is not the Panchen Lama."

It was so simple to explain to people: a real-life Harry Potter, kept in his cupboard, made to go to a muggle school, and taught that anyone who calls themselves a wizard is full of superstition, until he believes himself that he really is a true muggle and is offended and frightened by his own people, who tell him that he is really a wizard. I imagined him learning about "the Motherland" and the glories of Communist China. Shame about all the monks that had spent their lives waiting for him or lost their lives for his previous incarnation. The Chinese government should be protectors of these people.

Lost in my thoughts, I heard the click of my tape recorder and looked up to see Samdhong Rinpoche waiting patiently for my next question.

"Your tape, I think, needs turning." He smiled politely. I flipped the tape.

"Tell me," I asked, "about the Tibetan organizations in Europe and the United States. In your opinion wouldn't it be better if they worked with you in seeking genuine autonomy?"

"We are grateful for any support that we receive, no matter what the policies of the separate organizations are. We just ask them all to continue. We don't interfere."

There was a pause. I looked at him. He looked at me. I waited for him to say more. I looked up at him and smiled. He smiled back. But that was obviously the end of that topic. Change of subject.

"I wanted to ask about Tibet House in London. They are so overworked. How can you expect two people to cover Tibetan matters in the whole of northern Europe? Wouldn't it be possible for you to send another member of staff to London?"

"We are thinking of closing some of the offices in Europe in order to save money. Our funds can only sustain three offices in Europe, so we are thinking, for example, of closing offices in perhaps Paris or Prague and having more people in London. It is very expensive for us to run these offices. Sixty percent of the funds of the Tibetan government-in-exile go to maintain these offices. It is too expensive."

This was not good news. I hoped that these plans would be ditched before he came to London.

"Europe is very big," I remarked with academic brilliance. "These places may look close on the map, but Prague and Paris are different countries."

He laughed, obviously overawed by my brilliant contribution.

"On a more personal note . . ." I jumped in at a relaxed moment. "I understand that you didn't want this job? Are you enjoying it now you are doing it?"

"It is a challenge for me. I have to do it with vigor. But actually I feel I am not oriented for this. This kind of political leadership, unfortunately, particularly these days, needs people who are flexible and compromising. I am from a religious background and a monk, and I cannot compromise. What do you think?"

He amazed me with his question. "You want to know what I think?"

"Yes."

"I was at the Gandhi exhibition in Delhi last week, and I read that he wrote, "I am on the side of right against might," and you have that. Your job also requires patience, which you have from your monastic discipline, and the only other quality that the job requires is humor."

He smiled. We stood up.

Still I didn't stop talking. "Oh and I need to ask whether you would like to give our new effort in London a commendation? I wanted to ask you rather than His Holiness."

"Certainly I will write something. You can pick it up from my secretary tomorrow."

I liked Samdhong Rinpoche very much. He was honest and open. Goodness, what a thing to write about a senior politician. I felt that with him there was hope through all this mess. That the unwilling leader could lead and would lead. That the skills that he had learned as a monk—discipline, diligence, a sense of perspective, and an unfailing commitment to the Buddhist principles of nonviolence whatever the cost—these were fantastic qualities to have in a political leader. I indulged myself in a little fantasy. Professor George Bush Rinpoche? Only allowed to lead his people because of his commitment to nonviolence and his determination to turning around the economic divide and to creating understanding between the West and the Muslim world. His one constant question: "How can we bring about more understanding and more respect for our different points of view?" Professor Bush would of course ban the gun in America as he believed in nonviolent resistance at all times.

On the radio recently I heard the story of a youth in the States who was recommending the use of the gun. As they do. The interviewer asked him, "And what about Gandhi's teachings about nonviolent resistance to evil?"

"Who?" he replied. He had never heard of Gandhi.

REHEARSAL WITH THE DEPUTY SECRETARY

So now it was the day before the day before the day that I was to meet the Dalai Lama. First I had the briefing with one of his secretaries, Tenzin Taklha, a man who several people had mentioned to me as being one of the best-looking Tibetans around, the best educated, the most fluent in English, the most humble, and, of course, the most happily married. Ah, well, can't have everything. I made a ridiculously long list in my notebook of all the things that I wanted to discuss with him in preparation for my meeting with HH. I spent a day reading his *An Open Heart* and looking at the view from the Om Hotel balcony. I ate Tibetan momos and had an early night.

I woke almost as excited to be meeting the deputy secretary as I would be on the morrow. I donned my Tibetan *chupa* and set off with a new cartridge in my ink pen, a huge smile on my face, and a heart brimming over with happiness. I felt so undeserving and yet so blessed. How strange the world is sometimes. The sun shines on the unjust as it does on the just.

Tenzin Taklha must have been in his late thirties or early forties and with looks that took my breath away. I had to try to find a way to tell him about another idea I'd had of how to publicize the story of the boy Panchen Lama, who had not been on my banner. I sat in front of him with the most ridiculous enthusiasm and began, "Have you read *Harry Potter?*"

"Pardon?"

"*Harry Potter.* The children's book. Have you read it?"

Yes, I had just asked him the most unlikely question that anyone who had sat in his office had asked. That was evident.

"I have not." He enjoyed the moment for a second and then smiled at me. "But I've seen the film."

"Oh good. That makes things much easier for me."

He raised an eyebrow rather stylishly.

"You see, one of the things I wanted to do was raise the profile of Gedun Choekyi Nyima, and it struck me that there are so many parallels between Harry and Gedun."

He looked understandably dubious.

"Don't misunderstand me. I'm not saying for a moment that J. K. Rowling knows about Gedun but just that Gedun's case can be explained to the next generation so easily by talking about Harry . . ." I began to get into my stride. "Harry is born uniquely placed to help his people. He is special from the moment of his birth. As is Gedun. But they both become separated from their own people and live with another race that is suspicious of their powers and their potential. Both are locked up, by a people not their own, 'for their own protection.'"

He still looked rather dubious.

"In both cases their own people need them, and in both cases a special place is reserved for them in a kind of mystical school that they need to be educated in to develop their powers. In Harry's case, Hogwarts Academy; in Gedun's case, Tashilhunpo Monastery."

He began to look slightly less dubious.

"I could say that in the background are two supreme figures of goodness in Dumbledore and the Dalai Lama, both of whom refuse to resort to evil to fight evil, but that's not the main point. Harry's powers will never be realized unless he goes to Hogwarts, so he receives first one letter and then millions of letters. You remember the scene in the film?"

"I do."

"Now, Gedun has also been sent millions of letters and birthday cards by his people and by others from all over the world, but—and imagine explaining this to children everywhere—in his case not a single letter will get through. There is a real-life Harry Potter out there, but he will never be allowed to go to Hogwarts, Tashilhunpo. The muggles won't let him. He has been made to stay forever in his cupboard under the stairs."

"Isn't there a danger that the Chinese will say it is fiction?"

"Well, what I'm hoping is that the story could be used to explain about freedom and Communism and religious persecution. So it wouldn't really matter what the Chinese government said; children all over the world will know what has been done, and it is just possible that could made a difference. Gedun will never be told who he is. It's terrible. It's like Harry growing up and never knowing that he's a wizard and having to go to a muggle school and growing up thinking that he's just another muggle."

"Yes, that's what they will have told him."

"And the real-life version is even worse because of the other little boy who has been told that he is the Panchen Lama when all his people know that he is a fraud. And they'll never accept him. With this comparison it is easy for children to understand why the Tibetans won't accept the Chinese Panchen Lama. And if it is true that the Chinese are preparing the true Panchen Lama to come forward after his muggle education and say, 'I'm just a muggle,' if the children can be told the story they'll know what has been done to him, and they won't believe it . . ." I was excited by the parallels; they worked so well.

He smiled at my enthusiasm. "There is just one thing here. His Holiness will not have heard of Harry Potter."

"But he reads the papers. He listens to the BBC."

"Yes, he does. But he will not have heard of him, and he will certainly not have read it. I can assure you of that." He looked at me sympathetically. "He is a very busy man."

"But he'd have to read it. It's not such a crazy idea. If all the children who've read *Harry Potter* could learn about Gedun, that could be really effective." I paused for breath.

"You can explain all this to him. Speak slowly; his English is not perfect."

"And that's part of my problem. It's taken me ten minutes to explain it to you, and you've seen the film. I don't suppose that he'd have . . ."

"No. Do you know his schedule?"

"Yes, actually I do." I had read it in Mick Brown's brilliant book *The Spiritual Tourist.*

I flipped open my notebook. I had written it out at the beginning for inspirational purposes: "He rises at 3:30 a.m. and spends an hour meditating and does prostrations for thirty minutes. He eats a light breakfast at 5 a.m. and then meditates and prays until 9 a.m., pausing to listen to the 6:30 a.m. news bulletin from the BBC World Service. He spends an hour dealing with state and private papers. He spends his afternoons on government matters and in meetings. At 5 p.m. he drinks Tibetan tea and sometimes watches some television. His evenings are spent with scripture and in prayer. He goes to bed at 9 p.m., and he always sleeps soundly."

"Quite right. So as you are so well informed, you can understand . . ."

"Seems to me that he has a window round about 8:45 p.m. when he could fit in a bit of *Harry Potter?*"

He smiled at me.

"I suppose the chances of him popping out for a video aren't that high, either?"

He laughed. Come to think of it I hadn't spotted a video store on the temple grounds.

"Just say what you need to."

I hadn't come here to talk about Harry Potter.

"Also I'm worried that this will take up all the time, and I didn't come to talk about this. There were two more things."

"Yes?"

"I wanted to tell him about my project. To ask his advice. I'm trying to explore what one person can do to help. Any one person, to make a difference for Tibet. It would be crazy to come all this way and not ask him what he thinks."

"So you must ask him."

"Yes, but that wasn't what I want to ask him, that's what I feel I must ask him. What I'd actually like to ask him is different."

"What is that?"

"I'd like to ask him what you do if you have acquired one tiny, tiny bit of serenity to accept what you can't change and a smaller amount of courage to change something but zero wisdom to know the difference. I know wisdom is the Panchen Lama's department and the Dalai Lama's is compassion, but—call me optimistic—I think that he knows something about wisdom, too . . . so I'd like to ask him."

"You ask him that, too, then."

"And would it be OK if I record it all?"

"Yes, it would be OK."

"And a photo would be lovely."

"No problem."

"But how am I going to fit all this into fifteen minutes?"

"Don't worry. Everything will work out."

"Please, if you speak to him for two minutes between now and tomorrow, please explain why I'm bringing him a copy of *Harry Potter.* I mean, so that he knows I'm not crazy. Not completely crazy."

He didn't promise to do this.

"And I have a present for him. A photo from Lhasa. Does he receive gifts?"

"He will receive your gift, yes."

He stood up and held out his hand to shake mine. My briefing was over.

"We thought you were coming for a blessing."

"Oh. Sorry."

"That's OK. We'll fit it all in."

"Thank you." I walked away happy and then rushed back again. "Would it be possible for him to sign a photo for my daughter?"

"No problem."

I wandered into the sunshine with Yangchen. "How was he? He has a reputation for good looks and being a very kind person."

"It's all true." I was skipping on air. "He's gorgeous. And he didn't say no to anything."

PINCH ME, SOMEONE

Tomorrow I meet the Dalai Lama. Pinch me, someone.

Time had sped on towards this day without mercy. Why was I so ill-prepared? Why had I not spent more time here in silent reflection and study as I had intended?

Why had I spent days off chatting to Sue, Helen, and Ed? Why had I spent so much time browsing around the street stalls of Dharamsala, buying presents for friends, and so little time seated in front of the Buddhas?

Maybe what felt like my affection for HH was actually a lack of appropriate respect for the fourteenth Dalai Lama of Tibet. Maybe seeing my capacity for overfamiliarity he would be stern and distant with me to teach me the correct way to approach a spiritual figure of his stature. Maybe he reserved his friendliness for the lowly or those who approached him with trepidation.

Maybe he would speak just one sentence of irritation, and my heart would crumple. And then I remembered how he had been in my dream. Just there, so easily and so at peace with himself.

And so now here I am. And this is the present. And it's tomorrow. I pinched myself. Yes—it's tomorrow—it's a change of tense.

I have run the full gamut of emotions. I feel absurdly nervous. Not so much because of who he is, because I know that he will be kind and gracious, but because I'm afraid of messing up. I've been allocated twenty minutes, but I have at least forty minutes of things I want to talk with him about.

Ridiculously I really want to tell him that I was born on what is undoubtedly the most significant day of his life, the day that he left Tibet. Friends have joked that maybe I was one of the few Chinese soldiers who died and I'm having to do this project to pay back some bad karma. And of course it's pure ego, but I'd love to know if he thinks it's significant in any way. Or maybe he'll just smile and nod tolerantly and think, Why is she telling me this?

I have determined not to burst into tears, however wonderfully touched I am. So many people burst into tears. I saw a documentary of the Duchess of York meeting him. Poor Sarah had to walk straight out of the room with him and into a room of TV cameras. She struggled to voice her impressions to the waiting crew but just started to cry and took several minutes, under the cameras' full glare, before she could compose herself enough to speak.

Many people have told me that he just has to look at them and they start to cry.

So I kind of think that, were he not too gracious to allow himself such a thought, he might find all this emotion rather repetitive. And, anyway, I don't want to take him my pain and sadness as an offering. I like to imagine that I've almost dealt with that. I want to take him my joy.

I know in Buddhist terms he is profoundly holy and a being to be venerated and prostrated before, but there is a paradox. When he describes himself as "just a simple monk," he must almost be having a joke. I think he makes that statement when people assume he has mystical powers. Whether he actually has any or not no one will ever know because it is against the laws of Buddhism for anyone who has any highly developed abilities to make claims for themselves. I think it is safe to assume that he has, at the very least, what we could call a "highly developed sense of intuition," but he says he is "just a simple monk." Like all the others? I don't think so.

I still can't believe that I'm going to meet him. This figure around whom the entire Buddhist world revolves and, it would be possible to argue, has revolved for the past nine hundred years. This man who has taken some of the most obscure philosophical teachings of all time and summarized them into "My religion is kindness."

Maybe it will all be a big disappointment. Maybe he will say nothing, and I'll have to spend all the allocated time listening to the sound of my voice instead of being able to listen to his.

The wisest part of me didn't want to say anything at all but just go and sit and look at him and thank him for existing. For not repaying evil with evil. For being the one sane voice in the world. To say all that with no words. I wanted to thank him for all that he is to everyone in the world. To thank him for his laughter even though I'd never heard it.

It's 11:30 p.m. He's been asleep for two and a half hours already. Maybe it's time for me to sleep, too. The giddy flying sleep of a child before her most exciting day ever. So far.

HIS HOLINESS THE DALAI LAMA

I am wearing my red dress, and I feel more completely aware of the present moment than I have ever done in my life. I stand in a waiting room with walls covered with certificates from all over the world. A large portrait of Gandhi looks down at me. I try to take it all in. Tenzin Taklha appears, smiling. He shakes my hand.

"You have your gift?" I am clutching two gifts: one, the photo that I took in Lhasa, the other, absurdly, a copy of the first Harry Potter book for possibly the only person in the world who won't have heard of it.

"Should I leave my jacket on? Or take it off, do you think?" I ask. What a stupid question. How idiotically self-conscious I feel.

"As you prefer." He smiles gently. I suppose he must see people from all over the world reduced to this.

"Are you ready?"

Am I? Am I ready? No, of course I'm not ready. Will I ever be ready?

"Yes, I'm ready."

I walk out of a door and down a courtyard. Into a simple and elegant room with chairs and a low table. I look around and put my tape recorder down.

"Will His Holiness sit here?"

Surely he'll need space? He won't want to sit too close to the likes of me surely?

"No, he'll sit there. You sit there."

This seat next to mine? Not an inch between us? God, I hope the tape recorder works. I checked it five times this morning.

A door opens. A man walks in that I met briefly yesterday, the translator; he smiles at me. Then an older man, the senior secretary to His Holiness. He smiles and bows at me. Why is he bowing to me? I bow back. And then . . . a man enters with an energy I've not felt before. A huge energy. It really is The Dalai Lama. For a moment I feel a strange desire to run. But I can't run. There are too many people between me and the door.

What do I have to do next? The scarf, the ceremonial scarf. You bow and put it round his neck. Or do I? Do I just bow and hold the scarf? Does he take it? I bow, holding the scarf, wondering what happens next. I am panicing. He approaches me, smiling, and takes the scarf—I think, for I hardly dare look up. And, as I stay bowing, he puts a scarf around my neck. It is twice the size of the one I've given him. That can't be right. Eventually I look up. He smiles at me gently. He looks at me as if seeing me through binoculars the wrong way round. As if he is a long, long way away and there is a solar system of space between us. Yet his smile travels all this way and reaches me.

"Won't you sit down?"

I sit. Everyone sits. Except Tenzin Taklha, whom I see, from the corner of my eye, observing me with a broad grin on his face. There I was yesterday—so brazen; and here I am today—not a word.

I'm not one given to describing people's "energy fields." I don't see auras. I'm not psychic. But here is an energy that even I can feel. The man is huge. Physically I see an elderly Tibetan. He is approaching seventy years old, not thin, not overweight. He isn't particularly tall, and his face is, well, it is just as we've all seen it smiling from a million pictures. No surprises there. And he is warm and modest, just as I'd expected. But this energy . . . what is this? I feel myself lost.

Say something, Isabel.

"I've brought you a present."

I pass him the photo in the simple clip frame that I had wrapped so carefully in London. He looks at the paper of the dogs wearing silly hats, and I hear for the first time his low, deep laugh.

"Very funny dog." He chortles and fiddles with the tape.

Oh shit, why on earth did I wrap the thing so carefully? How thoughtless of me. He doesn't have fingernails like a woman; he's an old man who doesn't have time to mess with sticky tape. His secretary steps forward with scissors. I hear words coming out of my mouth.

"I took this photo in Lhasa at the Norbulingka. Of course you are not allowed to take photos, but I avoided the Chinese guards. I remember reading in *Freedom in Exile* that you particularly liked this room, and I thought that maybe you would like to see it again."

The secretary takes off the paper and hands it back to me. I remove the hardboard and the bubble wrap. It's covered with broken glass. I hadn't thought to unwrap it and check. I feel the ground fall out of my world.

"I'm so sorry. The glass is broken." I can't do anything. I promised myself that I wouldn't burst into tears.

"It doesn't matter." Tenzin Taklha speaks up, kindly rescuing me from my mortification. "We'll change the glass."

"I'm so sorry. It must have happened on the journey. I should have checked." Why had I checked everything else and not this? Why had I trusted the hardboard and the bubble wrap? I want to cry.

The Dalai Lama ignores the glass and looks at the photo.

"This *thangka* was not here when I was a boy. They have brought that from the Potala. I remember this *thangka*."

The broken glass has ceased to exist. "And this was not here." He points to a stool in the photo. I watch him as he looks. I have put things before his eyes that he hasn't seen since he was fifteen years old, and yet there is no emotion in his eyes at all. He doesn't seem either touched or grateful. He isn't moved at all.

I wonder if I've done something profoundly stupid in bringing some of that past back to him. That past that was so painful. Yet I know that this was a room that he had once loved in a palace that he designed and built himself. I watch his face for a flicker of emotion. There is none. He looks up from the picture.

"That is the past," he says, waving his hand in the air as if to brush it over his shoulder to the place where it belonged. In the past. Over. For a moment I am incensed. He dismissed the past with a wave of his hand and my present along with it. This was not the reaction I anticipated. I was hoping to touch him somehow. But I realize in an instant that this is a man totally devoid of sentimentality.

In a workshop I did once they spent a day talking about "putting the past in the past." And Westerners talked on and on about what had happened to them, how it had affected their present, how they could not function because of this or that event that had occurred twenty, thirty, forty years ago.

Perhaps because I still dream of the house where I lived when I was a child, I had imagined that the Dalai Lama might also be attached to his memories. I had forgotten that nonattachment is a key teaching in Buddhism. This was certainly a clear example.

I look up and there are his eyes looking at me. He doesn't need to say, "This is the present." His meaning is clear. It is a bit like having a bucket of cold water thrown over me or someone saying, "Wake up! The work is now." Only his eyes are warm—full of deep warmth.

He doesn't speak. But this is the most articulate silence I've ever known. I pull out the next present. This time, Isabel, open it yourself; don't waste any more of these seconds.

"I've also brought you a children's book. This may seem a strange gift, but I've brought it because I believe the story may be a way to help Gedun Choekyi Nyima." I tell the story. All the comparisons. All the similarities. I tell him that children all over the world have read this story, including children in China. He listens.

When I've finished he looks at me and says, "We must find out if the author has any interest in helping Tibet."

That was that. I stagger slightly under the clarity. It's like playing tennis with an expert. I'm surrounded by balls all on my side of the court. I'm running around; I can't even reach them to hit them into my own side of the net.

And yet this warmth. This love that I am being bathed in. Where am I?

"You wanted to ask me something?" He speaks first, seeing that I have quite forgotten who I am.

Where is my notebook? No, damn it—I don't need to look at my notes. I know what I'm here for.

"Yes . . . I wanted to ask . . . where Tibet is concerned . . . what can one person do?"

He sits back to answer and becomes more formal for a second. Maybe they have told him in advance that I would be asking this. That I am a "journalist."

"That's a difficult question. I think like Gandhi, who at that time made some impact. But I think that, even for humanity as a whole, Gandhi's nonviolence is truthful. He made a difference. In South Africa and India he made a difference. But not just him alone. Without millions of Indian public, without heritage of India, and without British imperialist rule of law, freedom of expression, without that, even at that time . . . with a totalitarian state, you can't do much."

He seems to be saying the same as Khenpo did in the Gandhi Museum.

"As a Buddhist we always look from the wider perspective. So in my own case—the Dalai Lama's name is something significant for Tibet but that does not mean that I do important things. The name of the Dalai Lama . . . at least for the past few centuries—many of the past Dalai Lamas have been able to make great personal contribution for Tibet. Today if Chinese Communists, right from beginning, had behaved like true liberators, then I think 'the Dalai Lama' could have found good opportunities. Under other conditions including other historical . . ."

"Circumstances," the translator interjected.

"Then yes, sometimes, one person can do some significant thing."

This is not the answer that I was hoping for. I'm not here to attack him for anything. Some journalists and young Tibetans may be critical of his nonviolent stance; I'm not one of these. Does his answer suggest that despite all he has achieved, he himself wishes that he could have done more? But the clock is ticking.

Wake up, Isabel. Make your question more specific.

"I was thinking more of the West. What can people there do?"

"Yesterday I was at the Tibetan parliament. I was just there. And we looked back on the last forty-three years, and we are very grateful for the international support, from the public. In 1959 and 1960 we didn't expect this much support. Unexpectedly we have achieved that. That achievement is much more than our expectation. Beyond our control, but somehow it happened. Along with some failures that I mentioned."

He chuckles. Maybe "some failures" is a trifle understated.

"So already I think Western nations, American and Western cultures—not Africa and Arab, the Asian is similar—the Europeans have good Tibet awareness about the importance of Tibet. They also have deeper awareness and a sense of concern about the environment, human rights, democracy, and religious and individual freedom. These are very high in their mind. So a person who already has that kind of . . ."

"Attitude," interjects the translator.

"When they saw the Tibet situation, then I think this creates sympathy and concern. So your work definitely will make a contribution. So, very useful. So I appreciate your intention to do something. To tell more people about Tibet. I thank you."

This is a man who sees everything from a map of the world. He sees from an international and historical perspective, and yet he still values small and seemingly insignificant actions of the individual. I am transfixed by the warmth he communicates. The words are almost insignificant. Except he's not saying, "So—what have you done, then?" He values my intention to do something, even though I feel I've achieved nothing at all.

The others in the room fade into soft focus. He sits and looks at me. It's so good just to have the courage to look back and breathe the moments and not to speak. I don't remember ever feeling loved like this. Tears start to prick the back of my eyes. I don't want to cry, so after a long pause I speak.

Absurdly, I say, "I wanted to mention that I was born on the same day that you left Tibet."

"I see."

"You and I were both on a big journey that day."

And then that wonderful laughter that I'd heard described that came from deep within him. "Ha ha ha. Yes, they were both complicated journey."

"Last question. In this prayer that I'm thinking about, it is written that you have to have courage to change the things you can."

"Courage is very important."

"But how do you know the difference? Between what you can change and what you can't?"

"Through experiment. Research. Calculate whether you can achieve on mental level, then experiment." He stops.

"Oh." So simple. "OK."

We both laugh.

"Otherwise it is very difficult. The result? What that is going to be? What kind of result come? So from the Buddhist viewpoint the action, whether right or wrong, ultimately much depends on motivation. Result not very sure. Your intention, something good. Good purpose, good goal. But some other factors, conditions, results may not go that way. So it doesn't matter. Your motivation is very sincere. The result is not predictable. Difficult."

So it didn't matter that I hadn't changed the world, then?

"Courage, determination are neutral. They can be constructive or destructive. The Nazis, Stalin, Chairman Mao—of course they had tremendous will, determination, and courage, but that used for destruction. But Gandhi, and many others, their determination became constructive. So it depends on motivation and wisdom also. Sometimes intelligence can be a most destructive force. Mao and some of the people I mentioned earlier, very smart. Mao I think was more clever than Stalin. He was a very clever man."

Fortunately most of the people I know are not Mao. I need to drag him down to my level.

"But for the more average person . . . If we assume that we are using wisdom for good things, then how do you gain more of it?"

"It's a kind of intelligence or awareness. It's thinking longer. Wider perspective. We also need something happiness, something good today. Animals only thinking immediate, not next year or next generation, but we human beings can think long-term and sometimes even we have the courage to sacrifice immediate things for long term and next generation. More spiritual sight, awareness, more inner values and thinking about mind and about conscious- ness and how it works. Understanding emotions. How it works. Destructive emotions, constructive emotions. Inner wisdom. So wisdom, you identify wisdom as a spirituality or something good."

Is he saying "Awareness of yourself is the start of wisdom and for things outside yourself, look at the big picture?"

But I don't move so he goes on patiently. "Marxism . . ." He's moving again from the personal and into the greater picture, "espe- cially Marxist theory, concern for desperate people, working-class people under exploitation of ruling class—the concern is very right. The majority of people under working class really suffer. Marxist economic theory, which is concerned not only with how to make a profit but how to distribute . . . very good. Therefore some of these ideas very positive. But because no inner value, compassion, a sense of concern . . . so result? Whole system become ruthless. Fear and suspicion everywhere. Lack of inner value."

"And the individual?"

"If the individual acts, society is changed. Society is a combina- tion of individuals. To change, whether right or wrong, good or bad, the start point, the initiative, must come from the individual. So it is good what you do. It is very important. Sometimes people feel a problem is a huge problem, and even though you see some- thing wrong, something that need change—then, they think too huge. One person can make a difference. It is very important."

"And Tibet?"

"With the Tibet issue, firstly in my mind it is a case of saving Ti- betan culture. Tibetan culture has some good thing to make all heart human being. All heart human being, compassion. Therefore the preservation of Tibetan culture is not only interest for six mil- lion Tibetan people but also to make happy human beings. That is something really worthwhile, to make happy human beings. Tibetan culture is dedicated to that. The Tibetan question is also about the environment because Tibet has a delicate environment and it needs taking care not just for Tibetan people but for India, for Chinese. This I would like to share with you, when you talk, it's not only a question of independence, of human rights, it's much more. Compassion."

"Yes. Simple kindness."

This is why I had wanted to be involved with Tibet and with their cause in the first place. Because of what he teaches. That we need to have simple compassion, one for another.

I glance at my watch. I have been with him for forty minutes.

"Thank you," I say. "For all that you are." He laughs his deep chesty laugh once again. He reaches out and clasps my hands warmly. We stand together to be photographed, the man who some consider a living Buddha and the girl from Battersea.

It didn't matter—it doesn't matter whether I succeed in what I try to do or not. My serenity to accept the things that I can't change comes now from knowing that I will not cease to take action. My courage to continue to take actions that may change something is no longer attached to my judgments about what counts as worthwhile. Maybe the divisions in the prayer itself are limitations. Perhaps serenity, courage, and wisdom are all needed in every action that we take. Maybe the wisdom lies in not having too much serenity and accepting the world as it is, and in not having too much courage and wanting to change the world all at once. If the Dalai Lama can tell me that the intention is more important than the result, then I'll just go on and on taking positive actions. Just like you will. Whatever change we want to bring about, maybe one day there will be a positive result. Who says you and I can't change the world?

He stands in the courtyard to see me out. I have to leave. I'm lost again. I don't know whether I can turn my back on him or not. Somewhere, I read that when he was a young man no one was permitted to turn their back to him. But has he dispensed with this custom or not? I walk backwards. He bows low as I leave, so I stop and bow low, too. Facing backwards and endeavoring not to trip over, I bow some more. He bows again, even lower. I attempt to bow lower until I am virtually horizontal. I glance around to try to navigate my reverse exit and see Tenzin Taklha grinning at me again. His laughing eyes give me the answer. There is only one way to face now.

WHAT CAN I DO?

There are many, many ways that you may like to support Tibet.
    You may like to support small grassroots organizations working inside Tibet. You could help build a school or support a health clinic or environmental project. Pick a small-scale project that feels right for you.

    Or you may choose to support a wonderful charity that has built an award-winning school in Ladakh where Tibetan Buddhist culture can thrive away from interference.

    You may like to support the education of a child through the Tibetan Children's Village in India.

    Or become a volunteer for a year in one of the many Tibetan communities in India.

    If you like to travel, you could consider visiting the Tibetan world either in Tibet or in ethnic Tibetan regions such as Ladakh, Dharamsala, or Bhutan. Or you could visit Tibetan refugee communities in India or Nepal.
    You could get involved with a program that supports former political prisoners, or you could work to secure the release of political prisoners still being held.

You may want to take on the political issue from an international perspective. There are groups that support Tibet all over the world, and they all need active support. The USA has one of the best Tibet support groups in the world—they are the International Campaign for Tibet. Phone 202–785–1515 and their website is www.savetibet.org.

If everyone who buys this book joins together we'd have the power to really make a difference to their organization. In my experience they are wise and worked positively and I recommend them. Kate Saunders, who you meet in the book working for the Tibet Information Network in London, now works for them in Washington, so you can phone them and ask for Kate.

How could you use your special skills?
Would you explore the possibility of meeting your representative or senator to ask about government support for the Dalai Lama and the Tibetan government-in-exile?

There are student groups in universities under the umbrella of the "Students for a Free Tibet."

If you come to London and would like to visit the Wednesday Vigil for Tibet, it meets opposite the Chinese embassy, Portland Place, W1, between 6 p.m. and 8 p.m. However, contrary to the views of the embassy, no one will pay you to attend.

As an individual, you may want to support one particular Tibetan scholar or artist in exile.

Information about what is happening in Tibet—the diverse views and concerns of Tibetans there—is essential for campaigners, governments dealing with China, scholars, journalists, charities, and the Tibetan community in exile. It is also vital for any process of conflict resolution and to the welfare of Tibetans in Tibet, especially political prisoners. If you would like to contribute to an information service, see Tibet Information Network at www.tibetinfo.net.

If you are involved with a school, a hospital, a church, a Buddhist center or other place of worship, or a business, you could implement a "twinning" program that you design yourself, in which you link up with a Tibetan school or hospital. Exchanges between hospital staff are especially valuable: You could invite Tibetan doctors for training here (cataracts are a huge problem in Tibet) or volunteer medical staff in your own hospital to travel to rural Tibet, where health care is very basic, if it exists at all. For a school, the possibilities are also endless: Send books (a school I visited in Tibet had not a single book), learn Tibetan, exchange staff? If you are part of a religious organization, you could twin your place of worship with a Tibetan Buddhist monastery and invite them to come and teach. How about supporting a Tibetan business enterprise within Tibet? How would business twinning work?

If you are a teacher, the organization www.rokpa.org has a program where you could go to teach in Tibet. See their website for details.

Scholarship programs exist to enable Tibetan scholars to study in the West. If you are linked to a university that does not have such a program, could you create one?

If you would like to take action yourself—no matter how large or small—please look at the website that is created with this book: www .actfortibet.com. Information about all the above and more will be found there. And you can leave messages.

If you want to reach me directly, I am at www.isabellosada.com.

READING BOOKS AND
WATCHING VIDEOS: TIBET

BOOKS

Here is some of the reading I've done over the last two years, in case you want to read some more yourself.

1. *My Land and My People* (Warner Brothers). The original autobiography of His Holiness the Dalai Lama's early life. First published in 1962.

2. *Freedom in Exile* (HarperSanFrancisco). The later autobiography of HH. This is the book that got me involved in all this in the first place. Essential reading.

3. *The Dragon in the Land of Snows: A History of Modern Tibet Since 1947* by Tsering Shakya (Penguin Books). A history that upset both the Chinese government and the Tibetan government-in-exile. Five hundred pages but surprisingly readable.

4. *The Dance of Seventeen Lives* by Mick Brown (Bloomsbury USA). I adore Mick Brown's writing. (He also wrote *The Spiritual Tourist*.) Here he tells the story of the Karmapa lineage and makes me want to go and meet the Karmapa. If you don't believe in reincarnation, read this book!

5. *The Search for the Panchen Lama* by Dr. Isabel Hilton (W.W. Norton & Company). In the first half Isabel attempts to explain the en-

tire Panchen Lama lineage, and it's quite hard work, but keep going because the second half, which describes what happened to the current Panchen Lama, reads like a thriller that is also a true-life tragedy.

6. *The Hotel on the Roof of the World* by Alec Le Sueur (RDR Books). Alec Le Sueur spent five years in Lhasa, working for what was then the Holiday Inn. A genuinely funny book full of compassion for all points of view. Reads like *Fawlty Towers*.

7. *Seven Years in Tibet* by Heinrich Harrer (Jeremy P. Tarcher). Still a classic.

8. *Tibet* edited by James O'Reilly, Larry Habegger, and Kim Norris (Travelers' Tales). Twenty-seven stories by different travel writers about their Tibet adventures. My favorites are "Tibet Through Chinese Eyes" by Peter Hessler and "Mestizo" by Robbie Barnett.

9. *Namma: A Tibetan Love Story* by Kate Karko (Hodder Headline Australia). The story of how Kate, who took Cultural Studies at Portsmouth Polytechnic, fell in love with and then married a Tibetan nomad and went to live with his family.

10. *Sorrow Mountain* (Kodansha) and *Fire Under the Snow* (Harvill Press). Real-life stories—the first the life of the Buddhist Nun Ani Pachen, and the second of the monk Palden Gyatso. Inspiring reads. How to spend your entire life in prison and be tortured, having committed no crime—and still not hate your enemies.

11. *Heartlands: Travels in the Tibetan World* by Michael Buckley (Summersdale Travel). This book is based on a series of trips to Tibet that Michael Buckley has made over a decade. He also writes of his adventures in Ladakh, Bhutan, and Mongolia. (He is also the author of the *Bradt Travel Guide to Tibet*.)

12. *Tibet: Turning the Wheel of Life* by Françoise Pommaret (Harry N. Abrams). One of those fantastically beautifully illustrated little gift

books that you have to buy for the pictures alone. But also readable and with copies of some rare and interesting documents of Tibetan history included.

13. *The Snow Lion and The Dragon: China, Tibet, and the Dalai Lama* by Melvyn C. Goldstein (University of California Press). American academic on the great debate. While the majority of the book is a very useful overview of the history (except that it skips over the Cultural Revolution), the final section is a set of political recommendations that have been described by other academics as "highly controversial." He also does not count Kham and Amdo as part of Tibet, which wouldn't please the Tibetans who live in those areas. Not for reading on the bus.

14. *The Struggle for Modern Tibet: The Autobiography of Tashi Tsering* by Tashi Tsering, William Siebenschuh, and Melvyn Goldstein (translator) (East Gate Book). Although this is clearly not an autobiography (it has three authors), it is the only English-language text that can be said to be by a Tibetan who lives in Tibet. An amazingly valuable life story that takes you to the next level of understanding the complexity of life in Tibet.

VIDEOS

If you are feeling too lazy to read or so enthusiastic that you want to read and watch videos, try digging out some of these. If your local video store doesn't have all of them, you could try to persuade them to buy them, or you could buy them yourself through the www.actfortibet.org website and amazon.com will give us a small donation. The website even has links to trailers for some of them.

1. *Kundun,* 1997. Directed by Martin Scorsese. The film chronicles the life of the Dalai Lama from his discovery at the age of two to post–World War II, when Mao-led China declares that Tibet is a Chinese province and forcibly annexes it, leading to the Dalai Lama's exile.

2. *Windhorse,* 1998. Directed by Paul Wagner. Based on a true story about a singer who must flee Tibet. At great risk, the director took video of actors on location in Lhasa. This "docudrama" was filmed in Tibetan and Chinese languages and stars Dadon, a famous Tibetan singer who escaped into exile in 1992 and now lives in the United States.

3. *The Cup,* 1999. Directed by Khyentse Norbu. My favorite. The first major movie directed by a Tibetan, a Rinpoche resident in Bhutan. It's about soccer-crazy monks at a monastery in northern India. Filmed in Tibetan and Hindi languages with English subtitles.

4. *Himalaya,* 1999. Directed by Eric Valli. A stunning French-Nepalese co-production about the nomadic way of life, with an all-Tibetan cast filmed in Dolpo, Nepal, in the Tibetan language. Stars Lhakpa Tsamchoe. Try to watch it on a large-screen TV as the landscape is stunning.

5. *Seven Years in Tibet,* 1997. Directed by Jean-Jacques Annaud. Some say this is not Brad Pitt at his best, but it's worth watching for the wonderful performance by the Bhutanese boy who plays the young Dalai Lama. It introduces Tibetan actress Lhakpa Tsamchoe, who also has a lead in *Himalaya.*

6. *Tibet's Stolen Child,* 2001. Produced by Garthwait and Griffin films. Narrated by Patrick Stewart. A young filmmaker searches for the truth about the eleventh Panchen Lama and explores the political motives for the abduction. Features interviews with six Nobel laureates as well as Chinese historians.

7. *Spirit of Tibet,* 1999. Narrated by Richard Gere. The life and world of the acclaimed Tibetan teacher Dilgo Khyentse Rinpoche, one of the primary teachers of the Dalai Lama.

8. *The Saltmen of Tibet,* 1998. Directed by Ulrike Koch. A Swiss documentary about the salt route caravans from Tibet to Nepal, a trade now mostly extinct. Filmed in Tibetan and in the secret salt language (with cryptic salt-language subtitles).

9. *Lojong: Transforming the Mind,* 1999. Co-production of the Office of Tibet (London), the Meridian Trust, Jukes Productions, and Mystic Fire Video. The eight verses on transforming the mind written by eleventh-century meditator Geshe Langri Tangpa Dorjey Sengey are one of the most important texts from a genre of Tibetan spiritual writings known as Lojong, literally "training" or "transforming the mind." The central themes of Lojong are enhancing compassion, cultivating balanced attitudes towards oneself and others, developing positive ways of thinking, and transforming adverse situations into conditions favorable for spiritual development. What we'd call "Use everything for your learning upliftment and growth!" The Dalai Lama gave these teachings in London, May 8–10, 1999. Approximately five and a half hours on four tapes.

10. *Gandhi,* 1982. Directed by Richard Attenborough. OK, so it's not a film about Tibet, but it is one of the most inspiring films that has ever been made. If you haven't seen it, then this should go to the top of the list, and if you have seen it, see it again. (Look out for the scene where he tells the man who has murdered a child and thinks he is going to hell how to get out of hell.) Just wonderful.

READING BOOKS AND
WATCHING VIDEOS: CHINA

BOOKS

And here are some books on China that have helped me understand the context.

1. *Wild Swans: Three Daughters of China* by Jung Chang (Anchor). You've already read this, haven't you? But if by the remotest chance you haven't, then this is simply the best and most readable book. It won the 1992 NCR Book Award and the 1993 British Book of the Year Award. I read it walking down the street—literally.

2. *Balzac and the Little Chinese Seamstress* by Dai Sijie (Anchor). A wonderfully written story, and if you read it after *Wild Swans,* you'll enjoy it even more.

3. *River Town: Two Years on the Yangtze* by Peter Hessler (Perennial). Hessler went to Fuling in 1996 to teach English literature and was one of the first two "foreigners" to live there since 1949. A wonderful read, sympathetic and sensitive.

4. *The Complete Idiot's Guide to Modern China* by Vanessa Lide Whitcomb and Michael Benson (Alpha). The title appealed to me, and yes, it's excellent. Explains the whole of modern Chinese history and a lot more besides in terms that a novice can easily

understand, and if you've read any of the above, you're not a novice anymore.

5. *Mao* by Jonathan Spence (Viking). My Chinese friend says that many Chinese consider Spence to have a better understanding of Chinese history than they do. He has an elegant writing style and is never far from the *New York Times* best-seller list. Fascinating.

6. *The Coming Collapse of China* by Gordon G. Chang (Random House). I was intrigued by the title and the fact that the author has a Chinese name and has "lived and worked in Shanghai for 20 years." That may be so, but he's as American as apple pie. He was obviously raised in the United States, and his book reads more as a diatribe against China; I found his arguments unbalanced and unconvincing.

7. *China Since 1949* by Linda Benson (Longman). A clear little textbook. Just over one hundred pages and very well put together.

8. *Soul Mountain* by Gao Xingjian (Perennial). The first Chinese winner of the Nobel Prize for literature. Like a French or Russian film—very, very slow. More like a dream than a story. Almost a portrayal of the subconscious. Five hundred pages. Lots of amazon.com readers hated it. I loved it.

9. *Eighteen Layers of Hell: Stories from the Chinese Gulag* (Cassell) by Kate Saunders, whom you met earlier. You've read some extracts from this already. Cheerful it ain't, but you will never see the phrase "Made in China" in the same way again.

10. *Ten Thousand Miles Without a Cloud* by Sun Shuyun (Harper-Collins). This is the true story of one Chinese woman's epic journey through Central Asia to India and back, following in the footsteps of the eighth-century monk Xuanzang. As we travel with her we learn about this Chinese hero and his faith in Buddhism while Shu searches to find her own Buddhist faith. A tale told with great humility and gentleness.

VIDEOS

1. *The Last Emperor,* 1987. Directed by Bernardo Bertolucci. A truly magnificent grand epic that tells the life story of Pu Yi, the last emperor of China. It follows his life story from his crowning at the age of three and his being worshiped by half a billion people, to his abdication, his reeducation in prison, and his release to become an obscure peasant. Filmed in the Forbidden City, it won nine Academy Awards. The first Western film to be made about modern China with the full cooperation of the Chinese government.

2. *Raise the Red Lantern,* 1991. Directed by Zhang Yimou. One of the great classics of world cinema, starring the actress Gong Li, who has been described as "one of the world's greatest actresses." She appears in the majority of the films below. This remarkable film tells the story of a feudal nobleman in 1920s' China. Gong Li plays an educated girl of nineteen who is sent to be his "fourth mistress." Utterly compelling.

3. *To Live,* 1994. Also directed by Zhang Yimou and also starring Gong Li. Here she co-stars alongside Ge You. This is my favorite of this selection. It tells the story of an ordinary Chinese family over thirty years of Chinese history. Very restrained, a good history lesson, and a tender story, too.

4. *The Blue Kite,* 1993. Director Tian Zhuangzhuang. Banned in China. Again tells the story of an ordinary family trying to get by in China in the fifties and sixties, this time through the eyes of a small boy who grows up during the Rectification Movement, then the Great Leap Forward, and finally the Cultural Revolution.

5. *Farewell, My Concubine,* 1993. Directed by Chen Kaige. Bizarre, very long, and sometimes difficult to follow, this is nevertheless an extraordinary film and was nominated for an Oscar for Best Foreign Film and for the British Academy of Films and Television Award (BAFTA). Based on the novel by Lilian Lee, it spans fifty years of

Chinese art, passion, and revolution as it follows the lives of two male stars of the Peking Opera and the prostitute who comes between them.

6. *Ju Dou,* 1989. Another Zhang Yimou movie, also starring Gong Li. Set in the 1920s, our heroine is sold to become the third wife of an impotent old man. The film was banned in China: It has been suggested that the leaders saw it as an unflattering metaphor for Chinese life, a society ruled by a coterie of aging, controlling men. If you have become a fan of Gong Li by now, you may like to see this, as once again she is extraordinary.

7. *Not One Less,* 1999. Directed by Zhang Yimou. Not an epic this time but a simple tale about education in rural China, which casts nonactors in documentary style. When a thirteen-year-old substitute teacher in a rural village loses one of her charges, she decides to go to the city to find him. A really beautiful film that put tears in my eyes while tackling some difficult issues in a charming way that cleverly gets around the censors.

8. *Suzhou River,* 2000. Directed by Lou Ye. And now for something completely different. Chinese film-noir set in modern Shanghai, this is a mystery thriller that has been compared to Hitchcock's *Vertigo.*

9. *Red Firecracker, Green Firecracker,* 1994. Directed by He Ping. Classic tale of forbidden love on the banks of the Yellow River in turn-of-the-century China. Marrying below your status was as impossible as unwed love, and neither would please the ancestors— bad news when the object of a girl's desire is the actor Wu Gang.

10. *Warriors of Heaven and Earth,* 2003. Also directed by He Ping. I haven't seen this one yet, but I'm told (by a Chinese friend who has seen the film in China) that it must be seen. Set in the Gobi Desert in China's Tang dynasty, it's an action film about comradeship and honor—but in this case some sacred bones of Buddha come into the tale.

p.s.: AND ON THE SUBJECT Of NON-VIOLENCE

1. *The Unconquerable World. Power, Nonviolence and the Will of the People* by Jonathan Schell (Penguin Group). Jonathan Schell is a Visiting Professor at Yale and the Harold Willens Peace Fellow at the Nation Institute. I also rather wish he were your president.

ACKNOWLEDGMENTS

All the people in this book are real. In rare cases I have changed people's names to protect their identity, but most appear as themselves so I would like to thank everyone who is mentioned and has played a part.

Special thanks are due to Kate Saunders, Kesang Takla, Alison Reynolds, Tsering Tashi, Robbie Barnett, Tsering Shakya, Michael Buckley, Dr. Isabel Hilton, Alison Cooper, and Emily Hunter for helping me to understand the complexity. Practical help and encouragement have been essential and were provided in bucketfuls by Steven Hands, Rachael Laine, Khenpo, Ian Cumming, Isabel Kelly, Katrina Moran, Ian Rowland, Jane Moore, David Turrill, Gavin Starks, Muzamel Mahmood, Tess Burrows, and everyone involved in the stunt, particularly those who left the ground. Thanks also to everyone who has supported Act for Tibet with sponsorship and advice.

The Tibetan government-in-exile was wonderfully kind to me in Dharamsala, and I would particularly like to thank Tsering Yangchen, Thubten Samphel, Tenzin Taklha, Thinley Norbu, Professor Samdhong Rinpoche, and His Holiness the Dalai Lama.

My agents, Jonathan Lloyd and Christy Fletcher, have demonstrated extraordinary patience and grace, and my editor, Renée Sedliar at HarperSanFrancisco, is an incarnation of energy, joy, and inspiration.

Closer to home I thank, once again, my daughter, Emily, who supports me always with her enthusiasm and unconditional love. And finally, those "without whom none of this would have been possible"—MB, JJM, and CM.